Treasures To Keep – Book Two
DELIGHTING IN THE LORD– Large Print Edition
© 2020 Edna Holmes   All rights reserved.

No part of this book may be reproduced in any form or by any electronic or mechanical means, including information storage and retrieval systems, without written permission by the publisher, except by a reviewer who may quote brief passages in a review.

All Bible passages taken from the Authorized King James Version. Permission granted.

Published by:  Max Holt Media
303 Cascabel Place,
Mount Juliet, TN 37122
www.maxholtmedia.com
On facebook at www.facebook.com/maxholtmedia

Disclaimer:  Names, characters, businesses, places, events and incidents used here are by permission.

Cover design by: © Max Holt Media

ISBN: 13: 978-1-944537-46-3

Delighting in the Lord

*Treasures to Keep*

Book Two

# Delighting in the Lord

**366 DAILY BIBLE DEVOTIONALS**

*LARGE PRINT EDITION*

**EDNA HOLMES**

Delighting in the Lord

Edna Holmes

# FOREWORD

Sometimes, when you meet a stranger unaware, she will become one of your closest friends. I was a young missionary wife with two small children when I first met Edna. This was in 1971, and she was the pastor's wife of a new supporting church. At that time, I had no idea Edna would become an important instrument in God's hands to teach, guide and encourage me through the next forty-six years. This would include holding my hand and helping me wade through a very dark period of depression. She would become a very dear friend.

Edna's forty years of personal experience in the ministry, in speaking at ladies' meetings and conferences, in counseling, and her personal struggles in spiritual growth have given her a deep understanding of women and the problems they face in everyday life. In a candid yet compassionate way, Edna shares personal experiences and Bible truth as she discusses marriage, raising children, prayer, suffering, loneliness, temptations, doubt, and many other topics we all encounter in striving to live a Godly life in an ungodly world.

The devotionals she writes are easy to relate to, give practical direction, and are always grounded in the word of God. They will help you focus your thoughts and develop a stronger relationship with Jesus Christ. Edna's previous devotional book, entitled SPOILS, which was later revised and renamed **Treasures to Keep**, has been read by women all over America and in Europe. It has also been taken into prisons where it has proven to be a valuable tool in the lives of believers. I have personally talked to women who use Edna's devotional book repeatedly, year after year, to give them insight and inspiration for their day.

I have been in full-time ministry in America and in Europe for fifty years and am a published author. Through the years I have heard many women speak and read numerous devotionals. Based on my knowledge and experience, I can highly recommend this devotion book to anyone seeking *down to earth*, Christ-centered, devotional reading material. This book is guaranteed to both challenge and inspire you in your spiritual walk.

Sandra Hastings - Missionary wife & Speaker/Author

(**Publisher's Note:** See Sandra's books at www.amazon.com)
  **Victory in the Storm** (Kindle & Paperback in English, Spanish and German)
  **Seeing God's Hand** (Kindle & Paperback)

Delighting in the Lord

NOTE: Each day's devotional is Date-Numbered, making a Table of Contents and page numbering unnecessary.

Edna Holmes

# ACKNOWLEDGEMENTS

I'm grateful for the encouragement to write a second devotional book. Otherwise, it wouldn't have happened. I was twenty years younger when the first one was written, under the title of **SPOILS**. Later, with a major revision and change of title and cover, **Treasures to Keep** came into being.

The Lord has used it to minister to many readers. Some of those, who are friends I've never met, have in various ways contacted me and asked for a second devotional book; they had used the first one several years, and desired a new one. Such urging motivated me to launch out again and write.

I pray that **Treasures to Keep-Book Two...DELIGHTING IN THE LORD,** will be helpful to many who desire to have a devotional guide for their daily time with the Lord.

Besides encouragement from my closest friends, my family has encouraged and helped me beyond measure. My husband allows me access to his library which is a treasure trove of helpful books and notes. In addition, at times, he has ready answers for me when I need information; it has saved research time

My son, Louis, knows the secrets of a computer which are hidden from older folks. I could not produce a book without his expertise in setting it up where my part is only to sit down and write! I am indebted to him.

My brother, Max, also my publisher, (MaxHoltMedia.com) is kind and helpful no matter what time of day and night I'm needing advice with my project. I'm so blessed with all the help.

Most of all my Lord and Savior enables me to do this good work.

*"The Lord is my strength and my shield; my heart trusteth in him, and I am helped."* Psalm 28:7

Delighting in the Lord

Edna Holmes

# January 1

*"Delight thyself also in the Lord; and he
shall give thee the desires of thine heart."*
Psalm 37:4

We must read and obey the Word of God in order to make the New Year successful, not just *turn over a new leaf* and hope for the best. This promise, in Psalm 37, is like a sparkling diamond ring a man gives to his beloved when she promises to marry him. Untold blessings will follow when we truly *delight in the Lord.*

How do we do that? *Time, attention,* and *thought* are given to whomever and whatever we delight in. *My husband and I corresponded by mail before we married. His letters to me were treasures. I delighted in reading his words and never tired of them. I eagerly worked and finished the chores so I'd have time for what I really wanted to do—write to the one I loved.*

Your attention to the Lord will be more than a dutiful time of devotions, *if you delight in Him.* You will think of ways you can do extra Bible reading, and the *"pray without ceasing"* factor becomes easy. Thoughts become prayers which God will hear, and answer. Remember, He is omniscient, *all knowing.*

Begin this year to *delight in the Lord.* Give time to Him. Have a plan to read your Bible, consistently. Mark the place where you stop and start there each day. Don't waste time deciding on where to read. That is a trap which hinders progress.

If you don't have a plan, start by reading the New Testament through. Having a general knowledge of the entire NT will be a great benefit for you, personally. *Delighting in the Lord* will bring more joy and blessings into your life than you can imagine. *"I love them that love me; and those that seek me early shall find me."* Proverbs 8:17.

Delight:   Psalm 143:8    Psalm 147:11

## January 2

*"Keep thy heart with all diligence;*
*for out of it are the issues of life."*
Proverbs 4:23

Our hearts are like gardens that must be tended for good things to grow. The Holy Spirit has planted the seeds of *the fruit of the Spirit,* described in Galatians 5:22, but it will not take root and grow unless it is cultivated. Its fruit is precious: *love, joy, peace, longsuffering, gentleness, goodness, faith, meekness, and temperance.* Christ in us patiently works to develop these qualities in our lives, which enhances the character by which we are known.

The devil plants seeds in our hearts also; he works to hinder growth of the good fruit that brings honor to Christ. So, in this New Year, dedicate yourself to keeping *your heart with all diligence.* An expedient reason is that our own hearts can fool us!

*"The heart is deceitful above all things, and desperately wicked; who can know it?"* Jeremiah 17:9

Our hearts are easily stirred by emotions. Our *feelings* are often our downfall; they cloud our judgment, and we can get entangled in a trap. Sin may *feel* right and good at the moment, but we suffer consequences which *always* prove otherwise. Examine every feeling and situation in the light of God's Word. Verses will come to mind when you need them, such as Thessalonians 5:22 *"Abstain from all appearance of evil."*

God warns us to not only avoid evil but keep away from the very appearance of it! If we are perfectly honest, we will admit to a vague uneasiness about whatever is tempting us to do wrong. The Holy Spirit warns us in that still small voice. Don't ignore it. Guard your heart! It will save you a multitude of heartaches and trouble in the *issues of life.*

Delight:   Proverbs 23:26   Psalms 119:2   Proverbs 3:5

Edna Holmes

# January 3

*"Let the high praises of God be in their mouth,*
*and a twoedged sword in their hand..."*
Psalm 149:6

The psalmist directs this psalm to be sung in the *congregation of saints* in verse 1. Praise of the Lord is the most beneficial thing for spiritual health, and physical health as well. It lifts the *spirit of heaviness,* which is akin to depression in our day.

Isaiah 61:3 tells us to put on *"the garment of praise for the spirit of heaviness."* Praise is expressing thanksgiving to God for His bountiful blessings poured into our lives and extolling Him for His honor and majesty. You can experience the "lifting of the spirit of heaviness" if you put God's word to the test.

As a Pastor's wife, I experienced a bout with depression. Fatigue was a factor, but I'd gotten *too busy* and neglected time *with him* in fellowship and prayer. That was the main cause. Isaiah's exhortation became real to me when I started writing down the blessings I could think of from the time I'd trusted Christ as my Savior. The *garment of praise* effected amazing results. The longer my list got, the less heavy and depressed I felt. Day by day I felt better and was relieved. I kept the garment of praise on thereafter.

And God's Word, *the two-edged sword,* protects us in spiritual warfare, *if we keep it in our hands,* hold it, read it, and obey it. It's the way of happiness and sweet fellowship with the Lord.

Have a blessed year. Determine to lay hold of God's Word in study and prayer daily. Write down at least one blessing each day. Wear the *garment of praise* with gratitude; see how God keeps His Word and gives you an uplifted spirit which will keep you healthy and happy no matter the circumstances.

Delight:   Psalm 148:13   Psalm 147:1   Psalm 135:1

# January 4

*"The fear of the Lord is the beginning
of knowledge..."*
Proverbs 1:7

We just begin to have good understanding and knowledge when we have proper reverence and awe for the Lord—the *fear of the Lord.* When common people are privileged to meet an earthly king or queen, they are given instructions beforehand. Strict rules of etiquette and decorum must be followed in the presence of royalty. Our thoughts and behavior are much more important in the presence of God. He is the King of Kings and Lord of Lords! No earthly monarch can compare to our King. He is ours by birthright, that is, *the new birth by faith in Jesus Christ.*

Through time, each generation has let down the standard by which they taught their children the fear of God, or to have proper respect and reverence, or even who God is and why we should worship Him. Sadly, it is very evident in the attitude of our present society. When are we in God's presence? In church is the most obvious place we think of. True. Jesus said, *"For where two or three are gathered together in my name, there am I in the midst of them."* Matthew 18:20. However, the *irreverence* displayed toward the house of God today is appalling. We can't make this generation *fear God and keep His commandments,* but we can be good examples for them to see.

Most importantly, God's presence is *in us* by the indwelling of the Holy Spirit. We should have the *fear of the Lord,* which is defined as *loving reverence and awe* that causes us to delight in Him and live in obedience to Him. Do we *fear the Lord* in the proper sense as the Bible teaches? What is your reaction when you hear the Lord's name used in a derogatory manner or His Word maligned? Does your heart cringe? Are you grieved? If so, then you have the *fear of the Lord.*

Delight:   Psalm 89:7    Psalm 33:8

Edna Holmes

# January 5

*"Thou art snared with the words of thy mouth,
thou art taken with the words of thy mouth."*
Proverbs 6:2

A good thing to do in the beginning of the year is renew the guard on our most vulnerable part, *our tongue!* Reading James chapter three regularly is a healthy *spiritual* exercise.

Sometimes we speak impulsively, committing ourselves in some way with a word, and later we regret it. Stress grips us in a strangle-hold as we work to fulfill an unnecessary promise. I've created my own misery in that way, making hasty promises which meant extra work, and all the time hoping to please other people. Eventually, I came to see the thing as it really was and my misguided motives.

God's Word is our best teacher and has the answer for all our weaknesses. Psalms 51:6 *"Behold, thou desirest truth in the inward parts: and in the hidden part thou shalt make me to know wisdom."* God will reveal to our hearts why we do what we do. We don't always know ourselves. In many cases, it is a desire for acceptance which is innate in all of us. Love and acceptance are longed for by every human being. Realizing what we have in Christ and basking in the love He has for us will satisfy those needs. The Lord is our Counselor, and His Word will always speak in love and wisdom to our hearts.

When we get into a snare, a *trap*, with our words, the Bible also gives us a *what to do* verse. Proverbs 6:3 in part says *"...go, humble thyself, and make sure thy friend."* In other words, swallow your pride and go tell your friend, or whoever, that you spoke impulsively without thinking it through; you cannot fulfill the promise you made hastily. *Please forgive me*. That will settle it and get you out of the trap. I've had to do that very thing. It is humbling to admit your limitations, when you desire to impress others by working to gain their favor. A touch of *pride* is involved. We are to minister as God leads us to do so, but we are His servants only and must live by His will, not our own or others' expectations.

Delight:   Proverbs 29:20   Proverbs 11:2

# January 6

*"The fruit of the righteous is a tree
of life; and he that winneth souls is wise."*
Proverbs 11:30

The most important work for the Lord is endeavoring to win souls. Now is the time to make a fresh commitment to pray for opportunities to witness and lead people to Christ.

A little cartoon character told her friend she convinced a kid in school that her religion was better than his. When asked how she did it, she replied, "I hit him with my lunchbox!" That's not the way to win souls, but certainly, when we witness to the lost, we can, and should *hit* them in such a way they will be touched and give thought to their need of salvation.

1. **Have an excellent personal testimony.**

What we are is obvious as sunshine on a clear day. If our priorities are in place, dedication to God will be a way of life and others will see that we are *real* Christians. People won't *hear* a word you say if they have *seen* something amiss in your life.

2. **Use God's Word, not just your own words.**

Only the Word of God has power in it to convince a person of his need of Christ and salvation. It is *the good seed.* Plant it every opportunity that comes to you. Have enough scripture in your own heart to witness to others and lead them to Christ even if you have no Bible at hand.

3. **Depend on the power of prayer.**

God gives power to win souls as Christians pray with genuine concern, love, and desire to see lost souls come to Christ.

My pastor's wife was a dedicated soul winner. She said the secret was prayer. *"The more time I spend in prayer, the more successful my soul-winning efforts are,"* she told me. Daily, we should pray for lost souls to be saved, and for God to use us in that good work. After all, that is God's first love, and it should be ours too.

Delight:   John 3:16   Romans 5:8   John 3:36

# January 7

*"Oh taste and see that the Lord is good:*
*blessed is the man that trusteth in him."*
Psalm 34:8

Some people are picky about what they taste if the food is unfamiliar to them. There is a criterion. Does it look good, smell good, and do others swear by its goodness? It also helps to know who the cook is; then maybe they will taste.

Many will not *taste and see that the Lord is good*; they have only experienced negative impressions observing the lives of Christians who are not good examples. That is one reason my husband was turned away from the idea of becoming a Christian for many years. The inconsistency of those who were in the church, *Christians,* were a stumbling-block in his life. Then his heart was stirred when he heard the gospel preached by a dedicated pastor who impressed him with his godly living. He *tasted* for himself and saw that the Lord is good just as the Word of God proclaims.

A good testimony is an important factor. God will hold us responsible for how we represent Him in this world. There is a common saying, *"If you were on trial for being a Christian, would there be enough evidence to convict you?"* That question should cause us to pause and take stock. Is there?

We are *epistles*, or letters, read by others that see us every day. The world watches Christians. *"Forasmuch as ye are manifestly declared to be the epistle of Christ..."* II Corinthians 3:3
We are, more or less, open letters. Our words, actions, and behavior are taken into consideration by those observing us, especially if they *know* we are Christians. That won't be troubling to us if it is settled in our hearts to live according to the guidelines in the Word of God. Settle it! Being a good example for Christ is the least we can do for our wonderful Savior.

Delight:   II Corinthians 3:3   I Peter 3:15

## January 8

*"...if there be any virtue, and if there
be any praise, think on these things."*
Philippians 4:8

God tells us exactly how we are to think! We don't have to wonder about that. The entire text of the verse is a list. It would be a beneficial exercise for every Christian to write it on a card and display it in a prominent place in the home. We all battle negative thoughts at times; some days are worse than others. Once I was inspired to put our text verse on a card and tape it to the bookcase facing me in my study.

God's Word truly has the power to turn our thoughts in the right direction, and don't we all need that day by day? Women are more prone to put their emotions into their thought process, and a day can turn into a total loss unless we quickly turn to the Word and let God deliver us from that trap. This verse has helped me so much.

*"Finally, brethren, whatsoever things are true, whatsoever things are honest, whatsoever things are just, whatsoever things are pure, whatsoever things are lovely, whatsoever things are of good report; if there be any virtue, and if there be any praise, think on these things."* Philippians 4:8

Take a good look at that. That is how we should think! To honestly try and follow these guidelines will keep your thoughts right and pleasing to God. He knew we would need help, so He graciously spelled it out for us. Another helpful verse is Proverbs 16:3.

*"Commit thy works unto the Lord, and thy thoughts shall be established."* This is a great benefit. It's a good *start-the-day* kind of prayer before negative thoughts beset us early in the day. It helps us to *keep our minds on our business* instead of running helter-skelter from one thing to another. Our faces betray us when our minds entertain unhappy thoughts, though we may dutifully wear a half-hearted smile. Take hold of God's unbreakable promise and allow Him to guide your thoughts. *Choose to be happy.*

Delight:     II Corinthians 10:4-5     Matthew 6:28

Edna Holmes

# January 9

*"But the very hairs of your head are all numbered."*
Matthew 10:30

    The verse after the text tells us to *fear not*, and it's no wonder. God knows every little detail about His children, and He tells us that to assure us of our well-being in this world. We should never hesitate to ask the Lord for our most insignificant needs or desires, for he loves us and delights for us to trust Him in everything. It's a great *growing* moment when we experience this personally.

    In my exercise walking one day at the fitness center, I found myself halfway around the indoor track, mostly closed in with not a stopping place along the sides. I suddenly had need of a tissue but had not a scrap on me. Nobody was on the track but me at the time. I sent up a sloppy prayer, not sure if I should bother the Lord for a tissue. *"Lord, I wish I had a Kleenex!"* I picked up the pace and moved on. As I rounded the next corner, I saw a tissue lying neatly on the floor by the wall as though it had been taken from the box and put there for me! I was stunned, and my heart filled with wonder at the loving-care of my Savior. That He did it for *me,* just filled my heart with praise.

    The Lord *"daily loads us with benefits,"* and for the most part, we are not aware. *"Blessed be the Lord, who daily loadeth us with benefits, even the God of our salvation. Selah."* Psalm 68:19

    The word *selah* means *pause and think of that.* We should do that in the midst of blessings He bestows on us. And as we journey through this world, the Lord looks after us in detail. He answers weak prayers, and some that are mere thoughts. Once I loaned two poem books, favorites, and valuable to me. After a lengthy time, I forgot who I loaned them to. I was desperate: *"Lord, where are those books?"* Afterwards I visited an elderly lady who was moving away. She asked me to look for photos in a box of stuff; I found my books! She didn't recall where she got them. God's perfect timing! We can trust our Lord; He loves us.

Delight:    Psalm 46:1-3    Psalm 23:1

# January 10

*"She looketh well to the ways of her household,
and eateth not the bread of idleness."*
Proverbs 31:27

We understand the analogy here very well. The ideal woman of Proverbs 31 took care of her house and was not lazy.

That is significant for all of us—wives, mothers, housekeepers. The way we keep our houses tells a lot about us personally, plus it has a lot to do with our being happy. Nothing gives us more of a sense of well-being as having things in order around us. I have heard a saying that the *condition of a woman's home shows the condition of her mind.* In that case, mine has certainly been scattered in disarray a lot in my lifetime!

Some women are naturally good at order and organization. They are *clean-ies* by nature, and it is easy for them to keep their houses spic and span. Then, some of us have to really *work* at it. If we get inspired and get the house in perfect order, it only takes a day or so to tumble it up again. Other talents and abilities are irrelevant when someone knocks at the door, and the house is not presentable.

Our first order of help comes from God through his Word when He tells us to *"Delight thyself also in the Lord, and he shall give thee the desires of thine heart." Psalm 37:4*

Having your *spiritual* house in order precedes everything else in your life. Every personal disposition is improved in fellowship with the Lord. Read His Word. Talk to Him. Relish His friendship.

God keeps all His creation in perfect order at all times. Does He help us with our housework? Actually, the Lord prepares the day and makes *everything* easier to deal with if we put Him in charge of it. I haven't learned that lesson permanently, for on a hectic day I may let impatience and panic come in and disturb my calm. We desperately need the Lord, every day of our lives. *"In all thy ways acknowledge him, and he shall direct thy path." Proverbs 3:6*

Delight:   Psalm 36:5   Philippians 4:13

Edna Holmes

# January 11

*"Lo, children are an heritage of the Lord:
and the fruit of the womb is his reward."*
Psalm 127:3

On this date many years ago one of my seven brothers was born. At eleven years of age I remember the two nurses in white moving about in our old rustic farmhouse; *like angels* I thought as they assisted the doctor tending Mother. I helped keep the other children quiet if they awakened in the night.

As a child, I could not have imagined what my little brothers would be in adulthood. All it meant to me then was more little shirts and pants to wash and iron. This one being born that day would distinguish himself in serving the country as a career officer in the military, being a pilot in Vietnam and many other deployments. Wherever he was, he and his wife served God faithfully, being a witness for the Lord Jesus Christ. After retirement from the Army, he would serve as full time minister for a Singles group in a large church, during which he wrote a book, *Every Single Devotional.* He is a noted speaker, author, and publisher today.

My parents were delighted with every one of their ten children. But, more than that, the Bible tells us that *"children are a heritage of the Lord."* God is delighted too! All children are blessed and full of promise in God's sight. Parents may not realize this without the wisdom which God imparts. With love from his parents and discipline as the Word of God teaches, a child can become the person that the Lord created him to be.

Every child is born with a purpose; make sure your children and grandchildren know that. Tell them how God loves them and keep them in Sunday School to learn about Jesus the Savior on their level of understanding. It will be the most rewarding thing you can do for them.

Delight:   Psalm 127:4-5    Psalm 139:14-17

## January 12

*"The ants are a people not strong,*
*yet they prepare their meat in the summer;"*
Proverbs 30:25

And ideal part of personal devotions would be to read a chapter of Proverbs each day. In a month you've read it. Do that each month, and you will find it to be a beneficial habit. It's a book of wisdom.

God again speaks of wisdom and gives us amazing examples in these little creatures He made. They are more than just wise; they are *exceeding* wise. We would do well this first month to look at such good examples and learn from them.

The *ants* are the most common to us. The lesson from them is *preparation.* Being *prepared* takes more stress from our lives than anything else. The main issue of utmost importance is to prepare for our eternity, *the salvation of our souls.* It is such folly to ignore God's love and provision for us to have eternal life with Him.

How is this Gift of God given to one wise enough to seek it? *"That if thou shalt confess with thy mouth the Lord Jesus, and shalt believe in thine heart that God hath raised him from the dead, thou shalt be saved. For with the heart man believeth unto righteousness; and with the mouth confession is made unto salvation."* Rom. 10:9-10

If you believe this truth, your heart has *"believed unto salvation."* It follows that you *"call upon the name of the Lord." "For whosoever shall call upon the name of the Lord shall be saved.* Romans 10:13

Be assured you are prepared for heaven when you claim this promise of God, for He keeps His word! I have those that I lead to Christ personally copy this verse in the front of their Bibles, and write down the day, month and year and a statement: "On this day I prayed and asked Jesus to save me," then sign it. That becomes their *New Birth* certificate. It has been helpful even to adults. *Be prepared!*

Delight:   Romans 6:23   Ephesians 2:4-5

Edna Holmes

# January 13

*"The conies are but a feeble folk,*
*yet make they their houses in the rocks..."*
Proverbs 30:26

Now God points out these little animals, the conies, as examples of wisdom. Why? *They make their houses in the rocks.* They don't run to the rocks for safety; they *dwell* there.

The conies are not like rabbits, though they resemble them, for their legs are short, and they have claw-like feet which are suited to their environment. They live among rocks where predators can't get to them. There is much wisdom employed by these *feeble* creatures.

We learn by the wisdom of the ants to be prepared. God's gift of salvation prepares us for eternity, and also gives grace to live on this earth under his loving care and protection. The feeble conies are able to survive because they stay in the rocks; we also must abide in Christ, the *Rock of Our Salvation.* We are safe on the Rock.

We must apply the wisdom of the little conies. The animals that prey upon them no doubt try to reach them many times. The growls and sounds of the larger animals can be heard prowling about trying to find a way in as the conies hover deep in their rocky shelters. It's frightening, but they are safe. Our enemy, the devil, is on the prowl and will attack when we least expect it.

I Peter 5:8 Be *sober, be vigilant; because your adversary the devil, as a roaring lion, walketh about, seeking whom he may devour."* We dare not wander out from under the umbrella of obedience to the Lord, and the safety of living close to Him in fellowship. The devil cannot penetrate the Rock, our Savior, Jesus Christ.

Take some time to reflect on the many times last year that God protected you. He will again this year. In your notebook of blessings, acknowledge it and thank Him each time for those moments He puts His hand between you and tragedy.

Delight:    Psalm 34:7    Psalm 125:2

# January 14

*"A merry heart doeth good like a medicine."*
Proverbs 17:22

This is a delightful verse, one of my favorites. People with *merry hearts* are happy folks, which are the spice of life for the rest of humanity plodding through this world.

Recently, two dear friends with *merry hearts and ready hugs* gave me an inspiring little card with this Proverbs verse on it. These are older ladies with disabilities who shower love and infectious smiles on everyone they meet. They have made this verse *theirs,* and one of them wrote a poem on the inside of the card, which I'll share in part:

*"We laugh a lot about things that happen to us.*
*The problems we have and how we try to solve them.*
*People tell us we are having too much fun when we are just*
*laughing at how much trouble we are having doing something.*
*Never is there a day that we are without*
*a lot of laughter…"* (Betty Aston)

My friends have discovered a wonderful truth. When we decide we are going to laugh and be happy, it is so good for us that it even affects our health. Researchers have found that even if people shape their lips into a smile, it sends a bit of cheer to their hearts. So even a *fake* smile is worth the effort. Smile often, and it will become a beneficial habit.

Christians have something to be happy about. Even when our hearts are grieved, there is a deep abiding joy because of what we have in Jesus our Savior. We have eternal life, heaven to look forward to, and the loving care of our *Shepherd* as we journey through this life. What more could we ask? Even cheerful smiles make a good testimony for the Lord.

*"Thou wilt shew me the path of life: in thy presence is fullness of joy; at thy right hand there are pleasures forevermore."* Psa. 16:11

Delight:   John 15:11   Isaiah 12:3

Edna Holmes

# January 15

*"Thanks be unto God for his unspeakable gift."*
I Corinthians 9:15

Jesus is the *Gift* of salvation. He becomes ours personally when we repent, *turn*, and call upon his name.

*"For whosoever shall call upon the name of the Lord shall be saved."* Romans 10:13

With that sincerely done, a Christian is born again into the family of God. New Christians hardly know what to do with that precious Gift at first because it takes a *lifetime* to unwrap the Gift, to know more about Him. The wonder, glory, and beauty of our Savior, Jesus Christ, won't be realized fully until we are in heaven with Him, but He allows us to *grow in grace and knowledge* as we study His Word and stay in fellowship with Him. Little by little in spiritual growth, the wrapping comes off, and we see more of His wonderful being, and our Christian character is developed to a greater extent.

Do we understand that He is the Creator? Read Col. 1:16.

To save fallen humanity, hopelessly lost in sin, Jesus the Son of God from all eternity condescended to come into the world by a lowly birth through a virgin, to redeem us with His own life's blood. This old song conveys a sublime message:

> *The Great Creator became our Saviour*
> *And all God's goodness dwelleth in Him*

Have you seen others who remind you of Jesus? They have unwrapped the Gift they possess. Some do not bother to unwrap the Gift; it is concealed lest they be uncomfortable in the company they keep. Jesus is not untouched by such ill treatment. Matthew 10:33 states *"But whosoever shall deny me before men, him will I also deny before my Father which is in heaven."* That is a solemn warning to those holding such a precious Gift as salvation but are ashamed to show it. Unwrap the Gift, and marvel at the beauty and wonder of knowing Jesus more and more.

Delight:   I Corinthians 8:6   Ephesians 3:9

## January 16

*"For the word of God is quick, and powerful,
and sharper than any twoedged sword..."*
Hebrews 4:12

God gave us His Word, wonderfully preserved through the centuries, for our life. By it we know the way of salvation. It teaches us how to live, it protects us when we obey it; it cleanses us from sin, and also keeps us from sin. Our text says *"For the word of God is quick..."* That means it is alive! The Apostle John said in his gospel, *"And the Word was made flesh, and dwelt among us..."*

The closest we can be to Jesus is when we are reading His Word and praying to Him. His Word prompts us to pray, *talk to Him,* when we are prayerfully reading to enrich our own hearts. It prepares us for each day. It gives us instructions on how to live. We will regret it if we neglect to take its wisdom into our minds each day.

*My sister and I would often drive together and go visit our mother in East Texas after our father died. It was my turn to drive and I had the privilege of driving our new car, one with more than the usual gadgets. On this occasion I had to get back for the weekend while my sister would stay awhile longer with Mama. I got up at 4:00 AM and headed out for the three-hour drive home. It was very dark and drizzling rain. I immediately realized the lights were on dim, and I desperately needed them on bright! I pushed every button I could find, and the lights stayed on dim. By the time I had driven two hours in darkness along very lonely stretches of road, I thoroughly regretted not reading the book that came with the car.*

Much more important is the Book that comes with each of us when we are *born again* into God's family. If we know what's in that book of books, it will save us a multitude of problems and heartaches if we obey it. Read it! The road of life can be dark and dreary. We need the *light of God's Word* to show us the way.

Delight:   Psalm 119:130   Psalm 119:105

Edna Holmes

# January 17

*"...let not those that seek thee be
confounded for my sake, O God of Israel."*
Psalm 69:6

In our words, the psalmist is praying: *Lord don't let me be a stumbling block in the way of anyone thinking about his need of salvation.* It would be a tragedy to turn even one away from Christ because of a poor testimony. Christians are not aware of how they are being watched by unbelievers. The Bible says we are a *peculiar people*. What makes us different? Another person--*The Lord Jesus Christ*.

It is the general consensus of the world that Christians don't have any *fun*. Why do they think that? Because we don't frequent the places they do or use cuss words? Or could it be that we wear our Christianity like a heavy pack on our backs? If we give the appearance of *not enjoying* what we have in Christ, no wonder the world labels our way of life dull and boring. *No fun!* Occasionally we need to *check-up* to see if our hearts are spiritually healthy, producing the things that make us happy *and it shows*.

Fruit is growing in us; it is the Holy Spirit's fruit. He came to live in us the moment we were *born again* into God's family. He makes the heart a garden. We are commanded in God's Word to keep our hearts so good fruit can grow. *"But the fruit of the Spirit is love, joy, peace, longsuffering, gentleness, goodness, faith, Meekness, temperance: against such there is no law."* Galatians 6:22-23. These traits never have to be restrained by law in our society. The *opposite* of these, *the works of the flesh,* certainly do!

If your heart has such things flowing out of it, everyone around you will see that you are a happy Christian, whether life is easy at the moment, or you have trials going on. *Smile!* That's the easiest, most encouraging manifestation of a peaceful, happy heart.

Delight:   Psalm 144:15   Isaiah 12:3   John 16:24

Delighting in the Lord

# January 18

*"...and there was a man whose
right hand was withered."*
Luke 6:6

Jesus saw this man when He went into the synagogue to teach the people. He told the man to *"Rise up, and stand forth in the midst."* The man obeyed without question, and soon after Jesus told him to stretch forth his hand. It was restored whole like the other. He must have gone home that day praising God for two good hands now to work and take care of his family. Two good hands!

My older sister had a stroke ten years ago, which greatly impaired the use of her left arm and hand. She had to learn how to do everything with one hand, which was very difficult. To have a *withered* hand is a serious handicap. Equally tragic is the condition of withered *spiritual hands.*

There are many, many Christians who will never lift a finger to serve the Lord in the Church. Usually, a few people do the work. So seldom do some use their hands of service; they become withered. That is discouraging to others in the church family.

When our hearts dry up from a lack of fellowship with the Lord, our hands become withered. The first priority is the Word of God; it is our life! By that we stay close to the Lord, which energizes us for service. We will be eager to serve in some way. Little things are *big* in the Lord's work.

*In the early years of our pastorate, the workload was heavy for both of us. At that time, we had to do everything. A young mother decided she could help me by cooking our family a pot of beans every Monday. She said, "At least I can do that to help." That simple act of kindness was a tremendous blessing to me. Adding a pan of cornbread and very little else made a good meal for us.* I was so grateful.

Delight:   Ecclesiastes 9:10    Psalm 90:17

## January 19

*"Whoso keepeth his mouth and his tongue  
keepeth his soul from troubles."*  
Proverbs 21:23

God would have us keep our mouths, that is, put forth effort to take care of them responsibly as the heart is tended. Why? Our tongues get us into trouble very quickly if we do not stay in control of them. The mouth is connected to the heart for *"out of the abundance of the heart the mouth speaketh."* Matthew 12:34. Whatever we feed into our hearts comes out in our speech.

How can that be done? James tells us the tongue cannot be tamed, and it is full of deadly poison. Chapter 3:8. The only power that can counteract that is God's power applied by His Word and prayer.

Some have no trouble *not talking* in a group or fellowship, while others can't hardly wait to give an opinion. We are all different. But God knows us and gives warning to be heeded about the detriment of the tongue. Marriages, homes, churches, companies, schools, and reputations can be destroyed by the tongue. An old saying is so true, *"Words are like feathers scattered to the wind,"* and you can't gather them back up. We all have wished we could at times!

*"Set a watch, O Lord, before my mouth; keep the door of my lips."* Psalm 141:3

Challenge yourself to be *absolutely* truthful for one week! We are not aware, generally, of how easily falsehood slips into our talk. It's a common way of life in our modern world. It rubs off.

Ask God for power to control the impulsive urge to speak. We cannot recall the words we say, though we may apologize for them many times.

Delight:   Proverbs 15:1   Proverbs 15:23

Delighting in the Lord

# January 20

*"Great is the Lord, and greatly to be praised;
and his greatness is unsearchable."*
Psalm 145:3

The Lord's greatness can never be searched out and fully known. It is too deep and profound for human discovery. The things that will be revealed to us in eternity could not be viewed in our human state. It's thrilling to wonder about it, and just think, we have the *Holy Spirit of our Great God* dwelling in our hearts!

Things experienced in daily life may prompt us to think about God's greatness. Our minds rarely wander higher than that.

*"It was told that early in the discovery of The Grand Canyon that a man rode up to the rim on his horse. He got off and stood spellbound gazing at the grandeur and beauty of that place. His horse's attention was to the ground as it grazed on the grass."*

As the horse had no capacity to appreciate a marvelous site as The Grand Canyon, so we are dull in understanding the greatness of God. We *know* He parted the Red Sea for Israel to pass over, but we didn't see it and can't imagine it. The children of Israel forgot the greatness of it soon afterwards, and they witnessed it!

There is no starting and stopping place in describing God's greatness, but we know it best in His limitless love for all humanity. How could He love us so? That Jesus would condescend to come to earth to redeem us is beyond all understanding. But He did redeem us, *bought us back,* paying the price of sin with His life.

*"For the Son of man is come to seek and to save that which was lost."* Luke 19:10

Search out verses that tell of God's greatness. Focus on that and you will not be easily intimidated by others in this world. We have a great God and Savior Who loves and cares for us.

Delight:    Psalm 145:10    Philippians 2:9-11

Edna Holmes

# January 21

*"Ointment and perfume rejoice the heart."*
Proverbs 27:9

Any day that you have the doldrums—you just can't get up and going—then go put on a dab of perfume! It works wonders for that blah feeling that can hang on and ruin the day.

If you still need a little boost, call a friend that always gives sensible advice. The second part of the text verse says *"so doth the sweetness of a man's friend by hearty counsel."* The perfume delights your senses; a good friend delights your heart. A friend who will share God's Word will encourage you. When that happens, our Lord is so pleased He does something else amazing. Remember that to *fear the Lord* means having awe and reverence for Him that makes one desire to obey Him.

*"Then they that feared the Lord spake often one to another: and the Lord hearkened, and heard it, and a book of remembrance was written before him for them that feared the Lord, and that thought upon his name".* Malachi 3:16

The Lord also is delighted when we speak of Him, and even *think* of Him. *He loves us!* Our Lord has a special book with our words and thoughts of Him recorded for Himself. So, added to your dab of perfume, and a word from a trusted friend, go one step further to make your day wonderful. Write the Lord a little note and tell Him something you are thankful for, and that you love Him. It will go straight to His heart, and He will keep it!

*"And we have known and believed the love that God hath to us, God is love; and he that dwelleth in love dwelleth in God, and God in him."* I John 4:16

That is why He keeps every little *scrap* of love we offer up. Praise His wonderful name!

Delight:    Deuteronomy 6:5    I John 3:1

Delighting in the Lord

# January 22

*"The entrance of thy words giveth light;
it giveth understanding unto the simple."*
Psalm 119:130

God does not speak to us in an audible voice, though sometimes when one gives us advice that saves a multitude of trouble, we say *"the Lord spoke through him."* He does speak to us through His Word. A problem may have you in a fog and you don't know what to do. Prayerfully read the Bible where you have found answers before. He may answer there or direct you to other verses that will give you help. He has clearly told us that His Word *giveth light.* Also, that it gives us *understanding.* We need the Lord's *light* every moment of our lives. Otherwise, our lives would be dull and drab and *colorless.* The realization that light effects color came to me once in the middle of the night.

*Awake in the night, and glancing around the bedroom in the dark, it dawned on me that nothing in the room had color! Though I knew everything had color, there were only dark shadowy shapes. I strained my eyes trying to make out the slightest tint of color around the room. Even the covers on the bed were void of the pretty colors that I knew them to be. Later, I searched out an answer and found out an amazing fact.*

Color: *The sensation produced by the different effects of waves of light striking the retina of the eye. We must have light to see color.*

God's Word sheds light in us when we read it. We see *spiritually* what we could never make out naturally with our own reasoning. The light factor makes our text verse come alive! *The Word goes in, the light comes on*! Jesus gives our lives color and beauty because He is the *Light of the world*, and He abides with us. We should never be wandering in the dark. *Stay in the Light!*

Delight:    II Corinthians 4:6    Psalm 119:105

Edna Holmes

# January 23

*"Examine yourselves, whether ye be in the faith…"*
II Corinthians 13:5

January is a good evaluation time. It better prepares us for the year stretching before us. Certainly, the most important test of all is to *examine ourselves to see if we really are Christians,* or just going through the motions. How is that done?

The Bible tells us the *spiritual birth* brings a definite change.

II Corinthians 5:17 *"Therefore is any man be in Christ, he is a new creature: old things are passed away; behold, all things are become new."*

Has your life changed since you asked Jesus to be your Savior? List some changes on paper where you can look at them. The first for me was the desire to read the Bible and learn all I could about God. I longed to know more about Him. Being a church member did not acquaint me with God; one has to be *born again* before he has any spiritual understanding.

Some *pretend* to be *born again* Christians, putting up a front that looks good. Indifferent Christians may also put up a front, *but God sees what's behind the façade.*

*A lady, walking through her neighborhood, decided to walk in the alleys for a change of scenery. She began to match backyards with houses she had noticed from the street. In the yard of a modest house she'd seen, there were beautiful flowers and a lovely lawn. Then, she came to the backyard of a lovely house she had admired from the street. What a shock! The backyard was a mess of weeds and assorted junk scattered about. The front had hidden the mess in the back.*

What does your *spiritual backyard* look like? There is peace and confidence in one who has nothing to hide in his life. God knows our secrets as well as we do ourselves. Keep a clean and clear conscience.

Delight:   I John 1:7-9    John 14:23

## January 24

*"God is faithful, by whom ye were called
unto the fellowship of his Son Jesus Christ our Lord."*
I Corinthians 1:9

The Lord does not leave us to ourselves to live as Christians. He knows us through and through and has loving patience to deal with our inconsistencies. True to his Word, which cannot be broken, He works in us to *grow us up* as children of God. He can see the *backyards* where we hide the junk, as well as the *front* we put up which looks admirable to people around us. If there is dirt and junk hidden away in our hearts, it will come out sooner or later and show up in the way we live. Sin always exposes its true nature.

I read an illustrative story of a little Indian boy who climbed a high mountain for an endurance test. It was warm at the bottom, but at the peak very cold. He reached the top and saw a poisonous snake shivering on the ground. It said, "Take me back down to the bottom, I'm so cold up here." The boy said "No, I can't do that, you will bite me" to which the snake replied "I wouldn't do that. If you will just carry me back down, I'll be so grateful." The little boy felt sorry for him and put the snake inside his shirt and took him down the mountain where it was warm. As he took the snake from his bosom, it bit him! The boy cried, "You promised you wouldn't bite me", to which the snake replied, **"You knew what I was when you picked me up."**

The world will give us help in rationalizing sin, but in the end, we are the ones who will reap the effects of it. We know that God will faithfully forgive confessed sin, but He *does not* cancel the consequences of it. We must remember that on our journey through this world. Sin will make all kinds of appealing promises, but if you *pick it up*, you will be bitten. Store that truth in your heart.

Delight:    Psalm 119:133    Psalm 119:11

Edna Holmes

# January 25

*"Cast thy bread upon the waters..."*
Ecclesiastes 11:1

The *Bread* we are to cast upon the waters is the *Bread of Life, the Lord Jesus Christ.* A large part of the world has not heard the gospel. It is our responsibility to *cast the Bread, to* fling it out to the world's teeming *billions* before time runs out. The Lord came to this world to *"seek and to save that which was lost."* Luke 19:10. The church now is to *"go into all the world, and preach the gospel."* Mark 16:15. Everyone is responsible to *pray for lost souls, and to support missionaries who do the going part.* That's one way we can "*Cast the Bread."* Also, our daily *manna* gathered for our own spiritual food, should be shared with others at home. *"Ye shall be witnesses..."*

## Cast Thy Bread
*Bread gleaned by your heart and hand,*
*With time and determination to gather,*
*Is rich with promise and strength for the day,*
*And like the manna, can't be hoarded away.*
*Cast thy bread. Multiplied numbers have never been fed.*

Be ready! We never know when that opportunity is going to suddenly be there, and you must seize the moment. Have the Word of God stored in your heart to share at any time. If you cannot think of any verses to share, simply tell about when *you were saved* and how you called on the Lord to save you. You can always do that much!

*Once, during a funeral my husband conducted, I noticed a young woman who seemed touched by the message. At the graveside I led her aside afterwards and told her about salvation. There among the tombstones she asked the Lord to save her soul. She went from the graveyard alive in Christ!*

Delight:   I Peter 3:15   John 6:33-35

Delighting in the Lord

# January 26

*"...for thou hast magnified thy word
above all thy name."*
Psalm 138:2

While preparing for the year ahead, something to rehearse in our minds and hearts is the power of our omnipotent God and the power of His blessed Word. He holds it *above all His name!*

Besides the wisdom we need, instructions for our daily lives, it is the *balm in Gilead* for the troubling things that disturb our heart's peace. One of my soothing scriptures is Proverbs 3:5-6. You know how our minds can race around like a hunted thing when we begin to fret about something. *"Trust in the Lord with all thine heart; and lean not unto thine own understanding. In all thy ways acknowledge him and he shall direct thy paths."* This is a comfortable pillow to sleep on at night.

Our own understanding is faulty. We cannot possibly know all the intricate details or what is going on as God works *all things together for good.* Better to trust Him and wait. The Lord's intentions are always for the good of His children, and He certainly has the power to carry forth His purpose and plans.

*"For I know the thoughts that I think toward you, saith the Lord, thoughts of peace, and not of evil, to give you an expected end."*
He spoke that through Jeremiah 29:11.

Once my daughter and her husband knelt by their baby's crib and claimed that verse as they prayed for that tiny girl to get well. It gave them peace of mind to invoke God's word and trust Him.

The Lord gives us all we need in this life; we have the sure promise of heaven. Think of that! His *unbreakable, all-powerful Word* is ours to read, obey, and rest on. Selah!

Delight:    Jeremiah 29:12-13    Psalm 119:49-50

Edna Holmes

# January 27

*"Where the word of a King is there is power:"*
*Ecclesiastes 8:4*

God can do as He pleases according to His divine purpose; no one can stop Him. His power is His alone and is unapproachable. He can raise a man up and give him a heritage in his family which will last forever. My father and mother were poor farmers, yet raised a family that would make the privileged of the world proud.

*Today many decades ago, another of my seven brothers was born. His life has been an interesting journey. He has many talents and even in his older age he took special training and became a lay pastor for his church, which he has served faithfully for several years. He has experienced the extremes in life, even the loss of his son who was in his prime. But through it all his faith rested in God, and his hope is still bright.*

We had many adventures together growing up. One was enjoying our *penny suckers* Daddy brought to us on Saturdays when he went to town. We sat on the well and dipped our suckers in a bucket of water, licking them slow, enjoying that little treat right down to the stick, making a lifetime memory--*for a penny.*

Though our world has moved into the electronics age, we should still keep simple things in our lives which will make lasting memories for our families. Conversation is almost a lost art and the habit of prayer is diminishing everywhere.

We should read God's Word consistently. There is power in it to guide our lives. Also, have family times together. Pray, read the Bible together and talk about what it means with your children or grandchildren. Let them ask questions and talk about daily issues that are important in their lives. Communication bonds family together.

Delight:   Jeremiah 23:29   Proverbs 31:26-28

## January 28

*"But do thou for me, O God the Lord,
for thy name's sake..."*
Psalm 109:21

Some verses make such a big difference—a help that goes on and on. This verse is a permanent prayer help that came to me. There are things on my prayer list, people or life situations, that I don't know how to pray for. The details are unknown to me, so I use this verse as a prayer. *"Do thou for them Lord...for your name's sake."* I wrote a poem inspired by that verse; it's one of my favorites.

Do Thou for me, Lord.
Help me to recognize and admit my own
Slothful neglect of devotion to You;
To gather my wandering thoughts
As I read your word, and pray;
To make your word a reality in my life:
The Song to sing,
The sword to swing,
The rock to keep me steady.

Do Thou for her, Lord.
Help her sort out thoughts and feelings
That may be churning in her heart.
Give her reassurance in prayer, renew her hope.
Reveal a new precious promise
To her heart from your word:
A song to sing,
A sword to swing,
A rock to keep her steady.

There is no greater help in prayer than the Word of God. It goes straight to our hearts and prompts us to pray. We also have the *power* bound up in the Word to work for us. It's there. *Use it!*

Delight:   Colossians 3:16   Hebrews 4:12

Edna Holmes

# January 29

*"Sing unto him a new song...."*
Psalm 33:3

We should endeavor to learn some *new songs* this year. That are things new and wonderful from God's Word as we read and discover nuggets of truth that thrill our hearts. Others know if we are into God's Word by the *songs we sing*, or what we talk about. We naturally want to share what we discover in His Word when it becomes meaningful to us. It's a *new song to sing.*

If the church choir sang the same song for fifty-two Sundays, people would be wishing they would learn something new. It would be boring if the special singers knew only one or two songs and repeated them every week.

Do we wonder how the Lord may be grieved when we don't read His Word enough to ever learn a new thing for which to praise Him. Of all the thousands of verses in the Bible, we know very few that we can share with someone. We keep singing the *same songs* over and over, and they are good songs; it's just that we stop short by not learning more of God's promises and having *new songs* of praise to sing about Him. In our society, we speak of people talking as *singing.* "They are *singing a different tune now...."*

If you can't actually sing a note of music, you can sing, *that is talk about* the goodness of God, His marvelous grace, and His love that could fill an ocean! Learn that kind of new song. We can all do that.

*I will sing the wondrous story, Of the Christ who died for me*
*How He left His home in glory, For the cross of Calvary.*
F.H.Rowley

Delight:   Psalm 138:4-5   Psalm 149:1

# January 30

*"Behold as the eyes of servants look unto
the hand of their masters…"*
Psalm 123:1-2

Servants were trained to focus on their master, to watch the movement of his hands and obey. Kings and the masters of noble estates did not directly speak to the servants; their hands gave the cue. The servants were compelled to keep their eyes on them at all times. *They were trained to obey without a word.*

The Holy Spirit gives us spiritual insight to detect when God is speaking to us in the issues of our lives. He echoes what God has conveyed to us from His Word about wisdom and discernment.

You may sense a need of caution about a person or situation that comes into your life. It is very wise to heed. We need God's wisdom because we are vulnerable. We want to be helpful and loving and draw others to Christ. There are *con men* who scheme to cheat and rob unsuspecting people all the time. God knows this and will warn us in subtle ways. We must heed and trust Him.

*Pastors have to deal with people who come by asking for money, food, or whatever need they think will sound convincing. My husband had to discern the sincere ones from the con artists who prey on churches. Once a young man called him, stranded at the Airport, needing a safe temporary place to stay. After a second urgent pleading call, my husband got him and brought him to the parsonage. As he walked in the door, I felt a sense of caution, a fleeting thing; I shrugged it off. I should have heeded the warning! He pretended to get saved at church, so he was "in" and settled down to 'freeload' indefinitely. We soon realized the scheme and ended it.* It was a costly experience, yet valuable for future reference.

Delight:   Hebrews 5:14    Proverbs 2:10-11

Edna Holmes

# January 31

*"For she said, If I may touch but
his clothes, I shall be whole."*
Mark 5:28

When this desperate woman heard of Jesus healing the people, I'm sure her hopes soared. What a woman normally deals with a few days out of the month, this lady had been coping with for 12 long years. She had sought help and got none. She *"suffered many things of many physicians, and spent all she had, and was nothing bettered, but rather grew worse."* v. 26

She heard about Jesus and went to Him. He was surrounded by a crowd as usual, but she bravely pushed her way through, determined to at least touch His garment. Her faith was strong though she was weak. She touched Him from behind and was instantly healed! The power that flowed to her from Jesus, *because of her faith*, was also immediately known by the Lord. What a moment it was when Jesus turned to find her in the crowd. The woman fell down at his feet and told him everything. He spoke the words her heart needed to hear.

What a blessed day for this woman. She could put the *filthy rags* out of her house and her life. She would need them no more. No doubt her joy at being *clean again* knew no bounds.

*I have a friend who is so happy in the Lord, she talks about how wonderful He is in every conversation. Knowing Him in salvation and daily fellowship keeps her heart full of gratitude and joy. Over her front door she has a neat little sign that has one word: Forgiven.*

We should have hearts full of joy and thankfulness. Those things may be missing because we won't break through the *crowd* of hindrances to *touch* Jesus. We desperately need Him to restore our spiritual health. He has unlimited help and blessing to give, and *He loves us!* Push through every obstacle and *touch Him, every day.*

Delight:    Psalm 51:10    Ephesians 1:19

## February 1

*"This is my commandment,
That ye love one another, as I have loved you."*
John 15:12

    This month is noted for Valentine's Day. Some call it the *"love"* month. Many hope for a token of someone's love and affection on Valentine's day. One of my treasures is a valentine sent to me by my husband from Japan, then my *pen pal,* in the late *1940's.* I'd never seen one so elaborate. Three years later, I would marry my *valentine* man. I got him, and I've kept the valentine!

    Human love cannot come close to the love of God. We are incapable of unconditional love. We love those who love us back! The vows spoken at the altar of marriage are often forsaken after a short time. But God declares: *"…Yea, I have loved thee with an everlasting love: therefore with lovingkindness have I drawn thee."* Jer. 31:3

    John 3:16 is the ultimate statement of love. It has twenty-five words in it. Counting from the first word, the thirteenth word is Son; counting backward, the thirteenth word is Son. Everything hinges on the Son of God, and by Him God proved his great love for the world of humanity by Calvary. *"For God so loved the world, that he gave his only begotten Son, that whosoever believeth in him should not perish, but have everlasting life."*

    God has provided salvation for all who will believe. Now He has given us the commandment to love. We know what He is saying, but *who can love like God loves?* We can't in ourselves. We must yield our hearts to Him. With God's love, we can show love and kindness to those who are unloved. Send a card to some old person sitting among his or her memories, wishing for a bit of attention.

Delight:    Romans 5:8    Ephesians 3:17-19

Edna Holmes

# February 2

*"He that loveth not knoweth not God; for God is love."*
I John 4:8

That's plain. If we don't have love in our hearts, then God is not there, for *He is Love!* According to God's Word, we have to confess we fall short. If we are saved, the love of God is there, but it isn't obvious unless we yield our hearts to Him. But it is there as stated in Romans 5:5. *"And hope maketh not ashamed; because the love of God is shed abroad in our hearts by the Holy Ghost which is given to us."*

How do we explain the seemingly total lack of love for God and others? Salvation, the greatest treasure, is planted permanently in us. So, what happens that Christians can be so mediocre as examples of God's amazing grace and love?

*My husband, in England, was privileged to visit the Tower of London where the Crown Jewels are on display. In addition to the matchless jewels, the crowns have been worn by generations of kings and queens. Priceless! They are displayed in a vault like room, dimly lighted, with bright lights on the objects of display. Armed guards stand by. People file by and gaze in wonder at the royal jewels.*

Just suppose that the keepers of that place came to work each day and piled their coats, gloves, lunchboxes and other items on top of the display case and just moved them aside enough for the people to get a little glimpse of the magnificent jewels. Unthinkable!

We often times toss bits and pieces of trash into our hearts and minds on top of the priceless Gift of salvation. Be careful of what you read, listen to, watch on TV and the friends that influence you toward the bad instead of good. If it weakens your testimony and obscures the love of God in you, it's trash! Do a sincere heart cleaning with Psalm 51 and pray verse 10. *"Create in me a clean heart, O God; and renew a right spirit within me."* Let God's love sparkle in your life!

Delight:   I John 3:1   John 13:35

# February 3

*"A soft answer turneth away wrath;"*
Proverbs 15:1

Love thrives where a *soft answer* is the rule. The verse also names the opposite, the cause of much heartache, *"...but grievous words stir up anger."* Early in our marriage of sixty-six years, the unspoken rule somehow evolved that we would not call each other derogatory names when we were upset. We never have, and it has been a wonderful factor in our marriage. I didn't know then how simple things such as speaking in a soft tone of voice could be so important in marriage, and with family, your friends, and neighbors. But that's what God says, we can count on it.

We see how Abigail, Nabal's wife, calmed David, the warrior. He and his men had protected Nabal's sheep and shepherds in the fields by night and day. When David requested food for his men in return, Nabal, a very rich man, was irate and mocked David classifying him as a runaway slave! David's temper flared and he marched to the estate to destroy Nabal and everyone else! A servant told Abigail, and she acted quickly to take food and go meet David to appease his anger. She met him, bowed before him, and *spoke softly, as she asked* forgiveness for the ill treatment he had received. She offered the food as a blessing for his hungry men. She spoke a personal blessing for David, which must have melted any anger he had left. *"...but the soul of my lord shall be bound in the bundle of life with the Lord thy God; and the souls of thine enemies, them shall he sling out as out of the middle of a sling."* I Samuel 25:29

She asked David to remember her, and He certainly did. When God's judgment fell, and Nabal died, David soon sent for Abigail to be his wife. Her *soft answer* won the heart of the future king.

Delight:   Proverbs 31:26   Proverbs 15:23

Edna Holmes

# February 4

*"A Virtuous woman is a crown to her husband..."*
Proverbs 12:4

A virtuous woman is known for her moral excellence, worth, right actions, and thinking. The Bible says in Proverbs 31, *"...for her price is far above rubies."* A genuine ruby is one of the most priceless jewels on earth, and very rare. *And so is a virtuous woman!* Any woman *can* have that distinction if she fully surrenders to God and allows Him to develop those traits in her heart. Proverbs holds many helpful hints about beauty for godly women. One season I searched out several of these *beauty secrets* for a Bible Study lesson. The Lord gives encouraging words of advice to help us *be beautiful!*

**Rejoice your heart.** Proverbs 27:9 *"Ointment and perfume rejoice the heart."* Since it does, put a dab on every day! And smile....
**Don't tear the house down!** Proverbs 14:1 *"Every wise woman buildeth her house; but the foolish plucketh it down with her hands."*
**Keep your mouth....shut!** Proverbs 21: 23 *"Whoso keep his mouth and his tongue keepeth his soul from troubles."*
**Correct your children.** Proverbs 29:17 *"Correct thy son, and he shall give thee rest; yea, he shall give delight unto thy soul."* A mother who has unruly children cannot rest outside or inside her home. It is a physical, emotional and mental drain trying to corral children who will not obey. Training must start when they are infants.
**Don't be a tattle-tale.** Proverbs 11:13 *"A talebearer reveleath secrets: but he that is of a faithful spirit concealeth the matter."* Passing gossip around will make your *beauty* vanish quickly. It is also a detriment to listen to a talebearer. They cause such grief and heartache in their wake. Remember that beauty has little to do with the outside appearance. Every woman can be beautiful.

Delight:    Proverbs 31:25    Proverbs 31:30

## February 5

*"Many daughters have done virtuously,
but thou excellest them all."*
Proverbs 31:29

Early in the morning of the day Jeanne got married, she walked into the room where I was sitting. I spoke the first thing that popped into my mind. *"Many daughters have done virtuously, but thou excellest them all."* As I looked at my daughter, all aglow getting ready for the biggest day of her life, I realized how I was going to miss her. She had grown into adulthood as the best friend a mother could ever have in a daughter. So sensible, and she maintained a "soft answer" way of communication. After college she had come home, got a job, then settled down...waiting. She wondered how and where she would meet her future husband if that was what the Lord would have for her life. We discussed it many times sitting on the steps in the evening with our glasses of tea.

That year, before her birthday in July, she prayed a fervent *'let me know something'* prayer to God. She asked Him to give her a rose for her birthday if He had that special someone for her. She told nobody; she knew friends or family would *help God* with the request.

We had a missionary family temporarily living in the mission's house. The lady invited Jeanne and several others of the College and Career Class over for refreshments honoring Jeanne's birthday. When Jeanne went in, she saw a single rose displayed in a Dr. Pepper bottle of water. The lady said *"Jeanne, that's yours! That rose kept waving back and forth outside the kitchen window, so I finally went out and got it!"* No one knew what that meant to my daughter. But something was settled in her heart. She met her husband-to-be a few weeks after that, and in the next year they were married.

Use your privilege of prayer often. Prayer changes things.

Delight:   Matthew 6:6   Matthew 7:7-8

Edna Holmes

# February 6

*"For there is nothing covered, that shall not be revealed; neither hid, that shall not be known.*
Luke 12:2

I won't forget when our son, Louis, brought Jan home from college the first time for us to get to know her. He had met her the first year, and after writing letters over the summer, then more dating at college they knew they were meant for each other. With the weekend visit coming I cleaned house with all my might! Starting at the front, I worked my way through giving each room a spic and span cleaning. I kept putting the trash together and pushing it toward the back door in Louis' room so it would be hidden if they came early. They did! And he brought that lovely girl in the back door of his room to enter the house. They had to step over that pile of trash I had hidden to get in! So much for hiding your dirt...

That illustrates how some Christians tend to keep a clean and polished *upfront* while keeping things concealed that would show what's really in their hearts. Even sinful thoughts can't be concealed for long, for in some unguarded moment they will be verbalized. It is useless for us to think anything is hidden from God though we may easily fool other people for a while.

*"For God will bring every work into judgment, with every secret thing, whether it be good, or whether it be bad."* Ecclesiastes 12:14

The best habit we can have is keeping our sins confessed *up to date*. None should be carried over to the next day. In that way we shall keep our consciences clean and clear. It is stressful to hide sin. The Devil will torment you with it. Jesus will forgive you and give you peace again, and how quickly the burden and guilt of sin melts away when we pray for forgiveness. The power in the blood of Jesus never ceases to amaze me. It's the *only remedy* for sin. Praise His name!

Delight:   Proverbs 28:13   I John 1:9

Delighting in the Lord

# February 7

*"My little children, let us not love in word,
neither in tongue; but in deed and in truth."*
1 John 3:18

We all like to hear words of *love* spoken to us, but God says that is not enough. His Word tells us to follow the words with proof in our actions. For some people, especially men, it is easier to do the deeds than to speak words of love. That is frustrating to wives, but we must consider that the raising and temperament of a man conditions him to be as he is. Some are never going to display much emotion, but they would give you the moon if they could reach it!

*I read of a wife who began to notice that her husband, a very quiet man, seemed be frustrated at every meal when he had to ask someone to pass the salt. So she got a set of individual salt and pepper shakers, and placed them directly in front of his plate. That's the first time she saw him react with emotion as he acknowledged his gratitude for that little act of kindness. That should stir our hearts when we think of little things we can do to make others happy, beginning at home.*

God's Word is full of love expressed for us; His actions also equal His Words. Calvary is the strongest display of love ever known as God gave Jesus to die for us. *He paid the "wages of sin" so that we could be saved and live forever in eternity with Him.* What love!

We should not only say we love the Lord; we should prove it. Pray each day, *"Lord, how can I serve you today?"* God's work takes many forms; be ready to show your love in any way. Take a treat to a lonely, shut-in elderly person; send a cheerful card to someone who's ill; take time to visit a prospect, and with opportunity, witness for the Lord. Greet visitors at church, making them welcome. *Show your love for God!* He will bless you indeed.

Delight:    James 1:22    I John 4:10-11

Edna Holmes

# February 8

*"But one thing is needful: and Mary hath chosen
that good part, which shall not be taken away from her."*
Luke 10:42

Mary loved her Savior, the Lord Jesus Christ. When she was near Him, she paid no attention to anything else; she only wanted to hear what Jesus had to say. Her family loved Jesus and often had Him and the disciples in their home. When Jesus was there, she sat at His feet and listened to Him talk. Whatever He said was music to her ears. Her sister, Martha, loved Jesus too, but she was also a busy person with things she felt had to be done. She complained to Jesus that Mary wasn't helping prepare a meal, but Jesus took Mary's part! He said Mary had chosen *the good part* which would not be taken away from her. What was the good part? It was what she gained by sitting at Jesus' feet and hearing His words. It was a great privilege to hear Him, and Mary gave up every other activity so she could do it. She had more spiritual knowledge because of her devotion. It was she who anointed His body for burial. When Judas objected to the expense of it, Jesus rebuked him:

*"Then said Jesus, Let her alone: against the day of my burying hath she kept this. For the poor always ye have with you; but me ye have not always."* John 12:7-8

Is it important to us to sit at the Lord's feet at our devotion time and take in His words? Do we guard that time, putting Jesus first? Time and attention to God's Word, and fellowship with our Lord is the most valuable time of our day. If we could only grasp that fact. He makes everything work *for us*. It amazes me when I am aware of what God is doing to smooth the way. Be a Mary sort of person. True, the work has to be done, but Jesus in turn will lighten your load when you put Him first. Try it!

Delight:   John 12:3   I Peter 1:8

# February 9

*"This is the day which the Lord has made;
we will rejoice and be glad in it."*
Psalm 118:24

It was this day in the year 1891, well over 100 years ago that the Weather Bureau was established. Of course, in that era, they didn't have the technology that is in place today. Now the information we get is amazing in its scope. But men have always been able to discern in part about weather. The Lord mentions it in the scriptures.

*"...When it is evening, ye say, it will be fair weather: for the sky is red."* Matthew 16:2

There are sayings about life tied to the idea of predicting weather, such as, "You *can tell how the wind's blowing in that situation.*" "*There's a storm brewing at their house!*" "*There's a flood of trouble coming at work.*"

God's Word instructs us so that our lives can be predicted. He told the children of Israel, as they passed over into the promised land, what their obedience to Him would do. It happened just as He said. The winds *blew softly* as they obeyed God for a few generations, then they gradually turned to idol worship imitating the inhabitants of the land before them. That's when the *storm clouds* gathered, and the floods of judgment eventually came upon them just as God said it would.

Obedience to God brings countless blessings—*showers of blessings!* If we *disobey* His Word, there will be a *dark cloud* hover over our lives and move with us wherever we go, always uneasy, fearing the *winds of adversity* that can blow us away. Spiritual weather is predictable and more important than the weather in each day. We can *rejoice and be glad* every day with the blessings of God raining down on us. Selah!

Delight:   Psalm 68:19   Deuteronomy 28:1-14

Edna Holmes

# February 10

*"Put on the whole armour of God, that ye may
be able to stand against the wiles of the devil."*
Ephesians 6:11

My husband is a Korean War Veteran. He often speaks at their events. We attended a meeting recently where he and others spoke of their experiences in the war. It was informative for all of us and therapeutic for the veterans. War veterans have unique stories to tell, for there is nothing like that experience which leaves a permanent impression in the minds and hearts of those soldiers.

I was reminded of the constant *spiritual warfare* Christians are engaged in from the day they become children of God. Older mature Christians can tell a lot about that war. They have learned to use our weapon, the Word of God, and can tell how the Word gave them the victory in major battles. One who fortifies himself with the scriptures has protection which nothing else can equal.

*My husband related to me how the soldiers were taught and drilled to know every little detail about their weapons and to keep them clean because their lives depended on it. They had to know how to take their rifles apart, and put them back together...in the dark, or blindfolded! It was crucial for their survival.*

The Word of God is our weapon. We must learn it and store it in our hearts for times when we will have to apply it when the way is dark. The devil often attacks us in a totally unexpected way.

*"For the word of God is quick, and powerful, and sharper than any twoedged sword..."* Hebrews 4:12

The Word of God is the most powerful weapon on earth; it rescued us from darkness and brought us out into the light of salvation. Now it protects us. We need its wisdom and strength for every day of our lives.

Delight:   Colossians 1:13   Psalm 119:11

Delighting in the Lord

# February 11

*"...and is a discerner of the thoughts and intents of the heart."*
Hebrews 4:12

You will remember verses in the Bible that have done something for you, personally. You had anxiety, fears, or were puzzled about a situation. You prayed that God would show you something from the Word to help you. The key is to open the Bible and read it where you have been reading each day, or in some of your favorite passages. If I don't know where to start, I graze through verses I've marked at other times when they spoke to my heart. You must be in it before God *can show you what's there for you.*

*One night, in our pastorate years, I could not sleep because a resentful attitude was stirring around in my mind and took both peace and sleep from me. Finally, I got up and went to the living room, picked up my Bible and told the Lord I was miserable; that I had taught women how that answers to problems of the heart are in God's Word, yet I had not personally experienced it myself. That's what my pastor's wife had taught me. I needed to know if it was really true. I started reading Psalm 119. There are 176 verses in it, that psalm being the longest chapter in the Bible. I had to read to verse 133 before peace flowed into my heart. Blessed relief!*

**"Order my steps in thy word: and let not any iniquity have dominion over me."** That verse became my first *wake-up* verse. I have more now, but it's a favorite because it gave me a victory that was sweet indeed, from misery of mind to perfect peace. I repeat a *wake-up* verse as I get out of bed. It's so important to put scripture in our minds the first thing. It's good ammunition for the spiritual warfare. Be armed early!

Delight:     Psalm 119:18     Psalm 119:49-50

Edna Holmes

# February 12

*"All nations before him are as nothing..."*
Isaiah 40:17

That verse is a little startling to us. God *is not* impressed with human governments and politics. His interest is in the souls of men and His *born again* children on earth. He works His sovereign will and purpose in the affairs of men, and down through history has chosen those who seem less qualified to lead nations during crucial times. Later, history would show such leaders were divinely appointed.

Such a man was Abraham Lincoln, who was born on this day in 1809. You will see it on the calendar. He led our nation during the Civil War when, as a result, slavery was abolished. He was a praying man and was known to confess that he was *driven to his knees* because he did not know what to do in difficult situations. He was a great man because he depended on his great God to direct him.

We are troubled because of the condition of the world, our nation, and society, which has sunk to a new low morally. It will comfort us if we search God's Word for verses that speak of His greatness and sovereign power over this universe. That will calm our minds that can so easily work up to a panic.

As we learn and grow, scriptures we discover in a time of need are personalized. We get a collection of favorites. Proverbs 3:5-6 is among mine. *"Trust in the Lord with all thine heart; and lean not unto thine own understanding. In all thy ways acknowledge him, and he shall direct thy paths."* That means trust God, because our understanding about everything is limited. *God sees the whole picture;* we only see a little corner. I will acknowledge that He is capable and leave it all in His hands. That gives me peace of mind. *Continual trust in God is the way of happiness in this world.*

Delight:    Psalm 104:1    Deuteronomy 3:24

# February 13

*"And patience, experience; and experience, hope:"*
Romans 5:4

We have heard it said, *"Experience is the best teacher."* It is true. Whatever we experience makes an indelible impression on us not easily forgotten. Those who have experience in any area of life can speak with credibility on the subject. When we patiently endure trials, it will yield us valuable *experience,* which also builds up strong *hope* for future difficulties sure to come. Though we do not have pleasure at the thought of it, trials often start a cycle of learning and growing. There are also humorous experiences in life which teach little practical things and make us smile.

My older sister gained much in experience raising four sons. When *my* son started to school, that first day I dressed him up like a catalog model, putting a long-sleeved shirt over his little tee-shirt underneath. The weather was too warm for long sleeves, but I wanted my little boy to wear his new clothes on that first day. My sister told me he would come home that afternoon dragging his shirt behind him. With experience, she predicted it exactly the way it was. Louis, six years old, walked home dragging his pretty new shirt behind him on the sidewalk!

Those *experienced* in spiritual growth have learned valuable lessons. They can serve God well by helping those younger in the faith. They can go back over the trail and encourage others along. There is a modern little saying alluding to experience: *been there, done that!* When I talk to a young pastor's wife just starting out in a pastorate, I'm qualified to answer some questions because I've *been there, done that.* Experience is a wonderful teacher. Use yours wisely.

Delight:     Galatians 6:10     II Peter 3:18

Edna Holmes

# February 14

*"Pray without ceasing."*
I Thessalonians 5:17

How can one do as that verse says? I soon learned the secret. When you communicate with God early in the day, the attitude of prayer is established in your heart. You pray without words, as your thoughts go to God throughout the day. He reads the thoughts and intents of the heart. That's what is important. What we desire may not come out in the words we say. But the Holy Spirit helps us pray. Romans 8:26 *"Likewise the Spirit also helpeth our infirmities: for we know not what we should pray for as we ought: but the Spirit itself maketh intercession for us with groanings that cannot be uttered."*

We prayed for my husband's cousin, eighty years old, for over fifty years! He lives in another state far from us, and we rarely see him. Much of it was that silent prayer from the heart, for we had the desire fresh in our hearts all the time, a burden for his soul. Finally, my husband sent him a gospel message on a CD and the Lord used that to direct his interest to the gospel. He started going to church and in a short while, was saved! Nothing is more thrilling than for a soul to be saved that you have personally witnessed to or prayed for.

If we can't do another thing else, prayer can be our labor of love for the Lord. I knew an elderly saint, living in a nursing home, who labored in prayer for her church and pastor. She was sorely missed when she passed on, *for there is power in prayer*! As my husband and I have moved into the elderly bracket, I've developed a way I can keep up a consistent prayer life to support the Lord's work.

I keep a *prayer list* which is updated every month. It blesses my heart to mark off answers and add new requests as needed. I can't work as I used to, but I can *pray and write devotionals!* PTL!

Delight:   Matthew 7:7   Luke 18:1

# February 15

*"...that ye should follow his steps."*
I Peter 2:21

In the days after my father died, Mother discovered his footsteps in their garden. She followed his footsteps around each day until rain came and washed them away. She felt close to him while she could see where he walked. It comforted her heart.

The text verse further tells us that Jesus is our example. He walked in this world, was misunderstood, hated, and was finally crucified to redeem us from the curse of sin. He bore it all patiently, with His heart full of love. Now we are to *walk in His steps* and be a light in this world for His honor and glory. The safest, most blessed place we can be is in the Light! Jesus is the Light of the world.

*"Then spake Jesus unto them, saying, I am the light of the world: he that followeth me shall not walk in darkness, but shall have the light of life."* John 8:12

As we walk through life in this world, we can easily follow the steps of Jesus. He won't lead us into dark places of sin. He walks the *high road* of righteousness, never the *low road* of immorality. With every plan and intention of your heart, if you can't see His steps to follow, then turn back! Don't go where He is not leading you. Keep a faithful eye reading His Word to see His will and way for you. Focus on Jesus alone, and you will never go astray.

Jesus tells us who is going to follow: His sheep! *"My sheep hear my voice, and I know them, and they follow me."* John 10:27 This is a *blessed assurance* verse of scripture. Do we *know* the voice of Jesus? Do we answer when He calls us? If we lag behind and stray off the path, there can only be trouble for us down the road. Stay close in fellowship with the Lord. Whatever He speaks to your heart, listen! Wherever He leads you, He will take care of you.

Delight:   Ephesians 5:2   Ephesians 4:1

Edna Holmes

# February 16

*"I will praise thee; for I am
fearfully and wonderfully made..."*
Psalm 139:14

We aren't aware of how our bodies function, unless we have aches and pains. That they are *"fearfully and wonderfully made"* isn't in our minds. We take it for granted, as we do the wonders of the universe and our amazing planet God made for man to inhabit.

Recently, as I waited my turn with the dental hygienist, it occurred to me that we are indeed *fearfully and wonderfully made.* The human body is so complex; every part needs a doctor in that particular field of study to take care of it medically. My podiatrist cannot fix my teeth; he spent years studying the feet! A cardiologist cannot fill a tooth cavity; he only deals with the function of the heart. Just think of the various kinds of medical people it takes to oversee our health in a lifetime. Amazingly, out of the dust of the earth, God made a human body so wonderful, so complex, it can never be fully understood by those who spend a lifetime studying it. We should pause and give thought to the wonder of our Creator who made us.

God's love is the greatest power in the universe. He made us in the beginning, and because He had set his love on us, He planned our redemption from sin before He formed Adam out of those particles of *dust* from the ground!

*"According as he hath chosen us in him before the foundation of the world, that we should be holy and without blame before him in love."* Ephesians 1:4

God loves us so much He sent Jesus to die for us! *Jesus, the Son of God!* Have you asked Him to save you? *He will! God loves you.*

Delight:   Romans 10:9-10, 13     Ephesians 2:5

Delighting in the Lord

# February 17

*"And whosoever shall give...a cup of cold water
only in the name of a disciple..."*
Matthew 10:42

This year could be your *"only"* year. It is little things that make a big difference in our lives, and with little things we can have influence as Christians. Here are some *little things* which seem big and special to the recipients of their blessing.

*Only* a few minutes with the Lord each day will do wonders.
*Only* a sincere little prayer can lift a load big as a mountain.
*Only* a few words can encourage another. *Always be positive!*
*Only* a smile can make someone feel special. *Practice smiling.*
*Only a* handshake can say *'welcome'* to a visitor. *With a smile.*
*Only* a greeting card can cheer up or comfort another. *Today!*
*Only* a little attention will make a big difference for someone.
The list of *only* things could go on and on. Make up your own and determine to make a difference this year by utilizing the little *only* things that are usually considered to be insignificant.

A very important one on the list is our *words!* Job 6:25 states *"How forcible are right words!"* Forcible means showing *force; strong; effective and convincing.* That is speaking *softly, or loudly.* Remember when someone spoke a little word to you that encouraged you? Try to say a positive, even complimentary word to someone every day. If you *think* it, then a word fitly spoken of it is being honest before God and that person. It is not flattery. There are a few *beautiful* people in this world, but most of us are in the common field as far as appearance goes. *Only* a little comment may give a lasting good impression.

The most *forcible* word is God's Word. Have it in your heart and mind to bless others when you have time for *only a word.*

Delight:    Psalm 119:172    Proverbs 25:11

Edna Holmes

# February 18

*"How forcible are right words!"*
Job 6:25

Continuing our discussion of *"only"* things that make all the difference in the lives of people, I'm reminded of the joy and encouragement our Church ladies gave missionaries by sending them cards for their birthdays, to just cheer them up. Our Church gave monthly support to more than seventy missionary families. Many were so happy to get a greeting card, they sometimes sent back a *'thank you'* card in return.

*Forcible right words* are plain and easy to be understood. Everyone's ears perk up at these words—*I love you.* That thrills the hearts of those who hear them spoken to them personally. The human heart craves love. It's only a little thing for us to open our hearts and let some love out in a spoken word.

Other *forcible right* words are: Please; Thank you; May I help? Excuse me; You look nice today; I'll pray for you; You did okay; Hang in there; You're a blessing! Of course, none are so forcible and right as the Word of God which should be present in our hearts to flavor all our communication with others. At every opportunity, let it flow out into your conversation to bless others. Only little things, and *forcible right words,* make the most impact. Anyone can do little things.

*"Only a handclasp, firm and true, Yet it gives me hope—and there are so few. Only a phone call across the miles; Someone remembered—someone smiles. Only an arm around my shoulder, Yet it means so much as one gets older. Only a letter from far away, But it says I'm loved—Hooray! Only a smile on a busy street, yet it shines like a beacon from some high peak. My "onlies" are many and when I am blue, I count them and for each pray "May God Bless You!"*

Delight:   Matthew 5:16   Galatians 6:10

# February 19

*"They that observe lying vanities
forsake their own mercies."*
Jonah 2:6

Jonah believed a lie. He thought he could out-maneuver God and disobey. He *observed lying vanities*, his own thoughts and plans, and got into a whale of a lot of trouble. Our own *lying vanities*, or prideful thoughts, can affect us in such a way that we are inclined toward strong delusions. By that we *forsake our own mercies.* God does not bless His children for disobedience.

*Early one morning after exercise walking at the mall before open hours, I came out the little side door of the huge glass front of the building. A little bird was lying on the ground as though it was asleep, but obviously it had flown headlong into those high glass windows, which reflected the sky and clouds, and perished from the blow. The reflection looked real, though it was an illusion.*

I was reminded of the *lying vanities* which crop up in our lives to tempt us off the path of obedience. If we don't practice discernment and the wisdom that God shows us in His Word, we too can be drawn away by a *lying vanity*. That is, "a*nything or act that is vain, futile, or worthless."*

Our society today is beset by *con people* and *scammers* who prey on others with *lying vanity* promises. They are experts, and ordinary citizens are fooled by subtle schemes they use to rob them of their money. *And they fork it over willingly!* They have been deceived into observing a *lying vanity*. Someone has wisely said, "If it sounds too good to be true, it isn't." God gave us His Word; it's true! Believe it and be saved, and then grow in grace and knowledge of His Word. His words and wisdom will protect you from lying vanities as you listen and obey.

Delight:    Psalm 31:6    James 1:5

Edna Holmes

# February 20

*"...for the things which are seen are temporal;*
*but the things which are not seen are eternal."*
II Corinthians 4:18

In a cartoon in the paper, a little boy had built a very elaborate sandcastle on the beach. It began to rain slowly, then escalated to a downpour while he sat helplessly watching his work of art melt away to nothing. He said, "There's a lesson to be learned here somewhere, but I don't know what it is."

We know. Our text verse tells us that everything we can *see* is temporal. Even our own bodies. The soul is saved and destined for heaven, but the body is going back to the dust where it came from. So the things we can see, are temporal. All will perish eventually.

But things we *can't see* are eternal. We can see *effects* but not the things themselves. *The new birth is the greatest thing on earth.* It is God's plan to save men from hell and give them eternal life. *We can't see it*, but when it takes place, lives are changed.

Many people prefer religion with elaborate buildings to worship in, and religious men dressed in pious garb. Christianity is simple, however, and that is why Christ was rejected when He came. What He brought to mankind was *the real thing*. He took on Him the form of a servant; yet He was and is the eternal Son of God. All man's religious doing, the sacrifice of animals, and strict rules of the law, were cancelled when Jesus said, *"It is finished."* He paid for our sins, so eternal life, *which is invisible,* is assured for every believer in Christ.

Many people stumble over preaching where a man raises his voice to proclaim the Word of God. But the Bible says that God chose *"the foolishness of preaching to save them that believe."*

Delight:     Matthew 6:33     II Timothy 1:10

## February 21

*"And walk in love, as Christ also hath
loved us, and given himself for us..."*
Ephesians 5:2

There is a unique kind of power and persuasion in love. The scriptures describe love to us, and yet it cannot really be understood until we have a demonstration of love. Our first understanding of love comes from God Himself. *"For God so loved the world that he gave his only begotten Son, that whosoever believeth in him should not perish, but have everlasting life."* John 3:16

Love *gives...and gives...and gives.* Our gratitude should overflow our hearts as God pours His bounty into our lives every day!

*"Blessed be the Lord, who daily loadeth us with benefits, even the God of our salvation. Selah"* Psalm 68:19

Our second understanding of love comes from others who love us. That is family, friends, our spouses etc.

*We attended the funeral of a sister-in-law where I observed the power and effects of love. This woman was marginal on the things that matter to people, physically and mentally. She had taken voice lessons, and had a nice singing voice, but that seemed to be all she possessed that might get her some respect, because of her handicap of being rather slow. But she had a loving heart! She loved people, and when she loved them long enough, they began to love her back.*

There were people at her funeral from all walks of life, and many beautiful flowers overflowed the place. *Amazing!* She had touched so many with her heart full of love. It inspired me to pray for God's love to fill my heart anew. We must stay in fellowship with the Lord Who gives us love. If it dwindles, our circle of people we love shrinks. We must reach out and touch the lives of others with kindness and love.

Delight:   I Thessalonians 3:12   John 15:12

Edna Holmes

# February 22

*"And the tables were the work of God,
and the writing was the writing of God..."*
Exodus 32:16

The Ten Commandments are fundamental laws for all mankind, though they were given through Moses to the Jewish nation initially. We find in our own country that when the Ten Commandments were removed from many public places and schools, lawlessness came in. Many tragedies have followed in recent years.

*I. Thou shalt have no other gods before me.*
*II. Thou shalt not make unto thee any graven images.*
*III. Thou shalt not take the name of the Lord thy God in vain.*
*IV. Remember the Sabbath day, to keep it holy.*
*V. Honor they father and mother.*
*VI. Thou shalt not kill.*
*VII. Thou shalt not commit adultery.*
*VIII. Thou shalt not steal.*
*IX. Thou shalt not bear false witness.*
*X. Thou shalt not covet.*

It is simple enough to understand. If God is not number one in our lives; we need to get rid of an *"idol."* We are not to set up any images of worship. We are not to use God's name loosely...it is disrespectful and unholy! The Sabbath turned to Sunday for us, as Jesus rose from the grave on the first day of the week. And a sweet promise goes with honoring our parents. *"It will be well with thee..."* Ephesians 6:3. Prisons are full of people who ignored, *"Thou shalt not kill."* And families are destroyed because of the sin of adultery. Don't steal! We all have to hang onto our purses in public. Don't lie! It's a way of life now in this world. Be content with what you have. It's the way of happiness. Only God could devise The Ten Commandments.

Delight:   Deuteronomy 6:5    John 14:23

Delighting in the Lord

# February 23

*"The Lord will perfect that which concerneth me."*
Psalm 138:8

We all may wonder at times if we are fulfilling our destiny, what God intended for us to accomplish in life, or if we have missed our calling. That depends on our yielding our lives to Him, holding nothing back. To *perfect* is to *complete in all respects.* God will do that and more. There is no limit to what a person can accomplish in the power and blessing of the Lord.

*On this day many years ago another of my siblings was born and, much to my surprise, it was a little sister that I'd longed for since I was big enough to realize all I had was brothers! The family was so happy about it, and she was a beautiful little girl. Our mother got a rocking chair, upholstered in pink satin, to rock this little prized baby. That chair looked rather out of place in our old rustic farmhouse, but it brightened things up.*

My sister grew up and became a dedicated school teacher. She is one of the best and loves that work. In fulfilling her destiny, she has helped to educate many children, many now grown who respect and honor her at every opportunity. She still thrives on teaching. God has *completed in all respects* the things that concerned her, her desires and goals for her life.

If you are a child of God, He is concerned about the things of your life. Consult Him today on the desires of you heart and the things you long to accomplish. Doesn't He tell us that He is *"able to do exceeding abundantly above all that we ask or think, according to the power that worketh in us."* Ephesians 3:20.  By His Holy Spirit in us, we have power available in our lives that we never think about. Jesus is our *Counselor*. Sit down with Him today and let Him search your heart to see what you *really* want, and ask Him to *perfect* it.

Delight:    Ephesians 5:17    Psalm 31:19

Edna Holmes

# February 24

*"Wherefore be ye not unwise, but understanding
what the will of the Lord is."*
Ephesians 5:17

Discernment is an advantageous quality to possess. We get it from God's Word and close fellowship with the Lord. The Holy Spirit gives us *insight,* which is the same as discernment. That is viewing things with understanding, such as circumstances, situations, other people, or one's self.

God is infinitely wise, and He tells us in James 1:5 *"If any of you lack wisdom, let him ask of God, that giveth to all men liberally, and upbraideth not; and it shall be given him."* He won't *chide us* because we haven't asked before; He just lovingly invites us to come ask for wisdom when we don't know what to do.

The important thing to discern is whether something is *good or evil.* The Word is strict because God is protective of us. For example, it makes perfect sense not to commit adultery; it destroys everything good in a person's life, starting with the family. The happiest one in any adulterous affair is the devil! If you are tempted, *stop and think of the consequences.*

I read of a pastor who was led to preach on the Ten Commandments. Each Sunday he preached on one, going down the list. When he came to *Thou shalt not commit adultery,* he protested to the Lord that the people did not need that, and he wanted to skip it. The Lord refused to let him off, and he reluctantly preached a powerful message on the evils of adultery. The following week, a young woman spoke to him privately and said *"Pastor, I'd made up my mind to give in to an affair, but Sunday your preaching brought conviction and good sense to my heart. That message kept me from sin and ruining my life!"* God protects us with *"Thou shalt nots"!*

Delight:   Psalm 119:9-11    Psalm 119:130

## February 25

*"As we have therefore opportunity, let us do good unto
all men, especially...of the household of faith."*
Galatians 6:10

The church is a family. Members can bring a lot of happiness to each other by displaying love and kindness. I encouraged the women of our church to pray for one another. In praying for someone, you are likely to feel inclined to minister to that person occasionally. As the Pastor's wife, whatever I could do to be a blessing to them, was done for everyone. My favorite thing was to write appreciative notes on their birthdays. Everyone likes personal mail, *handwritten!* They were so wonderfully generous and kind to me.

In over four decades in the pastorate, many individuals did things to help me in various ways which made a permanent impact on my life and ministry. One lady, who qualified as a professional seamstress, helped me tremendously to improve my sewing. My garments looked so homemade; everyone could identify them as such. But after she gave me some advice on technique and other practical helpful hints, my work was greatly improved. It was a big help when our daughter went to college because I made a lot of her clothing. I've always felt thankful that Joy helped me to become a better seamstress.

Ask the Lord how that you may show love and concern for those of your church, extended family, neighbors, or *anyone* of your acquaintance. So many long for a little attention and love.

Phone calls, letters, cards, and best of all, a *personal visit* once in a while are all excellent ways to bless someone else. Ask the Lord! He knows what would bring happiness to everyone you know.

Delight:   John 15:12    Ephesians 2:10

Edna Holmes

# February 26

*"A time to get, and a time to lose;
a time to keep, and a time to cast away."*
Ecclesiastes 3:6

On the matter of salvation, the *time to get* is urgent. Now! *"...behold, now is the accepted time; behold, now is the day of salvation."* II Corinthians 6:2. If you are not a Christian, stop and settle your eternal destiny now, today! Call upon the name of the Lord without delay. *"For whosoever shall call upon the name of the Lord shall be saved."* Romans 10:13.

It is also *time to lose* the world's influence over our lives. We have a world of evil at our fingertips. It will take control of mind and body unless we put up a fight! Prayer and the *Sword of the Spirit, the Word of God,* is our protection. Teaching children *from infancy* will sow the Good Seed in their hearts which takes root and stays there, though it may lie dormant for years. Men who were Prisoners of War have said they recalled verses they'd learned as children in Sunday School, and it comforted them and helped them to stay sane during the time of indescribable mental anguish and physical suffering. Take heart! The Word of God is powerful. By it you can *lose* the world's influence.

There are things *to keep*. One is *perspective*, the ability to see things in their true light—what is worthwhile and what is not. About disturbing things or situations, keep this motto in mind: *In view of eternity, what does it matter?* God is in charge of time and eternity. Whatever it is will work out ultimately for your good, if you love God. That's the qualification. Do you love God? *Re: Romans 8:28*

*Cast away hindering things, both good and bad, if it's in your power to do so.* Whatever keeps us from being faithful should be *cast away*. The Bible tells us to use time wisely so that we have plenty with which to serve God, and have a full, happy life.

Delight:   Ephesians 3:17-19   Ephesians 5:15-16

## February 27

*"...he is like unto a man beholding his face in a glass:"*
James 1:23

God's Word is referred to as a *looking glass,* or mirror. God does not waste words or meaning. The Bible is a miraculous book which does reveal to us what we look like...*to God!* That brings conviction to our hearts if we accept the truth God shows us in the *mirror, His Word,* and repentance follows.

We use a mirror every day to make ourselves acceptable even if we aren't going out. A mirror is vital, and absolutely necessary for us to have peace about our physical appearance. However, our mirrors reflect only the present moment.

God's mirror is *supernatural* and reflects my *PAST.* Every time I read my Bible, I see scriptures that I've marked because God did something special for me at that time. He delivered me from trouble; He enlightened me about a situation; He gave me counsel; He forgave my sins, as He promised in His Word. My heart fills up with fresh gratitude when I look in God's mirror and review the past.

God's Word, His *mirror,* reflects my *PRESENT* time, and exactly what I need for each day to fight a good fight! Spiritual Warfare faces us every waking minute. The scriptures are food, water, and the chief weapon for my soul to make me fit for battle. We can *win every battle* if we will faithfully look into the mirror of God's Word to see what God has for us to use for the day.

God's mirror of His Word also shows us our *FUTURE.* Read Revelation chapter 21 and anticipate the future! That became the most blessed comfort to an elderly lady that I read to in her last few months of terminal illness. She knew little about the Bible, and her heart was filled with joy to find out what was waiting after death.

Look in the mirror every day and do what needs to be done. Then look in *God's mirror* and fix your heart for the day.

Delight:   Psalm 119:130   James 1:23-25

Edna Holmes

# February 28

*"Let the words of my mouth and the meditation  
of my heart, be acceptable in thy sight, O Lord,  
my strength, and my redeemer."*  
Psalm 19:14

This is the *wake-up* verse I usually add in my devotional book when I autograph it. I have several, but this is a favorite that I repeat when I get up every morning. Nothing gets you set for the day better than running a verse of scripture through your mind. That is good preparation for spiritual warfare that you will be compelled to engage in the moment you are fully awake. The *wake-up* verse habit will give you an edge. What we say, and think about constantly, has everything to do with our spiritual condition.

*"A good man out of the good treasure of his heart bringeth forth that which is good; and an evil man out of the evil treasure of his heart bringeth forth that which is evil; for of the abundance of the heart his mouth speaketh."* Luke 6:45

Our words are just a tell-tale sign of what is going on in the depths of us. Once when I was bitter and resentful about a situation, I just talked on and on about it to my friend, who patiently endured. Later, when my heart was again right with God, I was grieved to think how I sounded rehashing things, analyzing, and rerunning the issues like a broken record through my mind and out of my mouth! I'd lost my focus on the Lord who can take care of all our problems and set my attention on the problem making it the priority in my thoughts.

Remember, the meditation of our hearts is our *thoughts.* That stays in the safe zone if we establish the Word of God as our priority to think about. When a verse speaks to your heart, put *Selah* beside it to designate it for meditation...thinking on it. On the next page we will see exactly *how* we should think.

Delight:    Matthew 15:18    Romans 10:10

# February 29

*"For as he thinketh in his heart, so is he..."*
Proverbs 23:7

Since our thoughts *rule the day*, to learn some verses in the Bible to run to for help is vitally important. Spiritual warfare takes place in the mind! We are not grappling with a tangible enemy, but one who is the Prince of the Power of the air! Satan is powerful and only God can overpower him. He gives us our ammunition to combat the enemy who will take control of our thoughts if we are unarmed.

The Lord has the Apostle Paul insert an awesome verse to help us with our thoughts. Philippians 4:8. I printed it on a card and taped it to my bookcase where I do my daily reading. A most helpful tool!

*"Finally, brethren, whatsoever things are true, whatsoever things are honest, whatsoever things are just, whatsoever things are pure, whatsoever things are lovely, whatsoever things are of good report; if there be any virtue, and if there be any praise, think on these things."* There we have the conditions—God's standard.

*TRUE*—Have we embellished what we are thinking by our attitude, or is it really facts we are processing in our minds? Whatever we take time to think about or meditate on, should be the truth.

*HONEST*—Is the subject we entertain in thought honorable, respectable, credible, and commendable and trustworthy?

*JUST*—Is our line of thinking proper, fitting, rightful or fair?

*PURE*—Are our thoughts free from sin and guilt, faultless?

*LOVELY*—Thoughts that fit in the *morally or spiritually* attractive bracket and are *gracious and beautiful in nature.*

*GOOD REPORT*—Does our thoughts entertain an *accurate, wholesome* account of things?

*VIRTUE AND PRAISE*—*Good* should define our thoughts, and all that we yield our minds to should honor God. We are His children!

Delight:    Philippians 2:5    II Corinthians 10:4-5

Edna Holmes

# March 1

*"Those that be planted in the house of the Lord*
*shall flourish in the courts of our God."*
Psalm 92:13

The month of March is the door of the spring season, and the exciting time for people who love to plant and grow things in gardens, on the farms, and in pots and flower beds. My neighbor brought me a sprig off an African violet planted in a cracked teacup! It had rooted and I soon transplanted it where it thrived and produced more starts until I had a lovely display of those flowers.

God does the *planting* in the house of the Lord. Those who are *born again* in the family of God are "set firmly as into the ground or fixed into position" by the Lord Himself to flourish and grow spiritually. That's the meaning of *planted*. What God has planted can never be rooted out, pulled up, or displaced in any way. We are safe in Christ! In John 10:27-29, we read of how absolutely secure we are.

*"My sheep hear my voice, and I know them, and they follow me: And I give unto them eternal life; and they shall never perish, neither shall any man pluck them out of my hand. My Father, which gave them me, is greater than all; and no man is able to pluck them out of my Father's hand."*

We are planted, and in the Father's hand, and in the heart of Jesus Christ, our Lord and Savior. Some people may feel at ease at church or with Christians, yet are not saved. But Jesus said plainly:

*"Every plant which my heavenly Father hath not planted, shall be rooted up."* Matthew 15:13

If you know in your heart that you are not saved, don't fool around about your eternal destiny. Ask today for God to *plant you* in His house, the family of God.

Delight:   Romans 10:9-10,13   Ephesians 1:13

## March 2

*"...that ye may know that ye have eternal life..."*
I John 5:13

Many are planted in God's family, firmly rooted in Christ, because that is the only way of salvation. Some do not thrive as others because of their fearful nature, and disbelief of God's Word. Not all take in and digest God's Word, our spiritual food, as others. It's like feeding babies. Some will swallow every spoonful their parent puts in their mouths; others spit out every bite until something they especially like is spooned in.

If a Christian is a fearful, doubting soul, they can be saved and yet be miserable because they can't lay hold on the blessed truth of eternal salvation, settled once and for all in Christ who sits at the right hand of the Father making intercession for us. Some have not been counseled properly and shown scriptures which would give them blessed assurance from the start. An unforgiving attitude will soon cause doubts to stir in the mind about your salvation. In the midst of trouble, temptations, and backslidings, assurance can slip away because a daily fellowship time with the Lord is neglected.

People, in their doubting thoughts, wonder if they "said the right words" when they called on the Lord for salvation. There is no set prayer everyone must say to be saved! God is reading the heart while a sinner "calls upon the name of the Lord." Romans 10:13

A young lady from our church attended Bible College and became a teacher. She called me from Florida one night, very distraught and crying in the throes of doubts. She wanted to know if I could remember *what she said* when she prayed to be saved. I didn't, and assured her that didn't matter—only that she *did pray* and asked God for salvation. Jesus said *"...him that cometh to me I will in no wise cast out."* John 6:37. The Lord turns the trials of doubts and fears to good, which we will address next.

Delight:   Hebrews 10:22-23   II Timothy 1:9

Edna Holmes

# March 3

*"For if our heart condemn us, God is greater
than our heart, and knoweth all things."*
I John 3:20

Jesus chided his disciples for their lack of faith. Once when they were in a boat with Jesus out on the sea, a fierce storm arose which threatened to sink the vessel. Jesus was asleep, and they awakened Him to save them!

*"And he said unto them, Why are ye fearful, O ye of little faith? Then he arose, and rebuked the winds and the sea; and there was a great calm."* Matthew 8:26. *Did* the disciples really think the boat would sink with Jesus in it? They forgot everything they had learned, momentarily, and reacted with the fear they felt of perishing in the storm. Afterwards, they said *"What manner of man is this, that even the winds and the sea obey him?"* Verse 27. That trial was a learning experience for the disciples. It taught them *Who He was.* He was God the Creator, and He could control the wind and sea that He made!

Doubts and fears may come into the minds of Christians who are really saved. It's *feelings* that come up and feed the fear and lack of assurance. There are various reasons, but the *main reason* is a neglect of daily fellowship with Jesus. When you neglect the Bible and prayer, you are an easy target for the devil.

Once I had a *major battle* with doubts and fears which clouded all the knowledge and sense I had of eternal security. It was a most miserable state and the only way out was to *find my roots in the Word of God.* I searched the Word, and it searched me! God never allowed me one good feeling, sign, or miracle of sorts; He made me find the answer in the Word. That is where assurance is. *"These things have I written unto you that believe on the name of the Son of God;* **that ye may know that ye have eternal life...**" I John 5:13. Read that little book often. It's the best medicine for peace in the heart.

Delight:   I John 4:15   Romans 10:13

## March 4

*"And truly, if they had been mindful of that country from whence they came out, they might have had opportunity to have returned."*
Hebrews 11:15

When we *truly repent* and God gives us the gift of salvation, we should face forward. Forsaking the old life altogether is the way of assurance and spiritual growth. Carrying the past of the "*old* "country in heart and mind will keep us astraddle the fence, and we won't be fully in either place. A *half-hearted* Christian is not happy on either side. He must make up his mind to be faithful to the Lord, and not linger close to the old life he had before salvation. Otherwise he may begin to doubt whether he is saved at all. The *old life* will be tempting him to come back. Jesus had strong words for those who gave excuses for not following Him.

*"And Jesus said unto him, No man, having put his hand to the plough, and looking back, is fit for the kingdom of God."* Luke 9:62

I'm a farmer's daughter; I know what happens when one is plowing and keeps looking back. You plow a very crooked furrow in the field. That makes a problem for planting the crop and cultivating it. Instead, you must keep your eye on an immovable object at the far end of the field and go towards that point.

We look to Jesus. He is immovable, the *Rock of our Salvation*. Looking to Him; we shall plow a straight row of faithfulness.

If you feel insecure in your faith, search out scriptures concerning the security of those in Christ. Soon, you will see it in almost every line you read! Go by the Word of God and not your feelings! When you awake each day think of what you *know* from reading God's Word, and not how you *feel*.

Delight:   Psalm 27:1   Psalm 34:4   Psalm 37:39

Edna Holmes

# March 5

*"...and be ready always to give an answer to every
man that asketh you a reason of the hope that is in you..."*
I Peter 3:15

We should be able to explain our experience of salvation in Christ, the why and how it came about, and where we stand now in Christian faith. Testimony! Is yours dusted off, polished, and ready to be presented? It should be *written down* somewhere. That will imprint the way to present it on your mind, making it easier. It is a little more difficult to convey to kinfolk. Does all your family know about your spiritual testimony? Recently, I wrote out my testimony like a story and read it to my siblings and their families at our big annual reunion. It is hard to convey these things to our relatives, more so than strangers. Why? They have known us all our lives *in the old life before Christ.* That impression is what remains until they see another lifetime lived *in the new life with Christ.* It is not the *telling* of your testimony that is going to convince your kinfolk, it is the *living* of your testimony that matters.

For others, we must be careful that our testimony comes across as an *honest and true* report. *Pride* will slip into our personal testimony if we aren't careful. The facts are, all are lost sinners needing a Savior. The sinner has to *know that and admit it!* He must realize that Jesus is the Savior who died for his sins, and come to Him with a *desire and willingness to turn from his sins*. That's repentance. His only hope is to trust Jesus to save him. *"For by grace are ye saved through faith; and that not of yourselves: it is the gift of God: Not of works, lest any man should boast."* Ephesians 2:8-9. The *blessed assurance* verse is Romans 10:13. *"For whosoever shall call upon the name of the Lord shall be saved."* God will never break a promise. *Never!*

Delight:   Romans 10:9-10   John 5:24

## March 6

*"...so doth a little folly him that is in reputation for wisdom and honour."*
Ecclesiastes 10:1

The text of this verse has always fascinated me. God's Word is simply astounding in its explanation of life.

*"Dead flies cause the ointment of the apothecary to send forth a stinking savour: so doth a little folly him that is in reputation for wisdom and honour."*

The apothecary was a *perfumer*. The ointment or perfume mixture would cease to have a pleasant odor if dead flies accumulated in it; it would stink! So will a Christian, long known for his good testimony, letting down his guard and *"acting like a fool"* in a mindless moment. The world will not let him forget it, and thereafter, he would *stink* in their estimation. That expression is common even in our present day. Someone who has lost the respect of people is likened to a foul odor—*he stinks!*

Christians may forget the world views us with a critical eye; one foolish moment can cost a lifetime of regret. Our flesh never changes. It is the spirit and soul that are made alive in Christ. If we venture out into the world our flesh will feel right at home. Therefore, we should *"Abstain from all appearance of evil."* I Thessalonians 5:22

I bought some special cleaner from a lady who brought it to me at church. The small brown bottle slightly resembled a beer bottle. It was in a sack, but a friend sitting near got a glimpse of it. He said, *"Tell me that is barbeque sauce!"* I told him it was only household cleaner, yet the *appearance* reminded him of something else. I took note of that. We must be discreet. God's Word reminds us for a good reason. It is important to have a good testimony for Christ.

Delight:   Proverbs 4:27   Proverbs 1:5

## March 7

*"Fear God and keep his commandments:*
*for this is the whole duty of man."*
Ecclesiastes 12:13

    Since this simple admonition is the main reason for living, in our generation most Christians are missing the mark! There is not much fear of God in this present day; it is as though the world of mankind has sort of detached from God, or their perception of Him, and have the notion that things are working okay without Him. We cannot imagine the final judgment, when in the end all the earth will humbly acknowledge Jesus as the King of Kings and Lord of Lords! *"That at the name of Jesus every knee should bow, of things in heaven, and things in earth, and things under the earth; And that every tongue should confess that Jesus Christ is Lord, to the glory of God the Father."* Philippians 2:10-11.

    To fear God is to have *an intense, deep feeling of respect, mingled with love and solemn wonder.* That often keeps us from sin which would grieve the Lord Jesus Christ.

    As with all good things, this attitude will weaken if we neglect God's Word, for it keeps our hearts clean and right before Him. We must never forget that to take in the scriptures is as important to us spiritually as eating food is to us physically. Many folks in our world today, especially our over-fed, over-stuffed nation, would panic if they found themselves in a place or circumstance where there was no food.

    Duty means *function.* So the whole *function of man* living is to reverence God and keep His commandments as set down in His Word. He will be blessed by God by his obedience. The devil works to keep that from happening. Set your attitude! Let God rule in your life. Function always for His glory!

Delight:    Colossians 1:10    Philippians 4:13

## March 8

*"For we wrestle not against flesh and blood, but
against principalities, against powers..."*
Ephesians 6:12

To know how to fight in spiritual warfare is a great element for Christians. If we are not ready for battle every day, the devil can keep us weak and weary so that we can't fight. I made up a list of helpful things to share about spiritual warfare. Every time we hear or read of something that encourages us in our Christian life and experience, we should take it in. We learn and grow that way. You may find these 10 reminders helpful. Keep them in mind, for the spiritual warfare takes place in the mind! We have mentioned that before.

**Spiritual battles are normal for Christians and will never cease. Don't think you will ever have peace with the devil. He hates Christ in you and will try to hinder you serving Him in any way.** Be aware that you must keep *the whole armour of God on at all times* to protect yourself. That is described in Ephesians Chapter 6. We especially need to fortify our minds with the Word of God, the Sword of the Spirit. The devil will confuse your thoughts, and weary you to distraction, so start *swinging the sword early in the day!* Quote God's Word to him and sing a song *out loud* about the blood of Jesus. Fight! That is the only way you will win and have peace of mind.

**Temptation is NOT sin! Yielding to temptation is sin.** God always provides a way of escape for us in temptation. I Cor.10:13 *"There is no temptation taken you but such as is common to man: but God is faithful, who will not suffer you to be tempted above that ye are able; but will with the temptation also make a way to escape, that ye may be able to bear it."* Look for it! God will do as He says.

Delight:   James 4:7   II Corinthians 10:4

Edna Holmes

# March 9

*"Redeeming the time, because the days are evil."*
Ephesians 5:16

Several things are very important in the realm of *spiritual warfare* of which we give little thought, *such as time.*

**Think of time as a treasure allotted to you to spend carefully. Don't waste it!** That has a lot to do with our preparedness in the spiritual warfare. Much can be accomplished in a day's time if we are time conscious and organize work accordingly. We will have time to spend with the Lord with no pressure to hurry, if we don't squander time elsewhere. One of the ploys of the devil is to entice us to do just that. It's disheartening and makes us feel like failures to come to day's end and we haven't accomplished important things. We are most vulnerable then. *"See then that ye walk circumspectly, not as fools, but as wise, Redeeming the time, because the days are evil."* Ephesians 5:15-16

**Be prepared for your responsibilities, anywhere, especially in your service for God.** The least little thing should be done with preparation. It is God we serve! He is worthy of our best. A great stress factor in our lives is *not being ready for things.* A Sunday School teacher should start preparing on Monday! If the daily chores are kept up, and added responsibilities organized in your time schedule, it will be a boon for your physical health along with your spiritual health! Frustration and worry are not healthy emotions.

Remember the devil is always ready for war, and he is watching and waiting for your "bad" days, in fact, he is working diligently to make all your days bad. Hours and minutes are precious treasures in your keeping every day. *Spend wisely and be prepared!*

Delight:   James 4:14    I Peter 5:8

## March 10

*"Thy word is a lamp unto my feet, and a light unto my path."*
Psalm 119:105

In Christian warfare, the main and most important factor is the Word of God. It is what Jesus used against the devil when He was tempted. With each attack, Jesus replied to the devil, *"It is written."* He then quoted scripture to defeat him. I call those three words spoken by Jesus, the *tip of the mighty sword*, which is God's Word.

**Make the Bible your rule to live by. God's Word is reality in this world.** Much of what we see and are tempted by in the world is fiction or passing fads. When someone entices a Christian with the familiar saying, *"It's not sin, everyone is doing it.",* he is speaking fiction. If everyone in the world was sinning in the same way, it would still be sin. Christians are a constant reminder to lost people of Christ, and it makes them uncomfortable. That's why the world tries to get Christians to lower their standards, and "have some fun in sinning!" It will give you peace and make you stronger in faith if you decide once and for all that the Bible is your rule to live by.

**Praying as you read your Bible is a powerful help in spiritual warfare.** This will help you with prayer more than any other method you will hear or study about. The Word stirs up your heart to pray and brings to your mind things you should pray for. How? Ask the Lord to speak to your heart as you read. When the scriptures bring a need to mind, stop then and *pray!* Then go on reading until the next stop to pray. Besides your personal prayer list, you will be surprised at the things God wants you to pray about. I've read of renowned preachers of generations past who did this, and I tried it! Prayer became easy, and talking to the Lord as He was talking to me through His Word was a pleasure to look forward to every day. *Try it!* It is a practice that will keep you strong and fit for spiritual warfare.

Delight:     Ephesians 6:18     John 14:23

Edna Holmes

# March 11

*"Acquaint now thyself with him, and be at peace:  
thereby good shall come unto thee."*  
Job 22:21

According to the scriptures all the treasures of wisdom and knowledge are hid in the Lord Jesus Christ. Colossians 2:2-3

*"That their hearts might be comforted, being knit together in love, and unto all riches of the full assurance of understanding, to the acknowledgment of the mystery of God, and of the Father, and of Christ; In whom are hid all the treasures of wisdom and knowledge."*

Searching for knowledge of Christ as you read the Bible, especially the four gospels, Matthew, Mark, Luke, and John, the better off you are going to be. You will be much stronger in faith to engage in spiritual warfare. Better equipped! Every *fiery dart* that is hurled into your thoughts can be deflected by what you *know* about Jesus the Savior. So the thing we should do to better cope with spiritual warfare is: **Pursue friendship and fellowship with the Lord. The better you know Him, the stronger you will be spiritually.**
Read the Bible consistently as much as possible for you each day. Much of our sense of failure comes because of that one neglect.

**Friendship with other dedicated Christian women is a good "weapon" in spiritual warfare. You can call and ask for prayer, and your friend understands what you are going through when you are having a big battle.**

Now we have "texting" with this amazing technology today. It was hard to learn how to use my phone, but, after learning, I just love the convenience of sending little notes and Bible verses to my grandchildren and others any time I want to, and its instant communication. Now I can ask my friends and family for prayer support when I have a particular need. What a blessing!

Delight:   Colossians 3:1-2   Colossians 1:10

# March 12

*"Put on the whole armour of God, that ye may
be able to stand against the wiles of the devil."*
Ephesians 6:11

The mundane duties of life are areas where we are vulnerable. The devil can attack your mind while you are doing dishes! While you are *doing* unpleasant chores, your thoughts can easily turn sinful.

**The condition of your home, the house, is an important factor in spiritual warfare.** We think more clearly if we are not covered up in clutter and disorder. It is depressing, and we can't *fight the good fight of faith* when we are depressed.

One thing that motivated me in keeping house, a church parsonage for forty-two years, is that I realized it helped me to feel better when things were clean, and chores were done. I had so many other responsibilities, it was very difficult to keep the house like that, but the extra effort rewarded me with a more cheerful attitude. If that is your weakness, then read some good books on cleaning house efficiently, and staying organized with a work schedule. Ask a Christian friend who is an excellent housekeeper to help you with advice, and how she organizes her house cleaning chores. A few little tidbits of advice may start you off on your own system which will make it much easier.

**Keep your heart with all diligence!** In Proverbs 4:23, the rest of the verse tells us why: **for out of it are the issues of life.** The only thing that will keep your heart right is God's Word. Your heart gives you a view of life which determines whether things becomes an *issue to you or not.* Most importantly, *keep sins confessed up to date!* That keeps our hearts strong for the battle. The devil will not defeat us if we have the power of God in our daily walk. Be a good soldier for The Lord Jesus Christ. *He fought a horrific battle for us, and won, at Calvary.*

Delight:     Galatians 5:22-23     I John 1:7, 9

Edna Holmes

# March 13

*"Make no friendship with an angry man;
and with a furious man thou shalt not go."*
Proverbs 22:24

The friends that we make also have a lot to do with the spiritual warfare going on in our lives. Friends who are Christians and want to live for and honor the Lord will be thinking along the same lines that we are; that is, unless he or she is an *angry* person. Unresolved anger and hatred cause a person to act unwisely. In an unguarded moment words may be said that cause deep wounds in someone else's heart. Permanent wounds. So, there should be a prayerful approach when thinking of cultivating a friendship.

The Lord has rules for friends and relationships for a very good reason. Our friends affect us whether we are aware of it or not. *Evil companions* have the most influence if we abide in their company and friendship. Because of *disobedience,* Christians are already weakened spiritually. The devil often sets this friendship trap for unsuspecting Christians. The only safe thing is to have your statement of salvation known to all with whom you associate, and refuse to compromise what you know the Bible says about how you should live. We are to love all souls that are lost, and hope for their salvation, but close friends who do not know Christ as their Savior will draw us away, before we can influence them.

Also, in our text verse, the second part says, *"and there is a friend that sticketh closer than a brother."* That friend is Jesus, of course. Only He loves us no matter what we do or say, or the unwise choices we make. He knows much more about us than our friends, even the things we don't tell *anyone* about ourselves, and *He loves us still.* He also knows our need of friends to satisfy the desire for friendship love and understanding from others. Ask Him to guide you in making friends.

Delight:   Psalm 34:1-3   James 4:4

## March 14

*"Favor is deceitful, and beauty is vain..."*
Proverbs 31:30

 *Beautiful Women in an Ugly World* is the theme I used for a Ladies' Retreat many years ago. As I studied out the lessons the Lord taught me more about things that matter. If learned and followed, such things will alleviate many disappointments for women in life.

 One thing, *beauty* has more to do with what's on the inside than the outward appearance. A lot of what is admired on the outside is makeup, expertly applied! When I was a young teen, I was enthralled with the pictures of movie stars I'd seen. I didn't realize at the time they used makeup, other than lipstick, which was always a bright red color. Once I babysat for my older brother and his wife. I ventured into the room where my sister-in-law had several lipsticks, all shades of red. I stood before the mirror and applied one layer of lipstick after another, hoping at some point my image would look beautiful! It didn't, and I regretted it for I had to scrub all that paint off my mouth before they got home.

 All the attributes of the Proverbs 31 woman were beautiful in that they issued from her heart: deeds of love and kindness for everyone in her life, beginning with her husband and family and household. Her husband was known as a *lucky man*!

 *"Her husband was known in the gates, when he sitteth among the eldesr of the land."* Proverbs 31:23.

 "She will do him good and not evil all the days of her life. V.12.

 *"The heart of her husband doth safely trust in her, so that he shall have no need of spoil."* V.11.

 This woman kept the house, tended the family, and spent money wisely. She was a beautiful wife! Trustworthy. Kind. The children grew up loving her and honoring her. A *beautiful mother!*

Delight: Proverbs 31:31 Proverbs 31:28

# March 15

*"She openeth her mouth with wisdom;
and in her tongue is the law of kindness."*
Proverbs 31:26

When we consider beauty as it applies to a person, it is clear that the outside appearance doesn't count for much. Fortunes are spent by people who make their living by the outside beauty. In time skin wrinkles and beauty fades like an old worn garment, and there is nothing they can do about it. Mankind cannot control the wind or weather. Neither can he stop the body from aging. They try!

I'm sure the Proverbs 31 lady had her quiet time of meditation with the Lord. She spoke with *wisdom* and you get that from God. His blessed Word is full of it, and we only have to ask Him for wisdom, and read His words for that wonderful element to be in our hearts. Women have done amazing things because they were wise.

Abigail saved her entire household because she used tact and wisdom in appeasing David's anger. The Bible says she was beautiful, but David blessed her for *her advice*! Wisdom. Read this amazing Old Testament story in I Samuel chapter 25.

Have you established the *Law of Kindness* in your tongue? The book of James, chapter 3, says that the tongue is an *"unruly evil, full of deadly poison."* Though we say that we'd never use our tongues for evil, it could happen if we don't submit ourselves to God and ask Him to make our tongues an instrument of kindness and blessing to others. Beautiful women must have more than a pleasant outside appearance. Whether they are really beautiful or not comes out when they open their mouths and *speak!* Kindness speaks words that soothe troubled hearts, defuses anger with *a soft answer*, and often makes people think of Jesus. True beauty is using wisdom and always speaking with kindness, which comes straight from the heart.

Delight:    James 3:13    Proverbs 8:11

## March 16

*"And the Word was made flesh, and dwelt among us..."*
John 1:14

Why is Bible reading so important for our lives after we become children of God? We can't think *deep or lofty* enough to adequately explain the whole, but only that the Bible is the Word of God, *God-breathed,* and preserved through generations of being handled by human hands after God, by His Holy Spirit, moved upon men to write His Words for mankind to have. We know what we know about anything important by reading God's book. Jesus is there in it.

In the Old Testament, Jesus is concealed in types and figures of things. In the New Testament, He is *revealed* as Who He is, our Savior and Lord. God in the flesh! We learn of Him and know Him in a personal relationship by searching and reading His Word, the Bible. The Bible, then, is our spiritual bread, water, peace, comfort, and joy.

We get the most if we make some good habits. Think of it in this way: do I want peace of mind, joy that colors all my daily walk, guidance in my life, assurance of salvation, wisdom, and my heart to stay right with Him? The Word of God has that for you. We don't have those benefits because we won't give God time to speak to us through His Word. He won't beg for time during the commercials on television. *He is God, the Almighty, the Great I AM.*

**Make time to read your Bible every day.** If possible, set aside a regular time, and you will cultivate the habit.

**Read enough of your Bible at one sitting so that you develop some continuity of thought.** Read the New Testament, so much each day, and mark where you leave off to continue next time. That's best. However, marked key verses can give you a quick spoonful of spiritual energy when you need it. Verses that have touched your heart are valuable treasures. Underline, or highlight them. *Memorize them!*

Delight:   Psalm 119:130   Psalm 119:160

## March 17

*"I rejoice at thy word, as one that findeth great spoil."*
Psalm 119:162

I'm always glad to get helpful hints about Bible reading and prayer, our lifelines to God. We need help with the common distractions which plague Christians when they try to concentrate and read the Bible with the proper focus.

**Keep your mind on the subject.** That was difficult for me with so much to do every day. My mind ran ahead and made mental lists while I was trying to get food for my soul. But I found that having a pen or pencil in my hand, as I read, and underlining words or lines I wanted to emphasize really kept me more focused. Your mind won't wander off if you will do that. By all means, have a Bible that is easy to read, and one you can mark in. It is our spiritual textbook, *a learning tool,* and vitally important for spiritual growth.

**Read while your mind is alert.** The Bible is a *profound* book. That means *having depth!* So, we must also ask God to help us understand it, by His Holy Spirit in us, as we read. Because it is what it is, we should try to give a fresh mind to it early in the morning. To my dismay, I have dropped off to sleep at night reading my Bible which I didn't do early in the day. I had to change my ways. If you were invited to breakfast with an earthly king, you'd be wide awake early and get ready for such a special event. Jesus is the King of Kings, and Lord of Lords, Almighty God, and the *Great I Am!* Set the alarm just a few minutes earlier...for Him.

**If you have a little extra time, keep a diary.** A simple notebook will do to jot down your thoughts about what you've read, or anything God puts in your mind. You'd be writing your own devotional book! Most of all, carve out a permanent habit in your life—that of reading your Bible consistently.

Delight:   Psalm 119:151   Proverbs 16:3

## March 18

*"Commit thy works unto the Lord, and
thy thoughts shall be established."*
Proverbs 16:3

Everyone has trouble with their thoughts, some more, some less. Many are plagued with thoughts associated with the past that they would like to put away permanently, yet the thoughts persist. This is a good promise that God gave to us to help in the dilemma with thoughts that are embedded in our minds.

The word *commit* implies to deliver a thing into the charge or keeping of another. Shouldn't we do that with all our plans for each day? I have noticed when I think to do that, *commit all to God,* the day has a different ebb and flow to it compared to other days without thought of God being in charge of all my doings. You forget about the distasteful thoughts which take away a whole day's productivity if they take your mind first.

The *how to think* verse in Philippians 4:8 is the perfect guide to motivate us to keep our thoughts in line. It is powerful with conviction every time you examine your thoughts with that verse in front of your eyes. *"...whatsoever things are true, whatsoever things are honest, whatsoever things are just, whatsoever things are pure, whatsoever things are lovely, whatsoever things are of good report; if there be any virtue, and if there be any praise, think on these things."*

*True; Honest; Just; Pure; Lovely; Good Report; Virtue; Praise.* Check it out and see how valid your thoughts really are. Remember, our memories are *embellished* by our thoughts according to the attitude we have nourished associated with them.

Thoughts that drain your mental and emotional energy are a detriment, *not lovely*...throw them out! His Word can make our dreaded thoughts shrivel up and disappear. *What a blessing!*

Delight:   Jeremiah 29:11   Proverbs 12:5

# March 19

*"...no thought can be withholden from thee."*
Job 42:2

Whenever we are thinking our worst, God is witness to it because He certainly knows our thoughts. In Matthew 9:3 the scribes *said within themselves, "This man blasphemeth."* Jesus immediately confronted them about what they were thinking. *"Wherefore think ye evil in your hearts."* V4. That He knows every thought we have is a sobering fact. We should be more alert to what it is that sets us off to thinking in a sinful way.

Does the devil know what we are thinking? He is not as God Who is omniscient—all knowing. But he can read the outward signals of what is going on in our minds. Our attitude determines what our thoughts are going to be. An attitude will always manifest itself, whether you are happy, angry, jealous, sad, frustrated, discontent or any such emotions that beset us. The devil listens to us talk and watches our behavior. With these clues he knows where we are weakest, and attacks there.

Whatever you give your *mind* to, is going to affect every thought that you think, and God is monitoring them all! We should carefully choose books and magazines to read. The covers may be appealing, but the inside may be bad for the mind! *Once in the grocery store, I stopped by a rack of paperback books, and absentmindedly pulled one off and flipped to the middle part and read a few sentences. Mistake! I still remember the gist of those sordid lines I read, to my sorrow. I learned a lesson with that incident.*

God's thoughts are higher than we can think. *"For as the heavens are higher than the earth, so are my ways higher than your ways, and my thoughts than your thoughts."* Isaiah 55:9. Our ability to think is a precious gift from God. Use it *for His glory!*

Delight:   Isaiah 55:8   Romans 6:13

## March 20

*"Are not five sparrows sold for two farthings,
and not one of them is forgotten before God?"*
Luke 12:6

The sparrows are the most insignificant little birds. So common.
God knows them all, and notices when they fall to the earth and die. Jesus used them in teaching the multitudes that God takes care of all His creation. Even Christians worry about things needlessly.

Civilla Martin, the writer of the poem, *His Eye is on the Sparrow*, said she got the inspiration from the testimony of a dear lady, a Christian, who had suffered as an invalid many years, yet was so at peace and happy in the Lord. When asked her secret, the frail sufferer simply replied, *"His eye is on the sparrow, and I know He watches me."* The poem was written in 1902 and was immediately set to music. It has blessed several generations with its message of God's love and care for us. God would have us to know that as He takes care of an incalculable number of birds on earth, He is able to care for all living creatures and mankind, His highest creation.

God reads our minds, and so is aware of every prayer that goes up. Even the *"I wonder"* prayers are noticed.

*Every spring huge flocks of blackbirds come flying in like a cloud and land on the acreage across the street from our house. They feed, moving in little waves of flight from one end to the other. Just a thought ran through my mind, 'I wonder what God is feeding those birds.' I'd walked across that ground before and noticed only a few ants.* Soon, God brought to mind a certain book on my shelf with information that answered. The earth is *teeming with life*; it is amazing what is contained in a square foot of soil! Just below the surface of the ground is enough *"bird-feed"* to feed all the fowl of the air. The more we learn of our God, the more peaceful we will be. *Selah.*

Delight:    Psalms 34:7    II Chronicles 16:9

Edna Holmes

# March 21

*"He shall cover thee with his feathers,
and under his wings shalt thou trust."*
Psalm 91:4

Using common things known to man, God describes His care and protection of His people many times in the Bible. Who on earth wouldn't know about chickens, and other domesticated fowl?

*Many times, in childhood, I've gathered eggs off the hens' nests and watched out in the yard as a mother hen would gather her baby chicks under her wings when she was alarmed. That hen would have fought a bear to protect her little babies! Such is the fierce courage of a mother for her offspring.*

God's protection never fails us. If the provision of God is ignored there can be devastating results. The scriptures tell us in Proverbs 19:3, *"The foolishness of man perverteth his way: and his heart fretteth against the Lord."* Not consulting God and using *wisdom,* will get us into trouble! Then we *fret* toward God, when we should be repenting. When a man has a "do it my way" attitude, he has perverted, or twisted God's way for him. Then he can expect nothing but what his way produces. It's the height of foolishness to exclude God from our plans, *of any kind.* Pray *before* you outline a plan. Jesus said if we love Him, we would obey His Word. *"If a man love me, he will keep my words…"* John 14:23.

Jesus poured out his blood in the sacrifice for our sins, demonstrating His love. How shallow our love is for Him! Our hearts are deceitful indeed. The only thing to keep us faithful is to take in His Word, let it work in us to keep our hearts clean and obedient. Admit it when you get off track. You will know; Jesus' footsteps won't be there.

Delight:   John 15:3   Colossians 3:16

# March 22

*"We hanged our harps upon the willows in the midst thereof."*
Psalm 137:2

Israel had been defeated and were prisoners of their enemies. Being marched away from their homeland to another country, they were devastated. They quit singing praise to God, hanging their harps on the tree limbs where they were stopped. Their captors made fun of them. *"For there they that carried us away captive required of us a song: and they that wasted us required of us mirth, saying, Sing us one of the songs of Zion."* With their lives turned upside down, and their hearts grieved beyond measure, they said, *"How shall we sing the Lord's song in a strange land?"* V. 3-4

This world is a strange land that we live in. It didn't become so strange until we met Jesus and were saved. Now we see through different eyes, and hear with new ears, and altogether experienced a heart change. But we also gained an enemy that is relentless in trying to hinder us from being faithful to God.

When the devil can shut your mouth from singing and praising God, he has taken *"the high ground"* in the spiritual warfare that engages every child of God daily. One of the chief weapons to defeat him is *to sing*, especially the songs about the blood of Jesus that saved us and cleanses us from sins that beset us. If your mind feels unsettled and you can't get the day going right, simply sing aloud a song that praises God. I've done it and was soon lifted up out of the doldrums. At times I also keep a favorite hymn tucked inside my Bible to read or sing during my devotional time each day. Your Bible is your personal learning tool; use it, or anything connected, that enhances your private worship time and helps you to stay focused and fervent for the Lord. Keep to the *high ground! Keep singing.*

Delight:     Psalm 95:1     Ephesians 5:19     Colossians 3:16

Edna Holmes

# March 23

*"Train up a child in the way he should go..."*
Proverbs 22:6

It is an awesome fact that the way parents train their children affects them the rest of their lives. The verse further states: *"and when he is old, he will not depart from it."* Great responsibility is involved here. As children become adults, they are set in the way they are raised, both with the teaching of how to live and the example set by parents, making a permanent impact.

Today in the year 1902, my father was born. He also had many siblings, mostly brothers. His mother died when he was a child, and life was incredibly hard, yet our father grew up with many good qualities intact. He was also blessed with musical talent, which later was passed down to his own children. In my parents' generation, churches were sparse, and for many country folks, it was rare to have regular services to enjoy on Sundays. What little preaching and teaching they were privileged to hear was taken more seriously.

More by example than with words, our father taught his children *to be honest!* There was never any deceit in his dealings with other people. To always pay your debts promptly and tell the truth about everything was his way of thinking. It was much more common in my father's generation than it is in this modern world.

Another trait our dad held to is God's plain command: *Thou shalt not steal. My little brother took peanuts out of the barrel at the market, dropped them in his pocket without telling our father, and proceeded to eat them later at home. Daddy discovered what was done; he drove the ten miles back to the market and returned what was left and paid for the rest.* Children don't forget such an example of honesty and integrity. Parents can have peace and rest in their old age by simply obeying the Word of God in raising their children.

Delight:   Deuteronomy 6:6-7    I Timothy 3:4

Delighting in the Lord

# March 24

*"For the ear trieth words, as the mouth tasteth meat."*
Job 34:3

When we hear someone speak, we hear more than just words. Listeners hear the *mood, attitude, and disposition* of the one who is talking. The Bible says: *"Doth not the ear try words?" Job 12:1.* As we refer to reading between the lines of a letter or correspondence, so also in listening to others speak we may detect another message behind the words. The tone of voice, whether the volume is soft or loud are all elements that the listener's ear is *trying* without being aware of it! It's an automatic thing. *"Doth not the ear try works?"*

We should listen with all gravity to the Lord as we read His Word. Since the scriptures have such depth, there is always more than the mere surface that we see when we read. After we learn a verse to the very core, there will always be more blessing to find in it as we progress in our spiritual growth. The Bible is like a diamond field which has been mined of all that can be seen on the surface, then God peels back the covering and reveals another layer of precious, priceless gems. *Only those who will diligently read and study the Book will reap the riches!* The Old and New Testaments alike are all about the Lord Jesus Christ. And in Him *"are hid all the treasures of wisdom and knowledge."* Colossians 2:3

Sometimes, a Christian may feel dull, as though learning has stopped. At that point, start from square one! Start poring over the New Testament, and read it, especially the four gospels, again. A refreshing will come to your heart. Rehearsing what you know of Jesus *always* brings revival to the soul. Also, grazing throughout the Word of God, revisit the verses you have marked in the past. They touched your heart, you were blessed; you have shared them many times. The blessing is still there. *Gather them up again!*

Delight:   II Timothy 3:16   Psalm 19:8

Edna Holmes

# March 25

*"That at the name of Jesus every knee should bow,
of things in heaven, and things in earth..."*
Philippians 2:10

Once when visiting a relative in the Nursing Home, I took a book from the bookcase located in the waiting room. I was curious to see what kind of reading material was available for the residents.

The book was a novel and from the first to the last page every noun or pronoun referring to women was marked out! The words were not *lightly* crossed out but were *emphatically* blocked out by someone leaning heavily on a pencil. You could sense the intensity of anger or hatred which caused someone to deface an entire book in such a way. I wondered what was behind such strange behavior.

In our present generation, the efforts to blot out the name of Jesus, and all His lovely titles, has intensified in recent years. Satan has rallied the world into a frenzy of hatred for everything that pertains to God, His Word, and the Lord Jesus Christ. Jesus warned us about what's happening. *"If the world hate you, ye know that it hated me before it hated you."* John 15:18.

The world is no friend to Christians. People of the world are not comfortable with us; we remind them of God, and *"spoil their fun."* Of course, it is the presence of the Spirit of God and Christ in us which the world rejects just as vehemently as the poor troubled individual who furiously blocked out the reference to women in the book. It will truly be a shocking surprise to the whole world when the end time comes, and God will judge and close down this universe as we know it. *THEN, every knee will bow to Jesus and confess that Jesus Christ is Lord, to the glory of God the Father!* Are we anticipating that glorious day? We should redouble our efforts to reach the lost who do not understand what is surely coming.

Delight:   II Corinthians 5:11   II Corinthians 5:18

## March 26

*"For they have sown the wind,
and they shall reap the whirlwind..."*
Hosea 8:7

This is an awesome statement in God's Word to me, and very much akin to Galatians 6:7, *"...whatsoever a man soweth, that shall he also reap."* And with that the Lord said, *"be not deceived!"* There is always the danger of being deceived because we are vulnerable.

*There are windows across the back of our house and the birds are known to fly headlong into a window, thinking it is the open sky reflected in the glass. So far, they have only stunned themselves, and eventually get up and fly away. And that reminds me of the illusions that deceive Christians*

Sin can appear as a beautiful illusion of happiness. Some Christians fly full speed into it and bring grief to themselves the rest of their lives. We are free to choose the way that we want to go, but we will never, ever escape the consequences of our choices. The law of *sowing and reaping* comes into play and we can't stop it. It is a fixed law; it won't make any exceptions—even when the godliest persons allow the devil to tempt them into a moment of carelessly "sowing to the wind." And in the simplest matter, the law is as sure as the sun and moon over our heads.

If we don't plan, using time wisely, we won't accomplish much. There is failure and frustration. *We reap what we sow!* We must be diligent to get good results. Many times, I've gone to bed eager to leave the day I'd wasted and wanting to start the next one differently. Confusion and disorder will only produce more of the same. We need God's wisdom to sow good things, *especially His Word, and a good testimony* before others. The world watches.

Delight:   Galatians 6:9   Psalm 126:5-6

Edna Holmes

# March 27

*"Be not deceived; God is not mocked: for  
whatsoever a man soweth, that shall he also reap."*  
Galatians 6:7

In the Ladies' ministries in our pastorate, we called our group *The Sowing Circle.* It was a wonderful theme we worked under for many years. Everything in life pertains to this truth in the Word of God. We had three main goals:

**To Sow the Word of God.** *"So the faith cometh by hearing, and hearing by the word of God."* Romans 10:17.

**To Sow a Good Testimony.** *"Be not deceived; God is not mocked: for whatsoever a man soweth, that shall he also reap."*

**To Sow Things.** *"Give, and it shall be given unto you; good measure, pressed down, and shaken together, and running over, shall men give into your bosom. For with the same measure that ye mete withal it shall be measured to you again."* Luke 6:38

We sow the Word of God every time we give it out to others. There are many ways to sow. Even a greeting card with a verse on it is "sowing" as the scripture is planted in someone's mind. We found that to pray for God to give opportunity for sowing in all these categories, was a sure way for it to come.

We must live so that others can see that we are Christians. We will reap what we sow. Any deception in a Christian's life will bring trouble to him, for God said plainly, *"God is not mocked"*! Whatever is planted will show up, much more than what was sown.

It is a joy to sow of our *things*, that is, share of the bounty in our lives whereas God has blessed us. And *"it"* will always come back to you multiplied in some form or other. There is no limit to God's ability to enrich our lives when we simply obey His Blessed Word.

Implement the *sowing and reaping* principle in your life today.

Delight:    Colossians 1:10    Proverbs 3:27

Delighting in the Lord

# March 28

*"...and be ready always to give an answer to every
man that asketh you a reason of the hope that is in you..."*
I Peter 3:15

First impressions are very important in life, and especially for Christians. The Bible tells us to *be ready always;* put forth effort to prepare, so you can explain what The Lord has done for you.

As you learn, you can share more you have experienced since being a child of God. But that *first impression* is vital. When you make a good impression at first, you are *"in"* so to speak, and have respect and credibility with others. Opportunities will follow.

My husband and I had a *pen-pal* courtship for the most part. We started corresponding while he was stationed in Japan before the Korean War started. We had never met, but he was a friend of my cousin who was there also. It was he that suggested that Louis write to me, to see if I'd correspond. My cousin knew I loved to write letters. Nothing would have developed if I had not been very impressed with that first letter. I'd gotten another soldier's letter before and threw it in the trash. But my husband's first letter was different. He was neat, polite, and sensible in introducing himself to a stranger willing to correspond. An excellent first impression led to matrimony a few years later. Of all the letters I received in nearly three years of writing, I remember that first one most vividly.

Christians make first impressions as they meet and interact with others. Impressions go beyond us because we represent Christ. Bad *first impressions* can be made in weak moments, which may take years to correct. We should establish some rules to help with the impressions we make.

Keep our sins confessed, *up to date.* I John 1:9
Keep our hearts with all diligence. Proverbs 4:23
Keep a good attitude about life. Roman 12:3

Delight:    I Timothy 4:15    Psalm 19:14

Edna Holmes

# March 29

*"...and he to whomsoever the Son will reveal him."*
Matthew 11:27

Jesus makes an amazing statement in this verse. In full, the Lord said *"All things are delivered unto me of my Father: and no man knoweth the Son, but the Father; neither knoweth any man the Father save the Son and he to whomsoever the Son will reveal him."*

Jesus is explaining a vital truth to the multitudes. He had just been preaching in many cities where His message was rejected.

God the Father and Jesus the Son of God know each other, but no one can know either of them, personally, until he is born into the family of God. *Born again!* Jesus must reveal the Father to the heart before a person can realize who God is and his personal need of Him.

People can know of the existence of God. They may believe He is the Creator. They may pray to God, but they will never know Him personally and in reality until Jesus reveals God to the heart. Jesus is the door of acquaintance with the Father. There is no other way into that room of knowing. *"Jesus saith unto him, I am the way, the truth, and the life: no man cometh unto the Father, but by me."* John 14:6

There is no hope outside of the Lord Jesus Christ. The most solemn words of Jesus rebuked the religious people of that day who did not believe He was the Son of God. *"I said therefore unto you, that ye shall die in your sins: for if ye believe not that I am he, ye shall die in your sins."* John 8:24

Has your heart totally, emphatically been opened to the truth? First the heart will be troubled to the core when Jesus reveals the need of salvation through believing in Him. With that conviction, the sinner admits his need (I am lost, I need to be saved) and the New Birth happens as he *calls on the name of the Lord.* Re: Romans 10:13 If you have never done that, let this be the happiest day of your life. Make sure you have eternal life—the only kind Jesus gives.

Delight:   John 10:9   John 10:27-30

## March 30

*"Wisdom hath builded her house,
she hath hewn out her seven pillars."*
Proverbs 9:1

This verse tells us what wisdom does. I had not considered what it teaches until I studied about wisdom in the book of James and finally discovered the process by which wisdom is settled in us.

*"If any of you lack wisdom, let him ask of God, that giveth to all men liberally, and upbraideth not; and it shall be given him."* This verse in James 1:5, tells us *how* wisdom is obtained. It comes from God! Many times, I've prayed for wisdom and felt like I got no answer because I had asked, and wisdom didn't fall in my lap—*whatever it looks like.* Then finally, I understood when Proverbs 9:1 sank into my understanding. Christians may expect wisdom to be handed to them like a box, wrapped beautifully, and inside is the instant solution to their situations they are needing wisdom to handle. Instead, God gives us wisdom, and wisdom takes up an ax and starts *hewing* to build a permanent abode in our lives. That's the only way we can become known as *wise.* Wisdom has to stay with us long enough *to make us wise!*

Do trials and troubles shake your life at times? The mighty oak tree trembles and shakes when the ax chops away at the trunk to bring it down, but a beautiful pillar can be the result. Just so, wisdom hews out pillars, *or strong supports* which strengthen us and cause us to increase in faith and spiritual understanding. Wisdom has to be *instilled in us by knowledge and experience.* As precious and rare as real wisdom is, it is foolish for us to think of it as something akin to instant coffee! The Word of God tells us *"for wisdom is better than rubies; and all the things that may be desired are not to be compared to it."* Proverbs 8:11. The dictionary simply states: *"power of judging rightly and following the soundest course of action."*

Delight:     Proverbs 3:13-14     Ecclesiastes 9:19

Edna Holmes

# March 31

*"Wisdom is the principal thing; therefore get wisdom..."*
Proverbs 4:7

Continuing our thoughts on wisdom, it is important to know how to recognize wisdom when we do acquire it. The Lord tells us how those *pillars of wisdom* appear in our lives.

*"But the wisdom that is from above is first pure then peaceable, gentle, and easy to be entreated, full of mercy and good fruits, without partiality, and without hypocrisy."* James 3:17

What an amazing person wisdom makes! That sounds like the very character of the Lord Jesus Christ on earth, going about ministering to everyone of all walks of life. Jesus was approachable; He turned nobody away who came to Him. And we know anyone can be saved. Jesus said, *"All that the Father giveth me shall come to me; and him that cometh to me I will in no wise cast out."* John 6:37

The ultimate in acquiring wisdom is in our pursuit of Christ. In Colossians 2:3 it says in reference to Christ, *"In whom are hid all the treasures of wisdom and knowledge."* The better we understand the Lord, and enjoy fellowship with Him, the *wiser* we shall become.

Wisdom is likened to treasure that is hidden, and one must dig to find it. In the culture of the Bible days, the wealthy people would hide their money in the fields of their property to secure it from thieves. Sometimes a man died without telling where the treasure was buried. Someone had to dig until they found it! It was work, but they *knew* there was treasure to be found.

Likewise, we know, *if we are Christians,* that the Word of God is rich with treasure buried in its pages for us to find and gain rich benefits of wisdom and knowledge. It's an amazing thing that we must be motivated and reminded and coaxed to read God's Holy Word. Make a new commitment today. *I won't neglect the Word of God!*

Delight:    Hebrews 4:12    Luke 21:15

## April 1

*"Teach me thy way, O Lord, and lead me in a
plain path, because of mine enemies."*
Psalm 27:11

This verse was a welcomed benefit to me when I discovered it. It's a wonderful prayer for Christians that want to be sure they are on the right path, in the will of God each day, and not blundering about in the enemies' territory. The devil is the deceiver, and he is much more practiced in it than we are in withstanding his wiles. He deceived Eve! Never forget it. So, we need a powerful prayer verse to help us.

The prayer is two-fold. *Teach me, Lord,* and *lead me, Lord.* We cannot learn God's Word except His Holy Spirit teach us. The Holy Spirit *enables us to understand it.* Jesus said of Him, *"...he shall teach you all things, and bring all things to your remembrance, whatsoever I have said unto you."* John 14:26. Every time you open your Bible to read, ask the Holy Spirit to *teach* you. We forget to do that, and oftentimes don't get much from reading.

It is easy to be tempted off the *path of obedience*; there are so many distractions. Great men of God who have made their mark didn't do it by ignoring God's leading. They *prayed for the plain path and followed!* When a path is plain to us, we follow without hesitation. It's comforting to know the road when traveling. To come to a maze of roads that run in all directions can panic the traveler, especially if he has not noticed the signs a quarter of a mile back! We won't worry on God's path; He makes it plain for us...if we ask and intend to follow.

My friend, Diana Olson, wrote a telling poem about following Jesus. I've borrowed a verse with her permission. Do You Follow Jesus?

*"In the life you walk each day, Do you follow Jesus?
Salvation you may freely own, but do you follow Jesus?
He bids us daily walk with Him, Do you follow Jesus?
He lives to intercede for you, Do you follow Jesus?*

Delight:    John 8:12    John 10:27

# April 2

*"Even a child is known by his doings."*
Proverbs 20:11

We are often reminded of this truth by the behavior of many children out in public places. Children will scream and cry to get their way, and parents ignore them while they disrupt the peace, or give them what they want so they will shut up. It is a sad thing for parents who cannot control their children. Uncontrollable children are certainly known by their doings, often labeled as *brats.* The worst, however, is that the parents have failed in training their offspring.

*Many years ago, my sisters and I took a trip together. One evening, as we had dinner in the resort restaurant enjoying the beautiful view of the mountains, a small child at a nearby table started screaming. Not fussing, verbally protesting, or any such thing, the child screamed nonstop while the parents ignored him and ate their dinner. We all had a miserable dinner hour, and for myself, I was frazzled from the struggle of trying to ignore the screaming and concentrate on eating. I wondered how the young parents could allow their child to exhibit such behavior, disturbing the peace of so many others who were there for their evening meal.*

Between my childhood generation and today, there has been a great breakdown in the family structure and standards. The Word of God has been abandoned and the world's philosophy put in place for raising children. Children *must be trained*; they do not know what is right or wrong unless they are taught. In Proverbs 22:15, it plainly tells us that *"Foolishness is bound in the heart of a child; but the rod of correction shall drive it far from him."* Parents are wise who obey God in the matter of raising their children. Their offspring are more secure and prepared for life. It prevents heartaches later on. Prov. 29:15 tells us *"...but a child left to himself bringeth his mother to shame."*

Delight:    Proverbs 29:17    Proverbs 19:18

# April 3

*"One that ruleth well his own house, having
his children in subjection with all gravity."*
I Timothy 3:4

This was a requirement in the early church, that the leaders have obedient children and their households in order. Some would say that we live in different times, and now it is impossible to hold to such standards. Not so. God honors His Word which never changes in the results which follow obedience. I have met families with a large number of children; all were obedient and respectful of their parents. I know others with only one child, which they cannot control! The difference lies in the resolve and obedience of the parents to God and His Word on child raising. My father and mother didn't have all the benefits of this modern, *enlightened* generation, yet they knew a few simple rules from the Bible, and followed them with success. To raise ten children with little or no parental control would have been disastrous, to say the least.

*Once, my father brought home a whole stalk of bananas! It was hung up in my room, a small side room in the farmhouse where we lived. Now bananas were my favorite fruit from the first time I tasted one; it has continued to be all my life. It was very tempting with so many in reach, and the household asleep, to sneak one off the stalk. Who would notice? I was not a Christian at the time, but there was something in me that kept me from disobeying my parents. It was the training. We were not to bother that fruit. It would be given to the children at certain times.*

When children are lovingly taught to respect parental authority growing up, they will respect God and His authority when they learn of Him. That is the blessed result of heeding God's Word.

Delight:     Isaiah 38:19     Deuteronomy 6:7

Edna Holmes

# April 4

*"But my God shall supply all your need
according to his riches in glory by Christ Jesus."*
Philippians 4:19

This statement was written to the church at Philippi by the Apostle Paul. It is not just a promise for a church, however; God loves and cares for all His children the same. That particular church had given sacrificially for the ongoing work of the Lord, and care of the Apostle Paul while he was in prison in Rome. He said it was *"...the things that were sent from you, an odour of a sweet smell, a sacrifice acceptable, well pleasing to God."* Philippians 4:18. How blessed are the givers! We have personally learned that through the years of our knowing the Lord and serving Him.

The text verse may seem to be lofty and for a select few, but it can be a delight to learn otherwise. In unique ways God shows us how He supplies our need. It can be a need for insignificant things that you don't mention; it is just a wish or desire of the heart. It has become a joy for me as I now expect and wait for the Lord to provide for me in everyday matters. He has shown me several times that what I'm needing is already in the house!

We needed more space for books, then realized that our large bookcase had several shelves of bric-a-brac and clutter that could be reclaimed for books. We get used to seeing things one way and don't really see it anymore. The Lord can give us a fresh look at times.

I prayed for an idea of how to give my husband a unique gift; something extra special that money can't buy. An idea came from a magazine article. My need was a little journal book, and what amazed me was finding one I'd forgotten, new and untouched, on my bookshelf! In that I recounted things he had done for me personally through the years that meant so much. He treasured that little journal and has kept it. God is *rich* beyond words. He *loves* you. *Ask.*

Delight:   Luke 6:38   Luke 11:9

# April 5

*"Whoso findeth a wife findeth a good thing,
and obtaineth favour of the Lord."*
Proverbs 18:22

There is a saying abroad that marriages are made in heaven, but they aren't. They are made on earth between a man and a woman who are unique individuals. The journey of marriage is the ultimate adventure. Each one has the makings of a good book if only we had the wherewithal to write one! Blending two lives together into one smooth running unit is the ultimate goal, but that is where the adventure part comes in. There is always a little turbulence when the process really begins and occasional turbulence through the years.

*When on a mission trip to Germany we stood at the place where the Moselle and Rhine rivers join together and continue on as the mighty Rhine. There was much turbulence in the waters at the place when they became one, and a little downstream until the waters smoothed out into one magnificent river.*

I thought of how that happening illustrates marriage. At the period of time when marriage starts, *after the honeymoon,* there is usually a little, or a lot, of turbulence. They find out that each other is not perfect, that a couple can't live on love, that real life is rarely romantic, and they have to accept each other as they really are.

The wisest thing to do is make your husband your best friend and *cultivate* that friendship. Share your thoughts, ideas etc. So, he may not always like them...then listen to what he has to say!

Christians should form the habit of reading the Bible together a little each day and pray. That is a wonderful element for a good marriage. Many problems are solved before they become an issue. Let the Lord in on your marriage. He invented it! He knows every little intricate thing about it, and He wants yours to be happy.

Delight:   Ecclesiastes 9:9   I Peter 3:1

Edna Holmes

# April 6

*"...in the shadow of thy wings will I make my refuge,*
*until these calamities be overpast."*
Psalm 57:1

Marriage has its good days, and bad days. On the worst days, the first two verses in this psalm would be a good prayer. *"Be merciful unto me, O God, be merciful unto me: for my soul trusteth in thee: yea, in the shadow of thy wings will I make my refuge, until these calamities be overpast. I will cry unto God most high; unto God that performeth all things for me."* The spiritual battle is a real factor in marriage. It goes beyond a heated argument. The devil is out to destroy your marriage, and he takes great pleasure in arguments which are never resolved. Couples may carry bitterness in their hearts toward each other. Ephesians 4:31:32 is medicine to take for marriage! Take a good dose when you need it. I have.

*"Let all bitterness, and wrath, and anger, and clamor, and evil speaking, be put away from you, with all malice: And be ye kind one to another, tenderhearted, forgiving one another, even as God for Christ's sake hath forgiven you."*

One of the best decisions in any marriage is to *begin again!* Each day brings that opportunity. My sister, speaking on the subject, said "Stop rattling the back door; go forward with each new day." That is a good rule for happiness.

It is a great blessing to grow old with your spouse. We are privileged to have fairly good health so that we are still active in the ministry. My husband has opportunities to preach out, and I have occasional speaking engagements. We have no greater joy than to serve the Lord as He has allowed us to do. We would not be enjoying this fruit in our old age if we had not diligently tended our marriage in our younger and middle years. It doesn't happen by chance.

Delight:   Psalm 28:7   Isaiah 41:10

# April 7

*"And Cain knew his wife; and she conceived and bare Enoch..."*
Genesis 4:17

In our pastorate, my ministry centered around the women of the church and their needs. In teaching each week, I often had them give me their questions about the Bible, so I could address them in Bible Study. I loved finding answers to hard questions. It helped me, if I didn't already know, and they learned how to find and answer difficult questions from the Bible.

One of the favorite questions people in the world love to ask Christians, is *"Where did Cain get his wife?"* It is one of the *easiest* questions to answer! When people only hear about the Bible, but have not read it, the facts are unknown to them. Their ideas can be foolish and unfounded.

Adam and Eve were *created* fully grown. God had blessed them and told them to be fruitful and multiply. Genesis 1:28. By the time they were at an adult age, they had many children both boys *and girls.* The Bible doesn't record the birth of daughters, and names only three of Adam's sons: Cain, Abel, and Seth. However, Adam lived 930 years, and *begat sons and daughters.* Genesis 5:3-5.

In the first generations, brothers and sisters married. Of necessity, that would be the case. Even in Abraham's day, close relatives did marry, and we know Abraham and Sarah had the same father. It is evident that Cain married a sister and left that area to and started another civilization. *He could not have married an ape!* That foolish notion has been parroted for many generations. But God said that everything reproduces *after his kind!* An animal and human cannot cohabit and produce *anything.* *"All flesh is not the same flesh: but there is one kind of flesh of men, another flesh of beasts, another of fishes, and another of birds."* I Cor. 15:39. God settles it. Selah!

Delight:    I Corinthians 14:48    Genesis 1:25

Edna Holmes

# April 8

*"To everything there is a season, and a
time to every purpose under the heaven."*
Ecclesiastes 3:1

On this day in the year 1925, my father and mother were married. My sisters and I went to the ornate old courthouse and stood at the spot where they stood as they exchanged their vows. Mother had often told us details of "the happiest" day of her life.

A man is going to find himself a wife! When that *season* comes in his life, he is out courting. Evidently, God had a plan for my parents to discover each other, marry, and to produce the children they had. To have ten offspring, and all have successful lives is most remarkable. Others have done so in my parents' generation; it was more common in that era, but I'm especially thankful to God for allowing my parents such success with the many difficulties they faced in life. Several of their children have served in the ministry and others have spent their lives in other pursuits which honor the Lord.

Another *season* is referred to in God's Word. The Apostle Paul gave young Timothy a powerful charge: *"Preach the word; be instant in season, out of season; reprove, rebuke, exhort with all longsuffering and doctrine."* II Timothy 4:2. That applies to us as well. Whether convenient or not, we should be *instant* in serving the Lord. It takes an attitude that has already been set: *When an opportunity comes, I'm taking it!* In the various seasons of life, you can be the most effective if you are quick to be a witness for the Lord. I've missed opportunities because I was not ready. Now I'm resolved to be prepared to "sow in all seasons" of my life the *gospel* of the Lord Jesus Christ, and to teach and encourage other Christian women on the journey through this world. If He is our priority, the seasons will find us actively honoring Christ in that way.

Delight:   II Timothy 1:7   Colossians 4:5-6

# April 9

*"...This is now bone of my bones, and flesh
of my flesh: she shall be called Woman..."*
Genesis 2:23

We can't say enough about Eve, the mother of all living, the unique woman. Born full grown, as God created her out of Adam, perhaps the first words she heard were these uttered by Adam when he saw her. Seems he didn't have a speck of romance in him to start with. You'd think he would at least have said *"Wow!"* or *"She is beautiful."* He was certainly under her influence right away and wanted to stay in fellowship with her more than God! When Eve was deceived and ate the fruit, she *gave the fruit to Adam* and he ate of it. The Bible says he *was not deceived!*

*"And Adam was not deceived, but the woman being deceived was in the transgression."* I Timothy 2:14. Adam knew where the fruit came from and what God had warned about it. But he took it from Eve anyway. That is why God holds Adam responsible for the "fall of man" when he deliberately disobeyed.

What can we learn more from Eve? She was a woman just like us, except God granted her an extraordinary *long* life to propagate the human race. She was 130 years old when Seth was born. Then she and Adam lived hundreds of years longer having children. Gen.5:3-4

Eve was a *perfect* woman; yet she was deceived. She was fooled by the devil because she didn't take seriously what God said about the forbidden tree. She had not listened *carefully*. That's what we have to consider. Do we *know* what God has said, and do we deep down believe it? We had better settle that or we can be easily deceived. We must *listen* with our hearts when we read the Bible, and get it lodged there. It's the *truth that protects us.* Jesus is that truth!

Delight:   John 14:6   Psalm 119:11

Edna Holmes

# April 10

*"...and she shall be called Woman,
because she was taken out of man."*
Genesis 2:23

Like it or not, ladies, that is where we originated. That's how we know Eve was like us; all women have common traits. We know that only women can be mothers, no matter how the world tries to muddle that up with their depraved thinking.

Eve had more children than any woman who ever lived! She had a generation of children before Seth, whose birth was a turning point for the human race. With the birth of Seth's first son, it was *"...then began men to call upon the name of the Lord."* Genesis 4:26. So Eve lived with a very large family that had quickly multiplied into a tribe and nation who *did not live in accordance with God's Word.* She *knew* that sin had grave consequences. Thorns and thistles grew everywhere! She saw the sweat on Adam and her sons as they worked the soil to grow food. Some animals ate flesh now, killing other animals. Her keen perfect brain could easily remember the lovely garden of Eden, which she would never see again. Her sin must have grieved her all the *centuries* that she lived, though the sin sacrifice was made regularly. Adam knew to do that, and evidently taught his sons, but Cain did not believe it to be necessary. He sinned more by killing his brother because Abel was obedient to God. We can imagine Eve's suffering at that time.

But Eve's hope was the same as women today. There is a Savior! The promise was made, and Eve heard it herself. God said to Satan, *"I will put enmity between thee and the woman, and between thy seed and her seed; it shall bruise thy head, and thou shalt bruise his heel."* Genesis 3:15. That came to pass as Jesus died for our sins on the cross. He defeated Satan, redeeming us from the curse of sin; the heel of Jesus was bruised at Calvary as he was nailed to the cross.

Delight:     Psalm 130:3-4     Psalm 145:8-9

## April 11

*"...but is clean every whit: and ye are clean, but not all."*
John 13:10

The most amazing thing happened after the Last Supper when Jesus girded a towel around his waist and poured water in a basin and washed the disciples' feet. They were astounded! Peter objected strongly saying the Lord would *never* wash his feet. Jesus calmly replied that if He didn't, Peter had no part with Him. Jesus told them they would understand later it was a lesson in humility.

*"If I then, your Lord and Master, have washed your feet; ye also ought to wash one another's feet."* John 13:14. We are to serve the Lord and each other without an attitude of superiority. For Jesus to humble Himself showed how He loved them, and He taught them right up to the time he was taken to be crucified the next day. What love! Can we imagine how low our Lord humbled Himself to do what only the servants or slaves did in that time?

The Queen of England is the richest and longest reigning monarch in the world, and the perfect example of royalty. Imagine that she ordered all her stable boys to stop raking out the muck and come in and be seated. Then she gets a big towel and water and gets down on her knees and washes their feet. *Surely the world would stop turning should that happen!* That illustrates in a small way what it was for Jesus to wash the disciples' feet. *Their Creator!*

Jesus said they were *"clean every whit"*. He was speaking of their spiritual state, not their bodies. Every 'whit' means every small part and particle of the saved is clean; cleansed by the blood of Jesus once and for all. But in our daily walk, touching the world, we have need of the *washing of water by the Word.* Have you taken your bath today...with the Word of God?

Delight:    Ephesians 5:26    Psalm 51:2

Edna Holmes

# April 12

*"And straightway the damsel arose, and walked;
for she was of the age of twelve years."*
Mark 5:42

The Bible always teaches more than what we see on the surface. Here is the beautiful story of Jesus raising a little twelve-year-old girl from the dead. Her father had gone to Jesus begging Him to come and heal her because she was dying. When Jesus got there, the servants met Jairus and told them the girl had died, and not to bother Jesus any further. The Lord heard those words and told the father, *"Be not afraid, only believe."* Mark 5:36.

Jesus stopped all the crowd outside the place and took the parents and three disciples inside where the girl was lying. *"And he took the damsel by the hand, and said unto her, Tal'itha cu'mi; which is, being interpreted, Damsel, I say unto thee, arise."* Mark 5:41

We know what happened. The girl immediately got up and walked! The people were astonished beyond measure, and Jesus told them to give her something to eat. The child had been terribly sick, had been dead a little while, and now alive and well! Jesus said she needed some physical nourishment. *Give her something to eat!*

It was a thrill to my heart when I read that one day and saw something for the first time. Jesus had just raised her from the dead, and his first command for her was *food*. When He raises us from the dead, *spiritually,* His first command is that we take in spiritual food. *"As newborn babes, desire the sincere milk of the word, that ye may grow thereby; If so be that ye have tasted that the Lord is gracious."* 1 Peter 2:2-3. The only way we will "grow up" as Christians to be strong and faithful, is by feeding on the food of the Word of God. We were *"dead in trespasses and sins"* before Jesus saved us, giving us life. Now that we are alive in Christ, *we desperately need to eat!* Get your daily nourishment from the Bible; it is *health food* for spiritual growth.

Delight:   John 6:47-48   Ephesians 2:1

Delighting in the Lord

# April 13

*"Where no wood is, there the fire goeth out:
so where there is no talebearer, the strife ceaseth."*
Proverbs 26:20

A *bonfire* is a large fire built outside. As children in a large family, always living out in the country, we enjoyed bonfires. Special occasions for them were holidays, especially Christmas time when we had company. We burned up lots of wood at times, when our games and storytelling went on into the night; but for sure when we stopped putting wood on the fire, *it stopped burning!*

God states that fact in our text verse, then uses it to teach us a lesson. When people go about *as talebearers, or gossipers,* it creates strife, but that strife will cease if the talk stops! The trouble stirred by gossip can be very destructive to a church, or family, or company. It can burn high and hot, until *everyone* involved decides to stop adding wood to the fire! *Stop talking and pray!* Gossip is a respectable sin, but sin, nevertheless. Gossip is never innocent.

There is a game played in adult groups which perfectly illustrates why gossip is so harmful. In the game, people are seated in a big circle. The first person is whispered a brief account of something, and in turn whispers it to the next person, until it gets all around the circle. The last one to hear it then tells what he heard. It never resembles the first person's account! People, in retelling what they hear, are rarely exact with facts. Few people are expert *listeners*, and altered facts multiply in the telling. A gossip is defined as *a person who repeats idle talk and rumors, especially about the private affairs of others.* One of the strongest temptations is the desire to listen! Fortify yourself to resist by storing key verses in your heart.

Delight:   Proverbs 11:18   Proverbs 10:18

Edna Holmes

# April 14

*"The north wind driveth away rain: so doth
an angry countenance a backbiting tongue."*
Proverbs 25:23

A few decades ago, the First Lady in the White House started a saying for the youth of our nation encouraging them to resist the drug culture's efforts to get them addicted to drugs. The saying was, *"Just say no!"* That's very simple, and no doubt helped many children in that generation to make up their minds beforehand to say "No" when they were offered drugs.

The Lord tells us to resist getting involved with gossip when it surfaces for various reasons. He says *look angry* when gossipers come around to fill our ears full of the latest tidbits of news. In other words, *don't look delighted because you have an opportunity to hear it!* When you refuse to be involved in gossiping, telling it, or listening to it, the offenders will pass you by. Also, to avoid it protects you from being an accomplice; a gossiper uses *references* of people who listen, as those who approve and is party to the opinions expressed. Gossip is one of the most devastating things on earth.

A large thriving church got a new pastor. He and his wife were young and had several small children. They were dedicated and thrilled at the opportunity the Lord had given them to minister in that town. In time, a teenage girl offered to help the pastor's wife tend her little ones in church. She also began helping out at the parsonage, tending the children and helping the pastor's wife. The gossip started! It was relentless and got so bad the pastor finally took his family and left that place. The church, after many decades, has not recovered. Ruined by gossip! May God help us to be brave against it, frown at the very hint of it, and call gossip what it is. Sin!

Delight:   Proverbs 26:22   Proverbs 29:11   Proverbs 29:5

## April 15

*"Likewise reckon ye also yourselves to be dead indeed unto sin, but alive unto God through Jesus Christ our Lord."*
Romans 6:11

Another hard question is asked as to how Christians *know* they are "dead to self and sin". Is there some sure way they can tell?

When a young man asked his pastor that question, the pastor told him to go to the cemetery to the grave of a brother that had died and stand over his grave. Then verbally criticize and demean him terribly. The young man did it, then came back. The pastor asked him what the brother said. "Nothing," was the reply. The young man was told to go back, and in the same way shower the man with lavish praise and compliments, and flattery to the extreme. When he came back his pastor again asked him what the man said. "He didn't say anything!" the young man replied. The pastor then explained that that is how it is to be dead to self, and alive to God. Criticism does not affect you, and neither does praise. Your life is centered on The Lord, and nothing distracts or turns you off the path of obedience and service to God.

So, when criticism is directed toward us, we should learn what we can from it, then discard it and go on. Likewise, praise can be very detrimental to a Christian. We all like encouragement, but praise is sometimes a trap we should avoid. Read all of Romans 6, and endeavor to memorize it. It is a wonderful, powerful chapter to store in your heart. It will *deflect* those arrows of praise, or criticism the devil oftentimes shoots our way when we are serving the Lord with gladness and fervency of heart.

Are you "dead to self" and alive unto God? Do you get distracted when you are personally praised? Or does it discourage you when someone criticizes you? There's an old saying that describes the right attitude. *Take it with a grain of salt!* That means don't let it affect you one way or the other.

Delight:   Romans 6:6   Colossians 3:1-3

Edna Holmes

# April 16

*"Let us hear the conclusion of the whole matter:*
*Fear God, and keep his commandments..."*
Ecclesiastes 12:13

Recently, we attended the funeral of a dear elderly friend. Many times, I'd visited with this lady and listened to her account of life as it was back in another era. It was fascinating. Life was very different before modern technology changed everything to a fast pace, which is still a difficult adjustment to folks who grew up where neighbors visited with each other and sat on front porches passing an evening in pleasant conversation.

When it comes down to it, even a long life at the end appears as the Bible describes it, *"It is even a vapour, that appeareth for a little time, and then vanisheth away."* In reflection, many have said their life span seemed short, and they didn't accomplish what they should have. It tells me that we need to keep the Word of God fresh in mind, a daily intake, in order to keep our perspective about life. As our text verse states, *"for this is the whole duty of man"* in reference to fearing God and keeping His commandments. We can't keep life *real* and in the present unless our minds are settled in God's Word.

Many come to the final period of their lives with a sense of loss. When God has told us what the *"whole duty of man"* is, and we largely ignore it, then we can expect a sense of lacking at the end of our lives. There is a sobering reason why God warns about the duty of man. *"For God shall bring every work into judgment, with every secret thing, whether it be good, or whether it be evil."* Ecclesiastes 12:14. That is so overwhelming, we don't want to think about it. Taking in the scriptures daily will help reconcile your heart to the fact. God paid an unspeakable price to save us through the sacrifice of His Own Son, and He holds us accountable for how we live our lives on this earth. Start anew today; make your life count for Him.

Delight:   Romans 14:11-12   Ephesians 5:15-17

# April 17

*"...behold, a greater than Solomon is here."*
Matthew 12:42

    The Queen of Sheba was a wise woman. She heard of Solomon, the King of Israel, who worshipped the God of heaven and was noted for *his* great wisdom. She wanted to know about God and this wisdom He had given to Solomon, who also was the richest King in the world!

    So, this Queen made the arduous journey, 1200 miles, from her country to the land of Israel carrying kingly gifts. The description of those riches she brought staggers the imagination. To transport the Queen that distance in royal style with all the priceless gifts for the King no doubt took thousands of servants to serve and guard the royal entourage and look after the camels bearing the wealth. The Bible says it was *a very great train.* But she came!

    Reading the whole chapter of Matthew twelve, we hear our Lord tell the people that He was *greater than Solomon, and greater than Jonah, and greater than the temple!* And Jesus also said He was *Lord of the Sabbath.* All these were held in awe by the Jews. But many did not grasp the meaning of His words, that He was very God in their midst. They heard Him speak in person, but we also hear Him speak to us through His complete written Word; do we believe Him with all our hearts? If so, it will affect our lives.

    Do we have such a yearning to know Him that we would go to great lengths to be in attendance to hear the teaching and preaching about Him every Sunday? The Queen of Sheba puts most Christians to shame by her determination to know King Solomon and his God. Many Christians today will not bear hardship in order to be faithful. They may drive a few miles, or blocks, in a comfortable vehicle; that's the extent of it. Pray for a new desire to spring up in your heart to learn more about Jesus the Lord; He is far greater than Solomon!

Delight:    I Kings 10:1-10    II Corinthians 4:6

Edna Holmes

# April 18

*"...no good thing will he withhold from them that walk uprightly."*
Psalm 84:11

What a promise from the Lord! The Word of God cannot lie; it is a fact to be cherished by all of God's children. He will, and does, give us anything *if it is a good thing for us.* Some things would ultimately do us harm, so God won't grant our prayers if that is the case. We fret, but because He is a loving God and heavenly Father to us, he will not relent.

Connected with this promise in the Word is Psalm 31:19. *"Oh how great is thy goodness, which thou hast laid up for them that fear thee; which thou hast wrought for them that trust in thee before the sons of men!"* I've used this verse to pray for many, especially our children and grandchildren, because they do fear the Lord, and others *know* that they are Christians. Mark verses like this in your Bible and store them in your "toolbox" of prayer helps. God's Word is so powerful; He is pleased for us to pray His Word for He holds it above His very name! *"I will worship before thy holy temple, and praise thy name for thy lovingkindness and for thy truth: for thou hast magnified thy word above all thy name."* Psalm 138:2.

When my husband became a pastor over 50 years ago, I was just learning about prayer. I discovered verses that I could use to pray for him as he labored in the work that began to flourish. Much study for teaching and preaching was necessary, plus all the time it took to tend to the growing flock. I prayed from Ephesians 3:16, *"That God would grant him, according to the riches of his glory, to be strengthened with might by his Spirit in the inner man…"* That prayer was answered many times over as my husband matured into an exemplary pastor.

Delight:   Ephesians 3:17-19    Ephesians 6:18

# April 19

*"The law of thy mouth is better unto me
than thousands of gold and silver."*
Psalm 119:72

Every verse of Psalm 119, the longest chapter in the Bible, has to do with the Word of God. It is referred to as the word, precepts, law, statutes, commandments, judgments, and testimonies in this great Psalm which shows us the importance of God's Word to us.

Without it we would be adrift in this world with no protection. But God would not leave us so; He provided His Word, the Sword of the Spirit which is the ultimate weapon in spiritual warfare. That is why the devil tries to keep Christians from reading it. It is the *bread of life* to us. When we neglect it, we suffer loss and bring grief to our lives.

A friend shared some helpful information along that line about some things that happen when we *don't* read our Bibles.

**Your sin is distorted.** It doesn't seem so bad; we excuse it and take the edge off by giving it another name. Adultery is "an affair" and lying is "mis-speaking". Obscenities is "colorful language". The world has tried to take the word, sin, out of the picture altogether. But God's Word keeps us straight on it, so that we are not tempted to compromise its truth.

**Your desire to serve the Lord diminishes.** The Word of God keeps us thinking according to truth. We could never repay what the Lord did for us in redeeming our souls from hell. We owe Him our lives and all we could ever do for Him. The Word reminds us of that. If we do not read it, our desire to be faithful and honor Him will gradually diminish. God's Word keeps us spiritually healthy.

*An African woman was asked if she enjoyed reading her new Bible. She replied, "Sir I'm not reading the Book; The Book is reading me!"* That is why the Bible is doubly important to us. Read it for good health!

Delight:    Psalm 119:89    Psalm 119:117

Edna Holmes

# April 20

*"...I know thee who thou art, the Holy One of God."*
Mark 1:24

Jesus delivered a man who was possessed with evil spirits, and the evil spirits then spoke to Him. They *recognized the Lord Jesus from eternity past!* The demons and devils knew the Son of God in his human body, though He appeared to be an ordinary man.

It is a simple fact that Jesus cannot be hidden. Some folks think they can be saved but keep it secret. But when the day of salvation comes, they find that it is impossible to keep Jesus concealed in their lives and they don't desire to. Even in a very timid Christian, the new life will show itself in various ways. How can one hide the presence of Jesus? *He is the light of the world!*

One who says he is a Christian, but has had no changes develop in his life, does not have Jesus. How do we know? Because Jesus makes a difference. Even good moral people, unsaved, who may be church members, have changes in their lives which are evident *after salvation*. That was my case, and the experience of so many others I know who grew up thinking they were just alright with God because they were "doing good" and living like everyone else in church. However, it takes a *new birth* to get into the family of God. After that, the change that takes place *in the heart* begins to make itself known on the outside.

An important religious man in that day came to Jesus in the dark of night so he could slip in and out without being known. He started in saying nice things to Jesus, but Jesus told him right up front, "Ye must be born again." Nicodemus was astounded and asked Jesus how that could be. Later, we find him at the cross helping get the body of Jesus down and burying it. That was in the daylight, not the dark! What a change.

Delight:   John 8:12   II Corinthians 4:6

## April 21

*"If any man have ears to hear, let him hear."*
Mark 4:23

Jesus knew that many that were hearing His words were not taking them into their hearts. There is hearing, and then there's *hearing*. The first is just words that's enjoyed perhaps, then forgotten; the latter is the hearing that gathers in the words that are said to assimilate and benefit by them thereafter.

How many of us read our Bibles in a *non-hearing* manner; that is, we see the words, perhaps reading them aloud at times, and still we are not listening? At such times, we are not as close to the Lord in fellowship as we should be. We must *walk with Him* every day, and He certainly will point out what we need from His Word to sustain us, and oftentimes shows us answers to our prayers right there in the scriptures. Remember how Jesus rebuked two of the disciples on the Emmaus road when He appeared to them after His resurrection? *"Then he said unto them, O fools, and slow of heart to believe all that the prophets have spoken..."* Luke 24:25 Jesus had told the disciples several times that He would be killed, but after three days, he would rise from the dead. *They did not hear what He had said to them before when He patiently taught them day after day for three years!* They were going along mourning as though Jesus was dead and that the rumors they had heard of His resurrection were just idle tales.

We must *listen* to God's Word, when we read it and also when we hear it preached and taught. It should be our goal at church services and Sunday School, to get that special word that God has for us, personally. It's there, if we will listen while we hear it. It will nurture us, protect us, enlighten us, give us discernment and other treasures too numerous to mention. Give it priority today!

Delight:    James 1: 22-23    Psalms 119:130

Edna Holmes

# April 22

*"Turn not to the right hand nor
to the left; remove thy foot from evil."*
Proverbs 4:27

If we follow close to the Lord, focused on Him, we are less likely to be tempted off the path by enticing sins. We think we never will, but we forget how weak the flesh is and so we get into trouble. The safe thing, always, is *"remove thy foot from evil"* as the Bible instructs us to do. When you detect that sin has entered into the picture wherever you happen to be, *walk or run* away as quickly as you can. When my granddaughter and some friends went to another girl's birthday party at college, they soon smelled the odor of an illegal substance that some boys were smoking. They excused themselves immediately and left that party!

Recently, while on the walking trail very close to our house, I was walking briskly, not looking ahead, when I walked within fifteen feet of a *skunk* foraging for food around the base of a tree close by the walkway. Panic surged, but the Lord gave me calm enough to think. I veered off the trail *before the skunk saw me* and hurried across the green toward home as fast as I could safely go. I didn't want him stinking up the neighborhood, *and me*, if he was disturbed.

Later, I thought of how we should avoid sin, or any hint of it in our daily walk. If I feared the "stink" of sin like I feared the stink of that skunk, it is certain I wouldn't be fooled by it as much as I have. We desperately need to be fortified with the Word of God daily for wisdom and protection from temptations that come our way. Christians may endure teasing or scorning by worldly friends when they do take a stand against sin and simply walk away; however, the gain will enrich their lives. Sin is a devastating destroyer for everyone who is deceived by it. It only looks good when it is bidding you "taste" and enjoy its pleasures. The misery will come later without fail.

Delight:    Proverbs 4:4    Romans 6:12-13

# April 23

*"Therefore to him that knoweth to do good,
and doeth it not, to him it is sin."*
James 4:17

Many verses in the Bible do not register as we read them, or even hear them expounded on in preaching. Perhaps some think of it as a "neutral" bit of scripture altogether. But God is serious about every verse in His Word. That is, if we know that there is something good that we can and should do, in an opportunity available to us, *and we do not do it,* it is sin to our account! Everyone is held accountable to God. After what His Son and our Savior, Jesus, suffered in order to redeem us from the curse of sin, God will not excuse anyone who takes the gift of salvation, and His Word, lightly.

If this verse seems vague; it may be folks don't take it personally. What God says goes for all His children, however. There are many good things to be done that some may consider as "optional." All should support their church and the Lord's work; that is *doing a good thing*, and it is absolutely necessary for God's work on earth to go forward. And we all know we should do that!

Missionaries have to be supported so they can preach the gospel in all the world while we stay home. Foreign countries won't allow missionaries to work and make money in their lands. The support for them to live and do the Lord's work *must come from home*. Jesus gave the *great commission* to the church, and the church is the people! Do you do your part in this good work? You know it has to be done...by somebody. We have visited many mission fields and saw firsthand what the life of the missionaries is like as they labor to reach the people with the gospel. We came away with a deeper appreciation for these servants of the Lord; they are worthy of our support, not only financial, but with prayer as well.

Delight:    Luke 24:47    Matthew 28:19

Edna Holmes

# April 24

*"Fear ye not therefore, ye are of
more value than many sparrows."*
Matthew 10:31

    The Lord takes care of all His creation. Not even a sparrow can fall to the ground without His notice. Jesus relates this to the multitudes of people who followed Him and in this particular verse, to His disciples as he sent them out to different cities to preach the gospel to the people. He wanted them to understand they were not to worry about things of life. They wouldn't go hungry, and other needs would be supplied as they needed them. That's the case for all of us. We should have as much confidence in our God as the birds of the air do! Amazingly, God can even use the fowl of the air to teach this blessed truth: God is Almighty, and He will do what He says He will do.

    *A crew of men cutting back trees for a new roadway being constructed, found a bird's nest on a limb of a tree. They had the time to spare it for a while since it had several little eggs in it. They left them to hatch, and afterwards, decided to let the little birds mature enough to fly before they cut the limb off. Soon, they flew away. In cutting the limb off the worker called for the others to come and see what he found in the bottom of the nest. Intertwined in the structure of the nest was a Sunday School card like children bring home. It read: "We trust in the Lord our God."*

    God can use anything on earth to witness of His glory and power in taking care of His creatures. Why should we ever doubt that He is going to see that our needs are met? We would be the happiest people on earth if only we completely trusted the Lord in everything. Feeding daily on His Word helps us to keep that truth real to us. We forget so easily. We are to *cast all our cares upon Him* because He cares for us. Re: I Peter 5:7.

Delight:    Matthew 6:31-34    Luke 12:7

# April 25

*"For with thee is the fountain of life:
in thy light shall we see light."*
Psalm 36:9

Don't you love to find verses in the Bible which grab your attention, and gives you something to ponder the rest of your life? Such a verse for me is in I John 1:5. *"This then is the message which we have heard of him, and declare unto you, that God is light, and in him is no darkness at all."* No wonder our text verse tells us that He is the fountain of life, and "in His light shall we see light." There has never been a speck of sin to darken any part of God. He is Holy, and He is Light! That is why we could not see God in our present earthly bodies, and live. A part of that glorious light emanated from the person of the Lord Jesus on the mountain of transfiguration in Matthew 17:2, and His face shone as the sun! His clothes were "white as the light."

We must be reminded that our sins, the whole lot of them, is in the realm of *dark* and need to be confessed and forgiven before we will be easy coming close to God. Our respectable sins and also the *bad* sins which crop up in our lives, no matter how right and good we want to be, must be confessed and repented of. Our old nature is clever about trapping us into yielding to the flesh.

We will only have light to understand how to live in this world if we stay in the Light; that is the presence of God. How blessed that we can do this because He has given us the gift of salvation in the Lord Jesus Christ. How do we get that light? Psalm 119:130 tells us. *"The entrance of thy words giveth light; it giveth understanding unto the simple."* The Word of God reveals His light, His wisdom, and His blessed will for us. It is full of promises we can claim as we journey through this world of darkness. God lights the way for us!

Delight:    John 8:12    John 12:35

Edna Holmes

# April 26

*"Then spake Jesus again unto them, saying,
I am the light of the world..."*
John 8:12

Jesus followed up that statement in the remainder of the verse by saying *"...he that followeth me shall not walk in darkness, but shall have the light of life."* What amazing things the people heard as the Lord spoke to them. In simple terms, He let them know that He was God Himself, co-equal with God the Father, by claiming to be the "light of the world." No one could say that except God! Jesus came to earth to display God's love and grace by sacrificing Himself as "The Lamb of God" to save us. Mankind could never know God personally without Jesus. He lights the way for us...*to God.*

There are countless religions in this world whose followers do not have light that Jesus gives. They are being led without the light which will end in eternal separation from God in total darkness.

Jesus' followers are bound for heaven and will forever live in the Light of the Lord. And while we are on life's journey in this world, the Lord is with us *lighting the way.* We don't have to stumble at all if we go to the source of light and prepare for each day. Read the Word, pray, and ask the Lord to give you light. He can smooth the way, solve problems, and give you wisdom and discernment to know what to do about decisions. Most of all, He will be real to you in the spiritual battles which occur every day of your Christian life. *Never* think for a moment that you can "handle the day" and move Jesus down to the bottom of your list. You could waste the hours stumbling about in the dark trying to figure things out on your own. I've wasted days like that in the many decades I've known the Lord. Experience teaches us. One thing I've learned is that I'm absolutely dependent on Him for my well-being. Learn that! You will have peace and satisfaction in every day.

Delight:   II Corinthians 4:6    Psalm 84:11

# April 27

*"Teach me to do thy will; for thou art my God."*
Psalm 143:10

Many Christians struggle with the "will of God" factor and worry as to whether they are in or out of it! What does it look like; how can I know when I've found it?

Along the way I've gotten peace about knowing the 'will of God' and living in it. I know that the Bible, the Word of God, tells us how to live. *It is the will of God!* If you neglect to feed your soul on God's Word, He will convict you of sin because you will have gotten *out of His will!* Certainly, things will not go good for you in your life if you transgress in that way.

Sometimes, there is a praying and waiting time to discern what way God wants you to go in a specific matter. One thing for sure, you will not have peace if you head out in the wrong direction from God's will. The Holy Spirit of God will bother you and take away your peace of mind. *Stop! Listen to Him.*

Sometimes, the Lord moves all kinds of hindrances out of the way before we can see the path that He wants us to travel in His will, not ours. Selfishness is a culprit. We desire to have our own way, yet we are afraid at the same time to rebel against God's will in a matter. Just know that whatever God does with our lives is going to be the best for us. Only He knows the future and the things that will happen to us along the way. All humanity is subject to the same afflictions. The difference for us is *we have the presence of God with us.*

When I had to take medical tests involving big machines that close you in on all sides, I felt claustrophobic. It had to be done, so I repeated comforting verses remembering that *"goodness and mercy shall follow me all the days of my life..."* from Psalm 23. I knew they had followed me into that room and were with me. Comforting.

Delight:   John 7:17   Psalm 143:10

Edna Holmes

# April 28

*"Ye ask and receive not, because ye ask amiss..."*
James 4:3

When it comes to prayer, it is amazing how slow we are to get comfortable with it, to learn how to pray effectively, and finally settle into the good life of praying regularly and lovingly to our Lord. The fault lies with us; Jesus taught plenty about prayer, and even gave us a model prayer to begin with. It was a model, a *teach us how to do it* kind of prayer, yet it became a one size fits all which is repeated regularly in many congregations. However, the model prayer, which it was, was not repeated by any of the apostles and other Christians in the prayers recorded in the Bible. It was a *teaching tool* the Lord used to instruct them in how to pray.

Prayer is private conversation with God. Of course, public prayers are the custom at certain times, especially in the church. But the Lord instructing in prayer also said we should *"pray to thy Father which is in secret; and thy Father which seeth in secret shall reward thee openly."* Matthew 6:6. Prayer is a special time of worship, praise, and petitioning our Lord. Someone has said that the reason Christians have troubles is because it makes them spend time privately with God. He longs to have fellowship with His children; we are the reluctant ones.

We do *ask amiss* at times when we pray. We aren't listening to our own selves! *"Lord be with me."* Yet, Jesus has already said He *would never leave us or forsake us*. Re: Hebrews 13:5. We should thank Him because He abides, or lives, in us all the time.

Another thing we do is make our plans, and right before starting a project, we ask God to bless it! A wise person will ask God for direction *before* any move is made toward a course of action. We should keep to the guidelines in the Word as we pray.

Delight:   John 15:7   I John 3:22

# April 29

*"Hitherto have ye asked nothing in my name:
ask, and ye shall receive, that your joy may be full."*
John 16:24

Why is it important to pray in Jesus' name? Much can be expounded on this one thing; but briefly, I'd say that because He said to and He is our life-line to the Heavenly Father, the Door to heaven, and our Savior who has purchased us by His blood. He is our Life! We are totally dependent on Him for everything. So we ask *in His name!* Besides, He sits at the right hand of the Father just for the purpose of interceding for us and answering our prayers. Read a special verse in Isaiah 9:6, which is the prophecy of the coming of Christ to Earth, and notice the titles of the Lord that are listed.

*"For unto us a child is born, unto us a son is given: and the government shall be upon his shoulder: and his name shall be called Wonderful, Counsellor, The mighty God, The everlasting Father, The Prince of Peace."*

All of these names are meaningful and rich in blessing as we discover them for our own in prayer. Have you every wished that you could have a private Christian counselor that you could pour out your heart to, and no one would ever know you had such needs? Well, Jesus is there for us, and one of His names is *Counsellor*! You can share all your heart's deepest secrets with Jesus, and they are safe with Him. He *knows* already, so it's a comfort that we don't have to try and acquaint Him with the depth of whatever grieves and hurts us. When I realized Jesus is indeed my Counselor, as well as my Savior, it is as though I'd inherited a fortune! We are all rich beyond measure just to know the Lord personally in salvation, and then to have all of these blessings beside: *Wonderful...Counsellor...The Mighty God!* Pray in His name. He is Jesus; He is all we need.

Delight:    Psalm 91:15    Jeremiah 33:3

Edna Holmes

# April 30

*"Most men will proclaim their own goodness:
but a faithful man who can find?"*
Proverbs 20:6

Man has a natural inclination to consider himself good; he has always, in various ways, proclaimed it! That's why the preaching of the Word of God is the only hope and power in this world. It is like a plow which breaks up the hard ground and uproots the wicked notion in the heart that man is good, *without God.* It is a fatal premise to suppose one's own goodness will be an advantage in the last judgment before God's throne. It won't. God tells us what our goodness, *or righteousness,* is really like in Isaiah 64:6.

*"But we are all as an unclean thing, and all our righteousness are as filthy rags; and we all do fade as a leaf; and our iniquities, like the wind, have taken us away."*

Scholars, who study the depth of meaning in the original language in which it was written, agree that the *filthy rags* in the text actually refers to menstrual rags used in past generations before the modern era began. If that doesn't let us know how utterly hopeless we are without the cleansing by the blood of Jesus, then whatever would? A faithful man will confess that the goodness that he possesses comes directly from the Lord Jesus Christ. He has trusted in His shed blood to save his soul. A faithful man is willing to admit the truth about himself.

With a parable, Jesus rebuked the religious leaders who declared their goodness openly. One prayed in the temple naming his good qualities, and even compared himself to a lost man who stood next to him praying also. Read Luke 18:9-14. Jesus said the "faithful" man, who admitted he was a sinner and asked for God's mercy, went home justified. Saved! Let us proclaim God's goodness, and not our own. The truth is sweet to the soul.

Delight:   Matthew 6:2   Romans 5:1

## May 1

*"For by grace are ye saved through faith;
and that not of yourselves: it is the gift of God."*
Ephesians 2:8

Salvation is a gift! If it were not so, we would all be hopelessly lost, for we were *dead in trespasses and sins.* God had to stir our hearts and bring us to Christ. We did nothing to merit salvation and we could never pay for it. It is a gift, by the grace of God.

However, *after* salvation has been bestowed by the new birth into God's family, the gift is apparent in us according to the choices we make in everyday life as we live it. *Our lives advertise for God!*

Some folks are like a huge billboard sign full of bright lights flashing on and off in a blaze of color! They advertise boldly that they are Christians. Others could be characterized by a little homemade sign on a post among the weeds at the corner of a lot with a faded out "Jesus Saves" printed on it. Most of us are somewhere in between, more or less.

God made pastors to feed and teach and look after the sheep of His pasture. Bold Christians need to be guided in their zeal, and the timid, fearful ones can be shown ways they can serve the Lord. There are many small tasks that must be done in the church. Many!

We should never be ashamed to advertise for our Lord. Jesus advertised His love for the whole world, lost humanity, when he endured the suffering of the cross for our sin. That day the planet turned dark at midday by the horror of it and shook as the earth quaked.

Read His Word and talk about it! By that we sow the Good Seed in people's hearts, and constantly refresh our own.

Keep a healthy attitude. It comes by the Word of God and prayer time with Him each day. Light up your corner. *Advertise!*

Delight:    II Corinthians 9:17    II Corinthians 8:24

Edna Holmes

# May 2

*"The heavens declare the glory of God;*
*and the firmament showeth his handywork."*
Psalm 19:1

I've repeated the first few verses of this psalm so much as I've walked early or late in the day and viewed the wonder of the heavens with the effect of the sun's rays lighting the morning or evening sky. Abraham Lincoln once said that he could understand how a man could look at the earth and be an atheist, but he could not understand how a man could look at the heavens and say he didn't believe in God.

It is no wonder that an unregenerate man can't see God in creation. Spiritual knowledge and understanding comes by a personal relationship with the Lord Jesus Christ, *"In whom are hid all the treasures of wisdom and knowledge."* Col.2:3. It is a great blessing to my heart when I'm out observing the skies that I do realize that the Lord, my Savior, the Creator did indeed create everything I can and can't see looking up into the vastness of the heavens and space.

We *can't* see the air, yet it is absolutely vital for life, just as water and light are to living things. Man cannot make or control these elements, though they can build dams and devices to channel water, yet they cannot control the rain, wind, or the lightning and thunder, nor the tides of the mighty oceans! Modern technology amazes mankind, but God is not impressed with the knowledge He has allowed men to acquire and utilize. God was gracious to allow men to reach the moon, the closest heavenly body to earth. *However, they had to take earth with them!* They could not do without earth's air, water, and food. That's because God made the earth, fully equipped, for mankind to inhabit. We are here and our business is to honor God and show His salvation to the inhabitants of the earth who don't know Him. *Let's do our part!*

Delight:   Psalm 115:15-16   Isaiah 45:12

## May 3

*"...forgetting those things which are behind,
and reaching forth unto those things which are before..."*
Philippians 3:13

A hard thing to do is to forget the past when we have been emotionally involved with whatever lingers back there in our memory. Women struggle with it more than men do, because we relate so strongly to our emotional connections. In spiritual warfare, the field can be strewn with years of carnage, yet there is no clear-cut victory, and the battle still rages on as our feelings remind us again and again of things unresolved in our hearts. I read an interesting helpful hint addressing that kind of burden which hinders many who certainly desire to be free from the hold the past has on their lives.

Whatever things of the past, which are difficult for you to forget, *which are still grievous*, should be brought out into the light of the present; lay them out, and sort through them carefully and find the *real affect* those griefs have ultimately had on your life. We cannot change a particle of the past; it is gone forever. So put it to good use, think it through, and you may be relieved.

Those things from the past that grieved you have fallen out to make you a more discerning, caring person today, now able to offer encouragement to others struggling with past issues. Some were hurt by others, and some have made their own decisions which later brought heartache, some of which they deeply regret or wonder still how it would have been *the other way around, so they* can't let go of it emotionally. If some of my impulsive decisions had come to fruit, I might never have been saved. What a tragedy that would have been! I thank God because He changed the course of my life.

Today, will be your past tomorrow. Make it good! Let the Lord rule your thought life and be thankful for your blessings.

Delight:   Romans 8:28   Psalm 118:14

Edna Holmes

# May 4

*"Redeeming the time, because the days are evil."*
Ephesians 5:16

A good motivational article about time management was found in the wallet of a very successful football coach at his death several decades ago. The author is unknown.

The article is titled *The Magic Bank Account*. It likens seconds to dollars, and you have 86,400 in the bank to spend each day. What you do not spend can't be carried over, and you get the same amount the next day to spend any way you choose, but, again, *you have to spend it.*

If our seconds *were* dollars that we had to spend or lose, do you think you could make use of it wisely? When you spent all you possibly could on yourself, you would buy for those you love and others around you. We would consider that scenario the greatest of blessings and opportunity. Yet, the seconds, minutes and hours of time allotted to us each day are more precious than money, or any other earthly treasure we could compare it with. *Time is our life!*

I have written above my prayer list the words: *Don't waste time.* That reminder helps for a while until it is too familiar. It seems that we all cease to *see what we have seen constantly over a long period of time.* It takes focusing on your goals until it's a habit to perform your daily duties. When I rewrite my prayer list each month, my little reminder *to not waste time* comes back into view; I'm more alert and diligent...for a few days, anyway. But if we do *nothing* to spur us on to get things done, the precious time God has given to us can be entirely wasted. We need motivation, and the best place to get it is from the Word of God! Read from the scriptures first each day, pray plainly and simply for what you need to get done, committing it to the Lord. He will smooth the way as you work through your daily chores.

Delight:   Proverbs 16:3   James 4:14

# May 5

*"The fear of man bringeth a snare..."*
Proverbs 29:25

How many times have we taken a certain course of action because we feared what someone else would think? The approval of others is so important that some may compromise their convictions in order to be accepted. That ties into man's greatest fear which is rejection. The only thing to help us out of that dilemma is by realizing our position in Christ our Savior.

If you have been *born again* into God's family, you are now and forever will be a child of God. In Christ, you are ready for heaven. Why should we ever be afraid of anyone or estimate their opinion of us as important enough to trouble us. *God loves us!* We are under His omnipotent protection and bountiful daily blessings.

*When I was a small child, occasionally Daddy would take us to town with him on Saturday. It was a small country town, yet to me it was a huge bustling city. It was an awesome experience just to cross the street, but I felt secure if I could hold to Daddy's finger! His hands were big; I could only grip my hand around one of his fingers as we crossed the street. I was never afraid of anything or anyone when my Dad was nearby. And what others thought of me didn't matter in the least.*

In childlike faith, we should be confident in the care of our Heavenly Father. In Psalm 46:1 the Bible declares *"God is our refuge and strength, a very present help in trouble."*

Psalm 27:1 gives us a powerful word about our fears. *"The Lord is my light and my salvation; whom shall I fear? the Lord is the strength of my life; of whom shall I be afraid?"* We don't hold to God's finger; He has us in His hand! Jesus said no one could pluck us out of His hand. Selah!

Delight:    Psalm 28:7    Psalm 31:19-20

# May 6

*"For ye were sometime darkness, but now are ye
light in the Lord: walk as children of light."*
Ephesians 5:8

Christians do not realize what their presence means to the world. Jesus explains it in the simplest of terms so that we can understand; but do we?

*"Ye are the light of the world. A city that is set on an hill cannot be hid."* Matthew 5:14.

Christians are lights because they reflect the light of Jesus. That is why the world recognizes a true Christian; he reminds them of Jesus by the reflection of that spiritual light. It cannot be concealed for long, even if you were trying; your speech, and attitude, and actions would betray you. And if in a weak moment we do *betray the Lord*, we should be like the Apostle Peter and go out and weep bitterly. Conviction and sorrow of heart settles in until we confess our sins and ask the Lord to forgive us.

Darkness is a formidable thing. It is scary; we can't see! It depicts the state of the unsaved, before the light that Jesus gives changes their state from darkness to light. That is the blessed miracle of salvation. *"Who hath delivered us from the power of darkness, and hath translated us into the kingdom of his dear Son."* Colossians 1:13. Once we were removed from the realm of darkness where the devil had control, it was inevitable that a telling change came over us. For the first time, I wanted to read and understand all about the Bible. My husband began to read the Bible every spare minute and instantly loved going to church and being involved. New Christians desire the *milk of the Word,* and are attracted always to the Light, which is Christ. It takes the power of the gospel to change the heart in such a way. *A supernatural power!* Has your heart been changed?

Delight:   John 8:12   Romans 13:12

Delighting in the Lord

# May 7

*"Wherefore by their fruits ye shall know them."*
Matthew 7:20

In a church recently, I saw a beautiful grand piano on the opposite side from the organ. When the musician sat down and started playing, it was apparent that it was not a piano at all, but only had the appearance. The inside parts had been removed and an electronic keyboard inserted in place where the piano keys had been. It was an empty shell of a once grand instrument. But until you heard the sounds that come forth, you naturally assumed it was the beautiful piano that it appeared to be.

Jesus boldly exposed the hypocrisy of the religious leaders who came to Him to find fault with His words.

*"Woe unto you, scribes and Pharisees, hypocrites! for ye are like unto whited sepulchers, which indeed appear beautiful outward, but are within full of dead men's bones, and of all uncleanness.*

*Even so ye also outwardly appear righteous unto men, but within ye are full of hypocrisy and iniquity."* Matthew 23:27-28.

Some seem like Christians, but their spirits are dark, and their hearts are empty because they have not been *born again* into the family of God. One must *call upon the name of the Lord* to be saved. (Re: Romans 10:13). We may fool others, but of what use is it to pretend? It will avail nothing in the day of death. I appeared to be a Christian for years, but I was lost. I had to admit I was a sinner and be *born again* by trusting in Jesus Christ. He is the Door to heaven. There is no other.

Many go through the motions, but they don't know Him. If there has never been a time when your heart was changed to know Christ, don't pretend it has. Be real; trust Him!

Delight:   Romans 10:9-10,13   Acts 4:12

# May 8

*"Commit thy works unto the Lord,
and thy thoughts shall be established."*
Proverbs 16:3

We defeat ourselves when we make our plans, which is the outworking of our thoughts, and then *afterwards* ask God to bless them. Since we need the wisdom of God to think right in the first place, we must not do as the old saying goes: *put the cart before the horse.*

Commit each new day to God and ask Him to guide you through it, so that it will be profitable for His honor and glory. The word "thoughts" here is translated "preparations" in verse one and means "plans." That is actually what comes forth from our thought patterns. I've made so many on my own and had a bummer of a day with nothing accomplished. As we grow spiritually, we learn to depend on the Lord and His wisdom instead of our own.

The brain is more complicated and marvelous than any computer on earth. Only God could create the human brain. It is the center control of the body and is a vast, vast storage bin of our whole life experience. The mind functions from that. Left to itself, the mind will drift from one thing to the next like an abandoned ship on the sea. It must be directed to work efficiently.

A great waster is negative thinking which slips in and gets stronger by the minute as the brain produces more data supporting the surge of dark thoughts filling our minds. Our emotions start stirring and then we are experiencing a bad situation all over again, sometimes decades after the fact. If we set our minds the first thing, we can avoid that. Regardless of your position in life, to start the day with a few minutes at least with the Lord is the wisest thing you can do. The Bible says of Christ, *"In whom are hid all the treasures of wisdom and knowledge."* Colossians 2:3. Never underestimate the value of even a few minutes with the Lord.

Delight:   Proverbs 4:23   Isaiah 26:3

## May 9

*"Lo, children are an heritage of the Lord..."*
Psalm 127:3

Growing up, the third one of ten children, I was Mother's helper with the young ones and did many chores. In my childhood our country area had no electricity. The washdays were a hardship, considering that we had no such appliances as a washer and dryer, and *disposable diapers had not been invented yet!* I felt knowledgeable because of my experience of tending babies. However, in adulthood, when I had my first child, I realized how much more comes with motherhood.

On this day of the year, several decades ago, our son was born. It was Mother's Day and as of 9:15 A.M. that morning I was the youngest mother in our church! But, of course, I couldn't go and receive the corsage given to the youngest mother present in the service. Nothing could dampen my joy, however; I was so thrilled to have my first child and my husband was walking on the proverbial *cloud nine!*

It is a *maturing* experience caring for your own new-born baby. God provides amazing grace for young parents and pronounces a special blessing. Our text verse says "…. children are an heritage of the Lord." It's a privilege to have them, a blessed gift. Therefore, it is an urgent matter to teach children early and thoroughly the Word of God. Parents must embed divine truth in their children's hearts because the world is waiting to corrupt their minds. Many parents have been grieved as their children became cynical about Christianity after attending college where atheistic professors endeavor to destroy their faith in God. *But we have our children first.* From the cradle, teach them to love God, His church, and the incomparable Word of God. That is the best protection you can wrap around their hearts and minds.

Delight:   Proverbs 20:11   Ephesians 6:1-2

## May 10

*"I lay it down of myself..."*
John 10:18

Jesus was not crucified because He could not prevent it. He was not arrested and subjected to cruel treatment and a mock trial because He was a helpless victim. Jesus was in complete control at all times. *He came to die!*

From all eternity, it was in the plan of Almighty God to redeem the human race from the penalty of sin. Adam, the first man, sinned and put all humanity under the curse that only God Himself could remove by the ultimate sacrifice. That perfect holy sacrifice was our Lord Jesus Christ, the Lamb of God that John the Baptist pointed out one day as he saw Jesus approaching. The Bible says that was what John was born for, to declare Jesus as the Lamb of God, publicly.

*"The next day John seeth Jesus coming unto him, and saith, Behold the Lamb of God, which taketh away the sin of the world."* John 1:29. Further in the chapter, again he points out Jesus publicly. *"And looking upon Jesus as he walked, he saith, Behold the Lamb of God!"* Verse 36.

The sacrificial lamb of the Old Testament had to be without a blemish; and so our Lord Jesus fulfilled that perfect type. He had no sin, for He was the eternal Son of God. The time had come, and Jesus the perfect Lamb submitted to the death of the cross, the cruelest way to suffer; death by crucifixion. We cannot fathom His suffering. When His Son actually *became sin* for us, God the Father, Himself, turned His back and pulled a curtain of darkness down over the scene. In reading it, I am always so relieved when Jesus cries out, *"It is finished."* His suffering was over! We should ask God to keep our hearts full of gratitude for what Jesus did for us, and *never* take it for granted. Have you thanked Him today for your personal salvation? Do it now.

Delight:   John 17:3   John 14:6

## May 11

*"...the borrower is servant to the lender."*
Proverbs 22:7

The modern craze of borrowing is rampant today. It's done mostly by using credit cards. It doesn't alarm chronic borrowers that each time they *charge* they are in debt unless the total bill is paid off at the end of the month. That seldom happens, so we have a lot of *borrowers* who are servants to the lenders, the credit card companies. Of course, interest is added to the bill each month, and the debt increases even as the borrower struggles to pay it off on a regular basis. *He must; or his credit will be ruined.* He becomes a servant.

Such big necessities as a house and car are considered acceptable reasons for going into debt. If that were all; it wouldn't be so bad. We are accustomed to making payments for those necessary things in our life. It's the many other optional purchases made with a credit card which runs up unnecessary debt. It adds up quickly. *"Use your card for convenience"* is suggested in advertising; but making the payments with interest added each month is a burden! The pressures of debt will take its toll on the family. The Lord admonishes us in His Word to owe no man anything, and that our only obligation should be to love others. Remember what Romans 13:8 says, *"Owe no man any thing, but to love one another: for he that loveth another hath fulfilled the law."*

The freedom you experience without debt is priceless. May the Lord give us that wisdom to be patient, and not impulsively spend ourselves into debt. If children are taught that concept, it will spare them much trouble later when they have the responsibility in adult life of managing their own money.

Delight:    Proverbs 22:26    Proverbs 23:4-5

Edna Holmes

# May 12

*"...let us lay aside every weight,
and the sin that doth so easily beset us..."*
Hebrews 12:1

Christians are prompted to get rid of the weight of sin, especially besetting sins. Sin sticks to us like glue and though we may say with heartfelt conviction "I'm *never* doing that again...*ever!*" still, it comes back. You may have prayed about a besetting sin at the altar, and when you got home from church, it was waiting for you.

*When we lived in the little parsonage behind the church, we had a stray dog come around one day and of course the kids were ready to take her in. Kids and dogs go together. But we had no place whatsoever for a dog, and no extra money for dog food. Still she wouldn't leave the friendly attention and table scraps we generously shared with Rosalie; that's the name we attached to our uninvited guest that decided to stay. However, we eventually had to make the decision to get rid of Rosalie because our front yard was also the gravel parking-lot for the church. She became a nuisance when people came in for the services.*

We took her off miles from the house and left her. We drove around for a while, then went home. There sat Rosalie by the porch waiting for us! *How did that dog get back before we did?* The next time, we took her on the other side of the lake near another little town and left her. In that way we had the lake between us that would deter her coming back.

To be rid of besetting sins, we must have something between which deters sin. *That's God's Word!* We must take it in daily. We are easily tempted when we neglect God's Word. That can be our worst besetting sin! Reset your priorities if you have slipped away from the habit of diligently reading the Bible. Start over by reading the four gospels, Matthew, Mark, Luke, and John.

Delight:    Psalm 119:11    Hebrews 4:12

# May 13

*"...the words of my mouth and the meditation of my heart..."*
Psalm 19:14

I often sign this prayer verse in the front of my devotional book. It is an ideal "wake-up verse" which I recommend when I'm teaching ladies. It gives us an edge to have some of God's Word fresh in our minds as we face each new day. Listen to the prayer verse in full: *"Let the words of my mouth, and the meditation of my heart, be acceptable in thy sight, O Lord, my strength, and my redeemer."* God's Word prayed back to Him is the best we could ever offer up; no one can express our heart's need better than God Himself. There are excellent books written about "praying God's Word." We can develop our own book of prayers. Copy down verses like these, and any that you love to pray, in a notebook and claim your own treasury of prayer verses.

We never know what will come up to trouble us in any day; we certainly need protection of this prayer that the words we do speak will be right and acceptable to the Lord. I've spoken hastily many times and regretted it, and at times had to offer an apology to someone. Very humbling.

Moods determine how we speak. Emotions govern our verbal expressions. That's why the *meditation of the heart* needs to be guarded by prayer. We know that out of the heart *"are the issues of life."* Proverbs 4:23. Mediation that we speak of means to give continual thought to, and solemn reflection on the Word of God. In other words, read and *chew on it* just as a cow lays in the shade and chews her cud after grazing all morning! I've seen that so much as a child on our farm. They get the good out of the grass or hay as they chew on it for hours. We get Spiritual food *at our devotional time;* then meditation should be practiced all day. God will bless the day as you think on Him. Meditate.

Delight:   Isaiah 50:4   Philippians 4:4

Edna Holmes

# May 14

*"He that answereth a matter before he heareth it,*
*it is folly and shame unto him."*
Proverbs 18:13

Much of Proverbs goes over our heads when we read it. It takes spiritual growth to appreciate and be settled in the wisdom of this wonderful book; God's Word has such depth. As soon as we feel we have thoroughly learned it, the Lord peels back another layer, and we are amazed all over again at what The Holy Spirit reveals to us, which we never noticed before.

I thought of our text verse as one who speaks impulsively, giving his opinions before he actually hears all the facts being discussed. He is not listening but only thinking of what he will say, given an opportunity. *Wise men talk when they have something to say; foolish men talk because they want to say something!*

We need the caution of the Word as we feel the urgency of voicing our opinion as others share their problems.

Be careful when *spiritual* problems are confided to you. Be careful when *financial* woes are disclosed for your input. Be *very* careful in listening to matters of *domestic or marital* problems. In many cases *people aren't telling the whole truth!* They aren't intentionally lying; they just aren't relating all the facts surrounding the situation. They share their own point of view. It is commonly said; there are always two sides to everything. Be careful and listen. *Let your words be few.* They may be a deciding factor in a case.

This does not mean we can't be a help. We can listen and pray more than anything. Sharing the Word is always a comfort. Direct them to seek expert counsel if you discern their problems to be more complex and serious. When a Christian glibly gives advice in a situation that's over his head, it is *folly and shame.*

Delight:   James 1:5   Proverbs 15:2

# May 15

*"Great peace have they which love
thy law: and nothing shall offend them."*
Psalm 119:165

When we stop looking to people and things and focus only on God as our source of fulfillment, then we begin to experience what this wonderful verse of scripture offers. That is great peace.

Why do we get offended at people, or situations? Is it because we are expecting to be fulfilled in some way, and they aren't coming through? We have disappointment if we look to the wrong source. We must take our eyes off of people and things and direct them toward God, taking strength and comfort always in the Word of God. It is referred to in Psalm 119 as *the law, precepts, testimonies, statutes, commandments, judgments, and the word.* Every verse refers to God's Word by one of these titles. It would be a great benefit to memorize it, storing it in your heart. My brother, who was a missionary in New Guinea for many years, told me he memorized Psalm 119, working on each section of eight verses at a time, and it was "life changing." God's Word has that effect—*life changing.*

In having the Word stored in our minds, we have the greatest protection and weapon in spiritual warfare. Remind yourself often of the power packed into God's Word. *"For the word of God is quick, and powerful, and sharper than any twoedged sword, piercing even to the dividing asunder of soul and spirit, and of the joints and marrow, and is the discerner of the thoughts and intents of the heart."* Heb. 4:12

It is easier to keep our focus on the Lord, when His Word abides in our minds continually. I have often prayed this verse and it gladdens my heart: *"Thou art my portion, O Lord; I have said that I would keep thy words."* Psalm 119:57. Make God *your* portion.

Delight:    Psalm 119:97    Psalm 73:25-26

Edna Holmes

# May 16

*"But it is good for me to draw near to God:
I have put my trust in the Lord God..."*
Psalm 73:28

There is a great benefit in staying in fellowship with God and enjoying that closeness to the Lord every day. One thing it does is make the assurance of salvation register in the depths of our hearts. For some, that is the most wonderful thing in the world! Some timid souls grew up feeling unloved, unwanted, and insecure in every way, so it is harder to grasp the truth of God's promises and words of love expressed to His children. But that blessed fellowship with the Lord sweeps away doubts and fears which sometimes crop up. It defeats the devil and strengthens the believers. What could give us more benefit and happiness than daily fellowship with our Lord? Close to God, there can be no fear of anything. He is our Heavenly Father who loves us, and watches over us as we journey through this world.

My father was never afraid of storms. He understood weather could be destructive, but he was not afraid in a storm. Once when he came from the field, it had darkened early because of the weather; so my dad had to go milk the cow in the dark with the wind blowing a gale, and lightning flashing every minute lighting up the place like daylight. Nine years old, I had to go and hold the extra milk bucket for him. We were in the open barn lot, with the wind so strong, he braced the cow with his shoulder as he milked her, and I stood behind him shielded from the worst and watching the constant lightning flashing. I felt no fear of the elements; I was close to my father, and he was not afraid. I *knew* I was safe with him.

How much safer and more secure we are with our Heavenly Father! There is hardly a worthy comparison. May the Lord give us a strong desire to seek His fellowship each day.

Delight:   I Peter 3:13   Psalms 91:5

# May 17

*"He that believeth on the Son of God
hath the witness in himself..."*
I John 5:10

That witness is the Holy Spirit of God, the Lord Jesus Christ Himself Who takes up His abode in us. That's what secures us as a child of God. Without the Spirit of God in us, we definitely would not be Christians. There is no way we could change ourselves, understand the Word of God, and choose to follow Jesus. We must be changed from the inside out, and only the Holy Spirit can do that.

Some may ask "What exactly is the 'witness of the Spirit'?" Bible scholars will tell us that the witness of the Spirit is the Word of God. He reveals its meaning and points out Christ to us. In that way we can know for sure that we are saved. The Spirit makes Christ real to us and reveals Him in the Word of God. Before I was saved, I had no interest in reading the Bible; even though I was a church member and very active. I could not understand it, but simply repeated what I heard others say in the course of visitation and teaching a children's class. Remember, a lost person has no capacity to understand the Word of God; he is *dead in trespasses and in sin.* Makes no difference how much you may pretend, without the new birth into God's family...you are lost. I fear that many people fall into that category, as I myself was for so many years. God's Word would penetrate my heart at times, but I pushed conviction away because of the pride that came quickly to the front to discourage any real consideration of salvation in Christ.

After salvation, the Holy Spirit revealed Christ to me in the Word, and I began to learn. That is the "witness of the Spirit". He makes Christians see and learn the things of God in His Word. When you read it, thank the Lord for your teacher—the Holy Spirit of God.

Delight:   Romans 8:16   Ephesians 4:30

Edna Holmes

# May 18

*"The fruit of the righteous is a tree of life;*
*and he that winneth souls is wise."*
Proverbs 11:30

    We who know the Lord personally in salvation can wield more power than any other people on earth. Why? Because we have the Holy Spirit abiding in us, and we are as a "tree of life." We can win others to Christ, thereby producing fruit that will abide forever. Everyone who is saved is full of gratitude to the people who told them of the Savior and led them to a personal faith in Him.

    It is wise to obey the Word of God, and much wisdom is gained by the varied experiences people have in endeavoring to witness and win the lost to Christ. In our early years in the pastorate, our soul winning efforts brought forth much fruit. The town was ripe for a harvest, and we were grateful that the Lord had chosen that place to put us in our first and only pastorate to serve.

    Early on, I accompanied my husband on visitation so that I could see to the children while he talked to parents about the Lord and invite them to come to church. I shall never forget one home we went to of a family just moved to town. They were very destitute, and it showed. They had only one chair, and they sat that in the middle of the room for the pastor. They spread a newspaper on the floor by the chair for me to sit on. The family sat on the floor. My husband opened his Bible and read to them about God's love, and His plan of salvation to everyone who will believe it. They listened attentively, thanked us for coming, and were in attendance the following Sunday! Everyone in that family was eventually saved. The grandfather, at 108 years old, was the oldest person the pastor ever baptized. It was a joy to watch that family turn a house into a home in their faithfulness to God. We can all be wise. In every way you can, be a witness for your Savior.

Delight:    Psalm 37:39    Romans 6:23

Delighting in the Lord

# May 19

*"The way of the slothful man is an hedge of thorns:*
*but the way of the righteous is made plain."*
Proverbs 15:19

We define the slothful person as being *lazy*! That is correct. It also means *indolent* which gives a broader sense of the slothful man, or woman. They dislike and avoid work, are idle and, again, are characterized as lazy. In this present generation, the *slothful* make up a large segment of our society. Lax parents have been slothful in raising their children, not teaching and training them to work, or being responsible for chores at home. Thus, they develop in them an attitude of slothfulness about work of any kind.

My father was not lazy. From a youth, he had worked and earned his own way. He taught his ten children to work and any other under his roof for any length of time. Once when a nephew was about to be sent to a correctional institution, our Dad asked the Judge if he could try to help this wayward boy. *"I don't think anyone has really explained things to him"* Dad said. The judge consented, and this rebellious cousin took up residence with our large family. The rules were explained to him, and he fell in step with the daily routine of work and family life. But he kept his attitude and soon rebelled. Dad patiently explained things again to him. Not liking the work routine, the boy again balked. It was explained plainly one more time. On the third incident of rebellion, Dad took him to the woodshed! From that day, he was a different boy. Soon, he went back to his family and grew to be a responsible person. Many years later, he came to see Dad just before our father died. He thanked him for changing his life. "Uncle Bill, you made a taxpayer out of me!" He is a successful man today.

Don't let slothfulness creep into your life. Have a list made of every day's work and work it off. The thrill of achievement is a great motivator for the next day...and the next.

Delight:   Proverbs 6:6   Proverbs 31:27

Edna Holmes

# May 20

*"The Lord is far from the wicked: but he
heareth the prayer of the righteous."*
Proverbs 15:29

Beyond the far reaches of the universe, in the eternal realm that we can't imagine, *God dwells.* In terms of distance, it is impossible to compute.

God is far from the wicked and near to the children of God. He actually hears the prayers of the righteous. And James 5:16 tells us, *"The effectual fervent prayer of a righteous man availeth much."*

Strangely enough, God graciously *hears* our prayers, whatever kind they be; weak, fearful, awkward or timidly spoken. The only thing that will hinder prayer is unconfessed sin in the heart. Prayer, which is talking to our Heavenly Father, our Creator, is the greatest privilege afforded to human beings on earth. Hardly anyone thinks of instructing new Christians about prayer. You are expected to know about that since being saved. However, a few instructions help to get one started in learning and, thus, enjoying communicating with their Heavenly Father. Jesus gave us a model prayer, which is commonly called The Lord's Prayer in Matt.9:9-13.

"Our Father who art in heaven." *Acknowledge who God is.*
"Hallowed be thy name." *Offer praise and thanksgiving.*
"Thy will be done in earth…" *Pray according to God's will.*
"Give us this day our daily bread…" *Ask God your requests.*
*Ask God for forgiveness of sins, and cleansing.* Psalm 51.

Consider that the Lord is your Savior who loves you and He will bless you according to His divine purpose for your life. It may take a while for us to understand that our life *is not* about us. *It is about Him.*

Delight:   I Thessalonians 5:17-18   Philippians 4:6

# May 21

*"Keep thy heart with all diligence;
for out of it are the issues of life."*
Proverbs 4:23

I've taught much about the heart, as spoken of in the Word of God; that part of us which relates to others and houses our mind and emotions and will. As we yield to the Lord in all our ways and do as He commands us to keep our hearts diligently, our lives will be a testimony for Him. A well-kept heart is filled with treasure.

*"A good man out of the good treasure of the heart bringeth forth good things..."* Matthew 12:35

There are outward signs of what is going on in the heart. We all have core *beliefs*. From our belief, an *attitude* develops. An attitude is our mental mindset. It means 'posture', or how we stand in opinion.

*Thoughts* come from attitude, and the quality of thoughts depends on the kind of attitude created by our belief.

*Feelings* are generated by thoughts. What we are thinking stirs our emotions, and the power of those feelings fed by what ultimately springs from the heart, brings forth *actions*! So we have the progression: *belief, attitude, thoughts, feelings and action.* If your life gets off track and there is a struggle going on, go back and check out your heart. *What are you believing?* A good "search" prayer is in Psalm 139: 23. *"Search me, O God, and know my heart: try me and know my thoughts: And see if there be any wicked way in me, and lead me in the way everlasting."*

When a dear friend shared these things with me about the effect of what we believe in our hearts, it shed light on other areas I'd struggled with. We forget that when we ask God for help, He helps!
He will show us in some manner the solution to our needs. *Just ask.*

Delight:   Psalm 138:3   Ephesians 3:20

Edna Holmes

# May 22

*"The backslider in heart shall be
filled with his own ways..."*
Proverbs 14:14

To backslide is defined as "to slide backward in morals or religious enthusiasm." Christians understand backsliding as neglecting fellowship with the Lord and the church. Sometimes backsliding is gradual; a Christian starts skipping Sunday School and Church. He stops reading the Bible for it bother his conscience and reminds him of the sin that has beset him. The habit of "forsaking the assembling of yourselves together" is easy to establish. Re: Hebrews 10:25. Staying away from preaching and fellowship with other Christians has a devastating effect. He may soon be drawn into the world which tempted him into his backsliding. If he ignores conviction in his heart by the Holy Spirit, he may slip away into the world and misery of heart will ultimately follow.

Many times in our ministry, we have witnessed what happens to backsliders. It is a grief to the pastor as he tries to rescue them, the sheep that wandered too far away from the flock, and now they are hopelessly entangled in that which lured them away from faithfulness to God. The pleasure of sin is *just for a season,* then sorrow will settle in the heart and stay until the backslider is drawn forward again by the love of God, and His amazing grace.

> The sparkle was gone from her eyes
> Which did radiate such happiness
> In days past.
> Even the dew of dormant tears
> Could not imitate it.
> How easily we wander from the way
> Into the place of sadness and regret.

Delight:     Luke 9:62     II Peter 3:18

## May 23

*"...he causeth his wind to blow, and the waters flow."*
Psalm 148:18

When I read this verse, I always think of windmills, which used to be a common sight on ranches and farms. When God makes the wind blow which turns the blades of the wheel at the top of the windmill, it generates power which pumps up water...*flowing water.*

In this Psalm, God lets us know that He is in charge of the weather on this planet:

*"He sendeth forth his commandment upon earth: his word runneth very swiftly. He giveth snow like wool: he scattereth the hoarfrost like ashes. He casteth forth his ice like morsels: who can stand before his cold? He sendeth out his word, and melteth them: he causeth his wind to blow, and the waters flow." V. 15-19*

Scientist can explain in detail what makes the weather, but it is still a mystery, and *they cannot control the least of its activity or power!* They have discovered how to utilize the power of the elements, such as wind, sun, and lightning, but they cannot control any of it. God has set down some basic laws of nature which govern the weather patterns on the earth. Certain changes in the wind flow and temperatures in the earth's atmosphere determine what can be expected in various regions of the earth.

Some folks have believed a myth about the seasons which started ages past, that someday the regular seasons of the earth will cease. God tells us plainly in Genesis 8:22.

*"While the earth remaineth, seedtime and harvest, and cold and heat, and summer and winter, and day and night shall not cease."* Even in tropical places where it is hot most of the year, the seasons are still accounted for. Seedtime is spring, harvest is the fall season, then the obvious summer and winter times come regularly.

Delight:   Genesis 1:31   Psalm 19:1

Edna Holmes

# May 24

*"A good name is rather to be chosen than great riches..."*
Proverbs 22:1

I first saw this verse in a newspaper which had the big "funnies" section of cartoons. In times past there was a more serious cartoon feature titled *Mrs. Worth*. A character in that cartoon quoted this verse which stuck in my mind though I was not a Christian then.

The Word of God is packed with power. It is the "good seed" which brings forth fruit unto eternal life. Anywhere you plant it, or drop it along the way, or *scatter it in the wind*, it has God breathed power to save souls. Some folks give out gospel tracts as a witness to others. One of the most interesting episodes of the power in the Word is given in *Treasures to Keep* on pp223.

*"Long ago, a Christian man stood at the dock and handed out gospel tracts to passengers boarding the ship to cross the ocean. One haughty man took a tract and when realizing what it was, tore it to shreds and threw it on the ground before proceeding to board with his friends. But later a tiny bit of the shredded tract fell out of the cuff of his shirt where it had lodged. It had a single word: eternity. That one-word message burned into his heart and he could not escape. It was the means of eternal salvation for his soul."*

The Word is amazing in its scope. God does the impossible for all else but Himself; He speaks to all ages with the same Word and it "fits" each one as though it was just for that generation. The Lord says, *when* you lose your good name, it is a great loss indeed. Nobody wants to have the same name as a wicked person commonly known in history. Was it not Shakespeare who said, "The evil that men do live after them; the good is often interred with their bones."?
As Christians we should be faithful to the Lord in all things and keep an impeccable *good name* for Him. He is worthy!

Delight:    Proverbs 22:4    Ephesians 5:1

## May 25

*"The spider taketh hold with her hands,
and is in King's palaces."*
Proverbs 30:28

Spiders are a menace to their fellow insects. They are savage little creatures, master murderers in the insect world! With all its terrible traits, the spider is also a master weaver. They are very ingenious in weaving their webs with a fineness and exactness such as no art can replicate. The silken thread is produced in their own bodies; anywhere he goes the spider is equipped for business. It expertly creates intricate webs to trap other insects to consume. Recently I was reminded of the instinctive genius of the spider.

*My husband and I sit next to the aisle at church, and on a recent Wednesday night, during preaching, we noticed a spider drifting down from the ceiling in the middle of the aisle. We didn't see it until it was down eye level because the thread was invisible. Neutral colored, the spider quickly disappeared on the carpet. Amazing! The ceiling at that place in the large auditorium is approximately thirty feet high, yet the spider came down on a single silken thread which it attached to the ceiling before it left!*

As the spider "taketh hold with her hands" and winds up in a king's palace, we can take hold with the *hands of faith* and someday dwell in the palace of the King of Kings and Lord of Lords! Not only that, in the present time we have the great privilege of knowing our Lord personally, and having access to Him by prayer and fellowship. *"Thanks be unto God for his unspeakable gift."* II Corinthians 9:15

Use the creative genius that God instilled in you to live and honor the Lord with your life, driven by love, not instinct.

Delight:     Romans 8:32     Psalm 139:14

Edna Holmes

# May 26

*"And, behold, there came a leper and worshipped,
saying, Lord, if thou wilt, thou canst make me clean."*
Matthew 8:2

I like to imagine this scene in the Lord's ministry. Leprosy was a loathsome disease. Lepers were excluded from society for they were unclean, and others could not touch them without also being infected. It was a lonely, miserable life as their bodies rotted away with incurable leprosy. But this leper approached the Lord *with faith and expectation!* He had a simple appeal*: "...Lord, if thou wilt, thou canst make me clean."* Jesus did the unexpected; He touched him! No one dared do that but the Lord. Jesus was not affected by that touch to the man's leprous flesh, but the man certainly was. Jesus spoke the word; the leprous flesh *immediately* was healed. *"Nature works gradually, but the God of nature works immediately; he speaks, it is done."* (M.H.Com.) Think of the joy and wonder of that healed man!

Leprous people lived under a strict code of conduct. They had to alert those who came near them by crying out *"Unclean, Unclean!"* to avoid any contact. Leprosy represents sin in the Bible. Sin is our undoing, and we were all born sinners. Nothing can help us in our sinful, *unclean* condition but the touch of Jesus. He touches us in salvation, and we are cleansed from our sins.

Once it was observed by visitors to a very old church in England that on one side of the front door there was a slit in the outside wall like a letter drop. It was called the "leper's squint"! That's as close as the lepers could get to the worship service inside. But thanks be unto God, Jesus came down and died for our sins so that we could be cleansed and be fit to come close, even into heaven to live with Him forever! *"In whom we have redemption through his blood, even the forgiveness of sin..."* Colossians 1:14.

Delight:   Ephesians 5:25-26   I John 1:7

Delighting in the Lord

# May 27

*"Let your light so shine before men…"*
Matthew 5:16

When one is fixed on a goal, staying focused, we could say "He is on a mission". Every Christian is *on a mission*. According to Jesus, it is plain what that mission should be.

**A Light.** Jesus said we are the "light of the world." We are lights because Jesus, our Savior, is THE Light of the world, and we reflect that light. *"Let your light so shine before men, that they may see your good works, and glorify your Father which is in heaven."* We reflect the light in the world with good works. People notice what we do; works are a powerful witness. *Our lives are on a mission!*

**Be as Salt**. Jesus said *"Ye are the salt of the earth: but if the salt have lost his savour, wherewith shall it be salted? It is thenceforth good for nothing, but to be cast out, and to be trodden under foot of men."* Matthew 5:13. The Lord would have us act as a wholesome restraining influence on a corrupt society. Salt preserves and is an antiseptic. Salt that has lost its savor, is fit for nothing. In that era useless salt was tossed out on the wayside where people walked. If we neglect fellowship with the Lord, we will lose our *saltiness* which attracts others to "taste and see" that the Lord is good. We need to stay salty!

*My Dad at times got a salt block for our cows. Cows need lots of salt to stay healthy and produce calcium for their milk. Lack of salt leads to disease. Dad positioned the block on a fence post and the animals went after that salt! They would lick out a big smooth place on one side, and it was a fun thing for the children to go out occasionally and lick on the salt block. The smooth side was our favorite place to lick!* Healthy farm kids, we were.

Delight:    Mark 9:50    Acts 26:18

Edna Holmes

# May 28

*"Now the we are ambassadors for Christ..."*
II Corinthians 5:20

If our lives are *on a mission* for our Lord, then we have another very important role in this world which is a great privilege.

**As Ambassadors.** Our text verse continues to tell us what we are to proclaim in the "foreign country" we are occupying until the Lord calls us home. *"...we pray you in Christ's stead, be ye reconciled to God."* That's the message we are to convey to the inhabitants of the earth. We are in Christ's stead, representing Him. Ambassadors! Those who are in foreign countries representing America stand out as *foreigners*. Their language, dress, and mannerisms easily identify them with their native land. And, likewise, Christians are soon known by the same things. If we are *salty* as we should be and reflecting the light of Jesus, we are pegged right away as Christians! Once traveling, we stopped in a place for breakfast. Before we had thanked God for our food, a waitress came over to our table and said, "you are Christians, aren't you?" We told her we were, and further asked how she knew it. She said, "You just look like it and act like it!" It reminded us anew that we are ambassadors for Christ, representing Him every moment.

**As Epistles.** Christians are on display on earth, and God through the Apostle Paul tells us how very open we are to the world's scrutiny. *"Forasmuch as ye are manifestly declared to be the epistle of Christ ministered by us..."* II Cor.3:3 He also said we are *"...known and read of all men."* v 2. Think of that! People just naturally love to read letters. And it is a delight to the world to observe Christians with a critical eye. So, they read with interest what comes from our hearts as we deal with the *issues of life.* Keeping your heart with all diligence, feeding it the Word of God, and fellowship with the Lord will make you worth reading. *Your life is on a mission!*

Delight:   II Corinthians 4:1-2   Colossians 3:1-2

Delighting in the Lord

# May 29

*"But ye shall receive power, after that the Holy Ghost
is come upon you: and ye shall be witnesses..."*
Acts 1:8

We don't have power in ourselves to be witnesses for the Lord. That comes from above, and so the Lord told the church to tarry at Jerusalem to wait for the Holy Spirit to come down at the day of Pentecost. After that, the Holy Spirit has indwelled everyone who comes to Christ and is saved. Christians will be bold to witness for the Lord, and effective if they are *"filled with the Spirit..."*. Many misunderstand that truth and we have a clear explanation in the book of Ephesians 5:18-20. Reading it carefully. *"And be not drunk with wine, wherein is excess; but be filled with the Spirit..."* That is a contrast. When one drinks wine till he is drunk, he is *under the influence of the wine, alcohol!* When a Christian is filled with the Spirit, he is under the influence of the Lord God! We are not containers, like buckets, and the Holy Spirit of God is not liquid. He is a Person, the third in the God-Head. We should be *filled* with Him; have Him in control of our entire lives that we be happy and fruitful for the Lord.

An apt illustration is marriage. The day I got married, my life was changed completely. Ever since that day, I've been keenly aware that another person shares my life and controls it in a blessed way.

*"Speaking to yourselves in psalms and hymns and spiritual songs, singing and making melody in your heart to the Lord; Giving thanks for all things unto God and the Father in the name of the Lord Jesus Christ..."* The Holy Spirit will put a song in our hearts, which will come out our mouths. Singing always lifts us up and rejoices our hearts. Then we will always be giving thanks to God for all the blessings and love He pours into our lives. We will love His Word more. We will be witnesses!

Delight:   Ephesians 5:8-9   Philippians 1:6

Edna Holmes

# May 30

*"...thou hast set my feet in a large room."*
Psalm 31:8

As a child I longed for a *large room!* Along with that daydream was the desire for a large house. With our big family, there never was enough room in the house to satisfy everyone. But in our era most farm folks had to be satisfied with too small houses and make do with what they had. It was when Christ brought me to Himself, and saved me, that I began to understand something of the *large room* I was really longing for.

Salvation gives us entrance into a very large room. There we breath the air of peace with God, fellowship with the Lord Jesus Christ, and discover new and wonderful things about the Lord as we can now understand the Word of God in that large room. We also discover that large room has other believers in it that we love instantly when we meet them. They are brothers and sisters!

There is protection in times of temptation in that large room and our defense is ready to protect us mightily. The large room is a blessed place. It is described another way by the Lord. Jesus said in John 10:9 *"I am the door: by me if any man enter in, he shall be saved, and shall go in and out, and find pasture."*

Jesus is the Door of that large room, and that explains the many wonders and blessings we find when we enter in. Also like a pasture, there is food, water, and multitudes of comforts waiting for us to partake of any time our hearts yearn for anything from the Lord. The Word of God encompasses all those needs, and our blessed Lord is more eager to pour out His blessings on us than we are to ask and receive! Be much in fellowship with the Lord in the *large room!*

Delight:   John 10:10   II Samuel 22:37

Delighting in the Lord

# May 31

*"Behold, thou desirest truth in the inward parts:"*
Psalm 51:6

In the powerful *cleansing* psalm prayed by King David as he repented of his sin of adultery, this intriguing verse causes us to pause when we read it and think on it.

God desires truth in our inward parts. *He already knows the truth about us from the time we drew our first breath of air.* So why did he tell us that? It soon occurred to me that it is only when we come to the real truth about ourselves, deep down in the inmost part of our being, that we can be healed from the things that hold us back from complete freedom in Christ. Jesus says in His Word, *"And ye shall know the truth, and the truth shall make you free."* John 8:32. Just knowing the truth about issues which affect our lives, especially those things that are buried in our memories, has a cleansing, freeing effect. The Lord *desires* that we be enlightened by His Word and acquire that blessed freedom. It is a delight to discover answers in the Bible as we read. One day it comes, and sometimes in a place where you never expected you would find an answer. There it will be and the affect that buried issue had on you is instantly canceled!

The power of God's Word is far more than we think of it. It is seed that can be planted in the heart of the vilest, most wicked man and sprout. He can be drawn to the Savior and changed immediately as the demoniac who was running through the tombs screaming and cutting himself. The Lord has such power that we can't comprehend it; rest assured when you plant His Word in the ears and hearts of people, it will affect them. We need it every day to keep our own hearts right also. Read it! It is your life.

Delight: Psalm 5:3    Job 42:2

Edna Holmes

# June 1

*"So ought men to love their wives as their own bodies."*
Ephesians 5:28

This month is known as *Bride's Month,* because more weddings occur in June than any other month. The Lord doesn't mince words when it comes to the subject of marriage. He performed the first wedding. He created Eve from Adam's rib and brought her to Adam and put these words in Adam's mouth when Eve was presented to him as his wife. *And Adam said, "This is now bone of my bones, and flesh of my flesh: she shall be called Woman, because she was taken out of Man. Therefore shall a man leave his father and his mother, and shall cleave unto his wife: and they shall be one flesh."* Gen.2:23-24 The second part is commonly used today in marriage ceremonies, first spoken in the beginning when only Adam and Eve were there. These words were for future generations that God knew would be created by the union of the first two human beings that He made. I might say also that they had a beautiful garden wedding!

Wives should feel secure in their husbands' love. Men are to love their wives as much as they love their own bodies! I'm sure this is not understood today by many, even by Christian men. It's a plain command from the Lord. Then a wife is to *reverence* her husband. That means honor him. God, speaking again to men: *"Nevertheless let every one of you in particular so love his wife even as himself; and wife see that she reverence her husband."* Eph. 5:33

*The* reason the Lord puts such emphasis on this subject is because the marriage relationship is a picture of Christ and the church. *"This is a great mystery: but I speak concerning Christ and the church." V.32.* Those of us who are married should pause and think on that. Does our home and marriage remind anyone of Christ and His salvation? A Christian is the object of Christ's love and care.

Delight:   Ephesians 5:25   Ephesians 4:31-32

# June 2

*"This is a great mystery: but I speak
concerning Christ and the church."*
Ephesians 5:32

A mystery is a *hidden* truth. The marriage of a man and woman portrays an example of the relationship between Christ and the church which is His "body" on earth. He is not here in body; we are here in His place doing the works of the Lord.

The picture of salvation should be seen in observing a marriage. Christ loves His own body, the saved ones, the church. He nourishes it and cares for it, protects and provides for all her needs. That's the way a husband is to be toward his wife. That's a big order in this corrupt world where the breakdown of the family is common and delights the world that hates Christ, as He said it would.

And in the same context, wives have their responsibilities. One is to *reverence* her husband, that is to honor him. Women may say, "The Bible does not say for wives to love their husbands!" God makes a strong point in that direction when He says in Titus 2:4 *"That they may teach the young women to be sober, to love their husbands, to love their children..."* That is the directive for *aged,* or older women. You can't teach what you don't know. Love begets love. When the wife is loved and cherished as the Word teaches the husband to do, her response will be to love. The world mocks this Bible truth, but the only place you can learn how to have a happy, loving marriage relationship is from the Word of God.

We were not Christians when we got married, but we knew marriage was serious, and for keeps. So in hard times, we just stuck with it. When the love of God and His Word changed us, it gave us a whole new perspective about every area of our lives.

Delight:   I John 3:1   I John 4:10-11

Edna Holmes

# June 3

*"And whatsoever ye do in word or deed, do
all in the name of the Lord Jesus..."*
Colossians 3:17

In the Gift of salvation, which is Christ, we have love packaged in various ways and means to be enjoyed and shared with all who are connected with us. *"God is love."* The Word of God keeps my heart prepared to sow love and consideration for others. Prayer gives power and direction to my heart for doing a good work for the Lord.

Salvation powerfully changes the recipients of God's grace. We are equipped to serve the Lord in any direction and capacity He chooses for us. He changes us completely! My husband was the first up close example for me of what God's salvation does. He had all the ones he loved in a very small circle. After he was saved, it was amazing to me how he began to love the church and be interested in others. God turned his life in the opposite direction that he has faithfully traveled ever since.

God has told us what to do as we occupy down here. *"But be ye doers of the word, and not hearers only, deceiving your own selves."* James 1:22. We are to obey the Word of God as we read and study it. We are His "hands" to do His work on earth. The basis of all His work is to get people to Christ in all the ways we can. Our hands are His to use.

### THE HANDS OF GOD

Yours are the hands of God—how did you use them today?
Did they crush or caress – did they ruin or bless?
How did you use them today?
Yours are the hands of God—use them well as you travel life's way.
Turn with love to each task—for one-day God will ask:
"What did you do with my hands today?"

Delight:   Galatians 6:10   I Corinthians 3:13-15

## June 4

*"...my cup runneth over."*
Psalm 23:5

There is a beautiful song titled, *Fill My Cup Lord,* which has a meaningful message. We should search our hearts to see where our expectations are really focused. *Cup,* is used figuratively often and means "the portion allotted to someone." From the scriptures, the *cup of God's wrath and cup of trembling* in Isaiah 51:17 have a clear meaning. Our text verse refers to the host *running the cup over the brim*, a signal to the guest that he is very welcome in his house. The Lord runs our *cup* over continually with His blessings.

We all have our cups: pleasure, grief, worry, and any such thing that's in our lives. But women have a *special cup* which they hold out to be filled. That's the cup of *expectation!* That is, we have a basic need to be fulfilled. If you are married, the husband is the first to be offered the cup! A Bride's expectation is at a peak when she says, "I Do!" to the wonderful man she commits to for life. He may fill her *cup of expectation* in part, but that is all.

The Lord is the One who satisfies the longings of our hearts. Open His Word and read; realize that every word and line of it is for us, His beloved children. No one can love us so and satisfy our needs but The Lord Jesus Christ, *"For in him dwelleth all the fullness of the Godhead bodily. And ye are complete in him."* Col. 2:9-10

When we married over six decades ago, it was two cultures joining hands. He was from Illinois; Texas was my home. He had never seen a cotton field! The first breakfast I cooked for him had homemade biscuits, enough for *ten people* like I was used to! I fully expected praise and admiration for those biscuits. He said, "Could you make just two?" I was stunned! I only knew how to make a big batch like Mama had taught me; *you couldn't make just two.* It took a while for me to appreciate his logic, *and also make a smaller batch of biscuits.*

Delight:   Psalm 62:5   Psalm 63:1

Edna Holmes

# June 5

*"My soul, wait thou only upon God;
for my expectation is from him."*
Psalm 62:5

There is always interest in teaching on personal relationships and especially on the subject of marriage. What do we expect? How are we to adjust, and still have our expectations satisfied? As in the devotional before, our fulfilment and satisfaction in life has to come from the Lord. Both husband and wife will thrive with spiritual growth. The Holy Spirit is your teacher; the Bible is your textbook. If a couple makes a habit of reading the Bible *together,* it will be a most beneficial practice; the best you'll ever make!

Women naturally identify with the bride's perspective concerning marriage. She envisions life with her beloved, who is near perfect in her eyes, as having all her longing for love, affection, attention, understanding, and strength poured into her cup of expectation. However, the husband not only doesn't fill her cup, he is apt to drill holes in the bottom of it with his insensitive actions!

It doesn't take long for a wife to understand that this wonderful man the Lord gave her is totally opposite of herself. Keeping that truth marked in her mind helps a wife very much. Women are emotional, and men are logical! My husband's cool logic has been frustrating at times, but it has also helped me greatly when I didn't know what to do. Someone has said Men think with their heads, and women think with their hearts. God made a husband and wife special suited for one another. Adams rib had to come back to him, and Eve had to have Adam rejoined to her to complete her. Marriage is a marvelous institution which God thought of first. Make Him the priority in your life, and your marriage is more likely to meet your expectations. *With God all things are possible!*

Delight:   I Peter 3:7   Colossians 3:18

## June 6

*"Thou therefore endure hardness as a
good soldier of Jesus Christ."*
II Timothy 2:3

On this day in 1944 the Allied Forces invaded Normandy and hastened the end of World War II. It was called D-Day. Our country and others rejoiced when that war came to an end.

The war that Christians are engaged in will never cease this side of heaven. It is Christian Warfare! Our war is with the devil. He commands a large invisible army of evil beings that are bent on hindering Christians from serving the Lord. It is warfare unlike anything else. It takes place in our minds and to those who love the Lord and want to serve Him faithfully, it is a tormenting struggle to keep our minds clear and on track.

We are soldiers. We must "endure hardness "and that means to have personal discipline and *grit* in our lives. God furnishes armor for protection. Eph. 6:11. *"Put on the whole armor of God, that ye may be able to stand against the wiles of the devil."*

All of God's armor is vital. There is protection for every part but the back. *We cannot turn and run!* There is no reason to retreat in the warfare with the devil. We resist by drawing close to God. James 4:8. *Draw nigh to God, and he will draw nigh to you."* This is not a study on the armor, but one part I will name is *truth*.

*The Truth* protects our minds. The Truth is God's Word. When the devil is trying to tempt you with a lie, quote what the Bible says about it. It will drive him away every time. Use the scriptures! It is your protection. Jesus showed us the "tip of the sword" which is: *It is written!* That's what the Lord used when the devil tempted Him. Jesus Himself quoted scripture saying beforehand: It is written! He didn't use supernatural power to scare the devil and defeat him. We have what He used. Load your heart up with the Word. Use it!

Delight:   Ephesians 6:14-18   Ephesians 4:27

Edna Holmes

# June 7

*"The entrance of thy words giveth light..."*
Psalm 119:130

The Word of God will absolutely give us light to live by, but do we see that light? Our minds may actually be engaged elsewhere even as we read the most powerful book in the world. The Bible holds the key to knowledge about God; that is what we should continually search the scriptures for and grow richer in our relationship with Him. Sometimes it's hard to decide what to do in a certain situation. You must make a clear decision. Which way is the right way to go? There are some things to consider based on the Word of God that is very helpful. It has helped me and many others.

>Can you ask God to bless your decision? Colossians 3:17. If we can say and do what we must with our decision *all in the name of the Lord Jesus, and give thanks to God,* we are on safe ground.

>Will your decision be a stumbling block to others? I Cor. 8:9. We must consider that some Christians, maybe newer in the faith, have not grown to understand as much as we do about the Word of God. There are "younger" brothers and sisters in Christ to consider.

>Have you thought ahead about the consequences of your decision? Galatians 6:7. One of the most sobering verses in the Bible is this one. *"Be not deceived; God is not mocked: for whatsoever a man soweth, that shall he also reap."* There are consequences to every single act that is done on this earth. Each person is the center of his own sowing circle. We sow, *or plant,* words and deeds every waking moment of our lives that we will be accountable for to God. We may only think of the negative side of this truth; but the positive side actively works also bringing joy and blessings into one's life. The world is a dark place; God's Word is light. Stay in the light!

Delight:     Colossians 3:2     I John 1:7

## June 8

*"For my thoughts are not your thoughts, neither are your ways my ways, saith the Lord."*
Isaiah 55:8

It is hard for Christians to grasp this fact. We are so sure that what we are thinking is so good that God is surely thinking along those same lines. He isn't! The Bible says in the following verse 9, *"For as the heavens are higher than the earth, so are my ways higher than your ways, and my thoughts than your thoughts."* We forget that God is Holy. I John 1:5 *"…God is light, and in him is no darkness at all."* There is not one speck of darkness in Him; He is the Light that is going to light heaven for all eternity. *He is Holy.*

Jesus startles our minds in His statement about thoughts in Luke 12:22. *"…Therefore I say unto you, Take no thought for your life, what ye shall eat; neither for the body, what ye shall put on."* Did the Lord really say that? *He did!* He said don't think about your life; and really, that is all we think about most of the time. We are to surrender and allow Him to control our lives. It's about Him, not us.

He also said don't worry about food. God will provide for us. I've heard so many testimonies of Bible College students, with families, struggling to get through, and sometimes not knowing where the next meal would come from. *But food always came!* They never went hungry as they trusted in the Lord for their daily food.

Then clothes! It is said that we wear only 20% of our clothes 80% of the time. Our closets are stuffed. Take some out and give them away! You will be blessed, and those who receive them will be blessed. Sit down and carefully read Luke 6:38 and think on it. It is an amazing promise of God, *which always is stirred into motion when you give!* Establish this verse in your mind, and act on it. You will be blessed.

Delight:    Luke 6:38    Jeremiah 29:11

Edna Holmes

# June 9

*"The Kingdom of heaven is like unto a certain king,
which made a marriage for his son..."*
Matthew 22:2

On this date sixty-six years ago, I was getting ready for my wedding. That is an exciting time for a bride. Getting ready meant sorting and packing all my things for traveling back to his home state right after the wedding. It was a hectic time. But I didn't mind; the next day I would say "I Do!" and be his wife.

Since Christians are the Bride of Christ, the church, there should be some preparation going on to be ready when the Lord comes for us. That is very important because we don't know *exactly* when He is coming. Matt.24:42 tells us: *"Watch therefore: for ye know not what hour your Lord doth come."* We must do all the things that will keep us prepared to meet our Savior face to face.

Daily fellowship with Him registers assurance and confidence in the Lord. The neglect of this one thing will keep us ineffective in the Lord's work, and a vague uneasiness in our hearts. It is a respectable sin which will defeat us and give the devil a victory in our lives.

Within that fellowship time, we must communicate with God in prayer. Talk to Him as you would your closest friend. We can tell the Lord everything in our hearts, and He can answer our prayers, and also reveal solutions to our problems. It has enriched my life since I've realized that Jesus is also my Counselor.

Are we going to be caught off guard when the Lord comes for us, His bride? Many Christians are side-tracked by the world that has crept into every corner of life, it is hard to keep in mind that the Bible is reality. What God has said *is going to come to pass!* There is so much fantasy portrayed in the world. In subtle ways doubt is cast in our minds about what is true and real.

Delight:   Titus 2:13   Hebrews 9:28

# June 10

*"Watch therefore, for ye know neither the day
nor the hour wherein the Son of man cometh."*
Matthew 25:13

Our wedding day! My soldier had come home unexpectedly from the Korean War. There was no instant communication then, but when he reached home, he called me. With only a month furlough, we put together our wedding plans quickly. If I'd only known when he was coming, I could have been ready.

The Lord gave us another parable about the necessity of being ready when He comes for His bride. The story is told in Matt. 25:1-13. Five of ten virgins were wise; they had oil in their lamps. Five were foolish and they had no oil in their lamps, so when the bridegroom came to get his bride, they were caught with no oil. The wise virgins lit their lamps and went out to join the bridegroom's procession.

In the Jewish culture, the bride and groom were betrothed, or engaged, for one year. During that year he prepared a special room for them on the family estate. When the day came to go get his bride, he, with a great procession of friends, marched to the Bride's house to escort her back to the wedding and feast. Her friends, the other virgins made ready to join the procession. It was a joyous occasion as this great throng of friends accompanied the couple to the wedding and the feast afterwards. But the foolish virgins didn't get ready for it, and so missed the once in a lifetime festivity for their friends.

It is our mission on earth telling others to get ready for eternity, or they will miss heaven and the bliss of being with Jesus forever and ever. It's a simple message. Jesus loves us; He died for our sins. He was buried and on the third day, He arose from the grave! That is the best news in the world, and anyone who knows it personally, can tell it.

Delight:   Romans 10:9-10   Romans 10:13

Edna Holmes

# June 11

*"And it was in the heart of David my father to build
an house for the name of the Lord God of Israel."*
I Kings 8:17

King David amassed the wealth it would take to build the magnificent temple that was erected during Solomon's reign over the nation of Israel. David so wanted to build the Lord a house to dwell in. The Tabernacle had been "the Lord's house" for generations. Now it was time. However, God would not allow King David to build the temple. *But God knew it was in his heart.*

God observes our hearts and sees what's there, instead of going by our words. Our love for Him and our motives for serving Him is what interests the Lord. God can and does get glory from the *behind the scenes* service that no one sees or pays attention to.

*In an earlier generation, a young man was accepted for Missionary service to Africa, but soon found out that his wife could not stand the climate. He was heartbroken, but prayerfully returned to his home and determined to make all the money he could, to be used to spread the gospel over the world. He eventually took over the family business and developed it to vast proportions. His name is Welch, whose family still manufactures grape juice. He gave a vast fortune to the work of missions.*

God can do miracles with a willing heart. What is in your own heart? Is there a longing to do something significant for the Lord? Perhaps you haven't told anyone, it just lies there in your heart desiring to get out, but you are unsure, so do nothing. Take it out today and give it to the Lord to do with as he sees fit. All He needs is your heart first of all. Ladies, our time is running out. We must do what we are going to do now...today!

Delight:    Psalm 51:10    Romans 12:2

# June 12

*"As ye have therefore received Christ Jesus
the Lord, so walk ye in him."*
Colossians 2:6

One sure identifying sign of a Christian is a new life. A permanent change comes over him. He walks with the Lord now. That walk implies *action!* The new life shows fruit of the indwelling Holy Spirit. We can't grow that fruit on our own in our hearts.

*"But the fruit of the Spirit is love, joy, peace, longsuffering, gentleness, goodness, faith, Meekness, temperance: against such there is no law."* Galatians 5:22-23 This fruit begins to show up in the new walk. It is developed in Spiritual growth. Meanwhile, the walk of a Christian continues in the new direction it has taken since he was saved. Walking implies *habit.*

Going to church quickly became routine for my husband after he was saved. He not only loved to go himself; he wanted to take others with him so they could hear the gospel too. He became an avid soul winner. The things in which we are consistent becomes a habit, and it is a good testimony before others.

*I read of a Christian family with the firm habit of going to church. They had invited their neighbors who were civil but refused to attend church with them. But each Sunday morning the unbelieving neighbors heard the four doors of the Christians' car open and slam shut, and they drove off. It both irritated and made them curious at the same time. Finally, one Sunday the neighbors of the Christians got ready and told them they were going with them to church!* "We want to see what causes you to go there every Sunday." A habit of a faithful walk is a very good testimony. How is yours today? Would it cause others to desire what you have as a Christian? You don't have to say a word to have an influence on others. *Just walk, and talk, with Jesus!*

Delight:    Ephesians 5:2    I John 1:7

Edna Holmes

# June 13

*"Therefore if any man be in Christ, he is a new creature:
old things are passed away; behold all things are become new."*
II Corinthians 5:17

This is a powerful verse, and a sobering one. The new birth that every sinner experiences when he comes to Christ, makes a new and different person out of him. The "new creation" happens on the inside, and then starts to show up on the outside. Some new Christians misunderstand our text verse. They expect to be perfect, and they aren't and never shall be in the body of flesh. We are perfect *in Christ* and that is our standing before God.

The Lord made provision for the sins which beset us. Jesus is seated at the right hand of the Father to make intercession for us. The "new creature" status we have makes us hate sin and try to avoid it; but we sometimes fail. I John 1:9 is one of our restorative treasures. *"If we confess our sins, he is faithful and just to forgive us our sins, and cleanse us from all unrighteousness."*

We have been *made alive* at the moment we trusted in Jesus to save us. We ought to be aware of when we went from darkness to light, spiritually. *"Who hath delivered us from the power of darkness, and hath translated us into the kingdom of his dear Son."* Col.1:13. Look what Jesus did! Aren't we aware of it? In searching our hearts during time with the Lord, it is good to list some things that have changed about our hearts and life. Write them down and feel the thankfulness well up in your heart like an overflowing spring.

The first telling change for my husband and myself was the interest in, and longing to know, the Word of God! I couldn't understand it before, now every word held meaning for me. What was the most outstanding change for your life? Write it down!

Delight:   John 5:24   Titus 3:5-6

Delighting in the Lord

# June 14

*"Being born again, not of corruptible seed, but of incorruptible, by the Word of God..."*
I Peter 1:23

The new Christian immediately longs after the Word of God. He longs after its sustenance as a newborn baby cries for its mother's milk. God's Word has many names that we cherish, and *the incorruptible seed* is one of them. It is pure seed that brings forth life everywhere it is planted. That's why missionaries, called of God, go all over the earth and plant that *precious seed* in the hearts of others. I've been to many countries with my husband visiting missionaries. We have seen them living in primitive conditions, doing without things which is unthinkable in this country, yet they are happily planting *that incorruptible Seed* of the Word of God. They plant, and water, and the Seed takes root; then spiritual life comes forth! That's what keeps missionaries going out and planting; the Seed brings forth eternal life for those souls lost without Christ.

After souls are born again by the incorruptible Seed of God's Word, thereafter, the Holy Spirit uses the Word of God to effect spiritual growth. It's more than our minds can fully grasp, that God loves us so much He gave Jesus to be sacrificed for our sins; thereby making our new birth possible. Then God gave us His precious Word to guide and sustain us through the duration of our lives on earth. *Amazing Grace* is the favorite song of millions because that's what God displays in countless ways to His children every day of their lives.

This acronym defines God's grace according to Ephesians 1:7. **G**od's **R**iches **A**t **C**hrist's **E**xpense. *"In whom we have redemption through his blood, the forgiveness of sins, according to the riches of his grace."* Let us never forget what Christ did for us. Be thankful.

Delight:   Ephesians 2:4-5   Colossians 2:6-7

# June 15

*"Though a host shall encamp against me,
my heart shall not fear."*
Psalm 27:3

David said he would not fear facing an army. He looked to God for protection. We read of such in the Bible when king Saul's son, Jonathan, was trying to get a breakthrough in the battle with the Philistines. He told his armor bearer, *"Come, and let us go over unto the garrison of these uncircumcised: it may be that the Lord will work for us: for there is no restraint to the Lord to save by many or few."* He had confidence that God could use just the two of them to rout the army. Jonathan engaged a few in combat, and they all jumped up and fled! So it happened.

I've been encouraged with the word, *restraint,* ever since I read that account in I Samuel 14:6. There is no restraint to God to answer our prayers, to save the souls we witness to, and supply all the needs of the missionaries we are praying for. I love knowing that for the Lord, *there is no restraint!*

Things and situations can make us afraid in this world. But we don't have to be. God is always very present with us.

*In my youth, we lived by a main highway and railroad. Vagrants sometimes stopped by asking for food. My mother, rocking my infant brother, was alone one morning, when she glanced up to see a woman standing in the dining room doorway. She asked her what she wanted. Food. Mama told her to take whatever was left from breakfast on the table. She gathered up the food and went out the back door the way she came in.* Mama was not a fearful person. It gave her an edge in such situations.

A daily *active* trust in the Lord will keep fear out. Focus on Him, not your fears. There is no restraint to the Lord. Selah!

Delight:   Ecclesiastes 12:13   Isaiah 8:13

## June 16

*"Better is a dinner of herbs where love is,
than a stalled ox and hatred therewith."*
Proverbs 15:17

Wealthy people ate meat! and the stalled ox indicated plans for a big feast with plenty of meat from a fattened ox. The poor could never expect such fare. They needed an ox for working their fields, eking out a living. They could not afford the luxury of eating him!

Those who have the Lord in their midst, whether rich or poor, are happy and content. It is the Lord Who makes the difference not their possessions, or lack of them. It's a fact: *"But godliness with contentment is great gain."* I Tim. 6:6. In the home with *godliness* there will be the sweet presence of the Lord, and therefore, love and peace and an attitude of kindness and generosity to those without. Wealth cannot produce those things, neither can poverty; it must come from the Heavenly Father through the Lord Jesus Christ. It is a *rich* family that has that treasure on display in their home and lives.

Growing up on a farm, our food was always simple, mostly homegrown, and varied with the seasons. The basic fare all year long was beans or peas, cornbread and biscuits, and the condiments on hand. The seasons brought variety, such as fresh vegetables, meat, and fresh fruits. Much was canned for winter. Every meal was fixed from scratch. No refrigeration, or even and an 'ice-box' was available in those days before electricity in the rural parts. Daddy came in from the field, hung his hat up, washed his hands, and sat down to ask the blessing before we ate. I didn't know it at the time; but we were rich!

*"Riches and poverty are more in the heart than in the hand. He is wealthy who is contented."* (commentary)

Delight:   I Timothy 6:7-8   I Timothy 6:17

Edna Holmes

# June 17

*"Wherefore God also hath highly exalted him,
and given him a name which is above every name."*
Philippians 2:9

Have you noticed that in the world you may talk about any and everything in conversation, but Jesus? Sports figures, TV and movie stars, books and authors, and the latest movies are acceptable subjects to babble on and on about…but not the Lord. He makes people "uncomfortable" and it creates an awkwardness or a stop to an otherwise lively conversation. It is not civil or acceptable in our society today to mention that blessed name of Jesus. Believers must seek the company of other Christians to enjoy the things of the Lord. The world does not want Him around.

Jesus is the Creator! He created our habitation, especially designed for man to live and discover throughout the ages the depth of riches in the earth. He created the universe and all you see and don't see when you gaze into the heavens. Then in the end times, He condescended to come to earth through the womb of a virgin, to identify with sinful men so He could redeem them from the sin curse. Our Lord did all that; *but we aren't supposed to mention it in the world*! It might embarrass someone to hear His name: Jesus. That attitude will someday come to an abrupt end. It is then that the world of mankind will be humbled beyond measure as everyone on earth and heaven will bow their knee and confess that Jesus Christ is Lord to the glory of God the Father. Phil.2:10-11. *"That at the name of Jesus every knee should bow, of things in heaven, and things in earth, and things under the earth; And that every tongue should confess that Jesus Christ is Lord, to the glory of God the Father."*
If you haven't done that; do it quickly! He deserves all our praise.

Delight:   Philippians 2:8-9   Colossians 1:16-17

# June 18

*"Wisdom is the principal thing; therefore get wisdom: and with all thy getting get understanding."*
Proverbs 4:7

People have different views of wisdom, what it is, and how you acquire it. The source of wisdom is God, and we get it from His Word. With the Holy Spirit in us to teach us, we soon learn so much of the wisdom that God has for us to enrich our lives. Wisdom has a simple definition. It is the *right use of knowledge.* That's simple enough for a child to understand. When we learn by experience that certain things hurt us, we don't do them anymore. That's wisdom!

A friend gave me a list of sayings which have been wrought out of experience and filed under the category of wisdom for future mediation. I'm grateful to the unknown author, whoever he or she may be. We can always benefit from shared wisdom.

1. *I have learned:* That you should always leave loved ones with loving words. It may be the last time you see them.

2. *I have learned:* That our background may have influenced who we are, but we are responsible for who we become.

3. *I have learned:* That it's not what you have in your life, but *who* you have in your life that counts.

4. *I have learned:* That you cannot make someone love you. All you can do is be someone that can be loved.

5. *I have learned*: That you can keep going long after you can't. It is a great element when, by experience, you learn this fact. *In pulling a long sack all day picking cotton or pulling bolls with family, I'd be so exhausted by quitting time, I felt I couldn't go another step. But we encouraged each other to reach the end of the row, weigh up our cotton, then head home for supper and rest. So I learned early in life that you can indeed "keep going, long after you can't!"*

Delight:   Job 28:28   James 3:17

## June 19

*"Get wisdom, get understanding: forget it not…"*
Proverbs 4:5

Continuing our list of simple but profound sayings; I am touched with the truth of them and they cause me to reflect on the experiences of my life. On the previous page, one said that *"you can keep going long after you can't."* You have worked on something; you are worn out and you're out of energy. You were ready to sit down and quit! Then an encouraging thought, or a strong motivation arose, and you felt energy infuse your body to get up and finish the task! You have learned there is always more strength reserved in you.

*Also, we can't make someone love us!* We can do all the female tricks in the book, but we really cannot make someone respond with love. We can be a person easy to love, but that is all. We must remember, however, that love has great appeal, and can influence an unhappy, difficult person to be an amiable friend. Other profound, yet simple sayings, were these:

*I have learned:* It is taking me a long time to become the person I want to be. In the Christian realm, spiritual growth is not an instant thing. We want to be mature quickly and know as much as the older Christians. Progress comes sooner if we pursue the study of God's Word. Then practicing what we learn is a major milestone.

*I have learned:* That true love continues to grow even over the longest distance. Nothing is equal to love in power and influence. Time and distance do not diminish its strength. The source of love is God. I John 4:16 *"…God is love; and he that dwelleth in love dwelleth in God, and God in him."* Those who have the capacity to truly love are God's children; they resemble their Heavenly Father.

Do you truly love anybody? Do you love God? He knows.

Delight:   I John 4:10-12   John 14:23

# June 20

*"Walk in wisdom...redeeming the time."*
Colossians 4:5

Again, the definition of wisdom is knowledge and good judgment based on experience; being wise. That means, simply, *the right use of knowledge.*

Christians are to use wisdom in their daily living, their walk. Those without Christ are watching, and they need to see something that will cause them to consider Him. Life is uncertain, and we are to redeem the time; that is, use it wisely. Many are lost in the world and time is running out. One day, the Lord Himself is coming back. What will we have to show for the talents and abilities He has given us to use for His honor and glory? And we should give solemn thought to the fact that we may be the only Christian that some others know. What are they seeing, and hearing in our lives?

Satan keeps our minds distracted and muddled up with worldly clamor to the point where these facts slip from our minds. Bring them back up into view on the screen of your mind and hold them there. Though timid, or shy, God will hold us responsible to be a witness for Him to reach lost souls. Time is slipping away, and most people in this world *are not saved.* Will this be their cry at the judgment: *"I looked on my right hand, and beheld, but there was no man that would know me: refuge failed me; no man cared for my soul."* Psa. 142:4

The greatest joy for a Christian is to win a lost one to Christ. You may bring a visitor to church, who hears the gospel and is saved. You may go out on visitation with another person and invite folks to church or share the gospel when you have opportunity. We don't open the doors, God does. We just obediently go. *"Salvation belongeth unto the Lord".* Psalm 3:8

Delight:   Colossians 4:6   Romans 6:23

Edna Holmes

# June 21

*"Every wise woman buildeth her house..."*
Proverbs 14:1

This verse continues to tell us that *"but the foolish plucketh it down with her hands."* There is a definite difference between a wise and foolish woman. Before I was a Christian, I was a young wife that often sat with the neighborhood women talking unwisely about their husbands. Though I said nothing disparaging about mine, some had a mocking way of describing things about their husbands and, younger wives, as I was, should not be hearing such discouraging talk about marriage. After I was saved, I had no desire to be in their company and hear them *plucking* their houses down more with their mouths than with their hands. Words from a woman with a scornful attitude about her husband and marriage is akin to germs which can spread and infect many. The "house" is the family, their happiness and well-being. When a woman is foolish, she disturbs the peace and tranquility of her home by airing her unhappy attitude.

Her husband cannot be totally at ease; he never knows what kind of foolishness his wife will display next. He knows her talk is detrimental to the family, and others know it as well. There is hardly a time when he can totally relax.

The Children are like radars, picking up signals that parents have no idea matters a whit to children. When my parents went through troubled times in their younger years, I was a young child, yet I *knew* when they were unhappy; it disturbed me and my sense of security vanished. Such is the impact of a home that has been "plucked down" even on a temporary basis, later to be built back again. Many are not! Faithfully following the pattern for home and marriage in the Bible will guarantee a loving environment for a family to thrive in. Your best company will be the *wise* woman; avoid the foolish *plucker!*

Delight:   Proverbs 14:7   Proverbs 15:1-2

# June 22

*"The heart of her husband doth safely trust in her..."*
Proverbs 31:11

Marriage is a popular subject to teach on to women. Every wife welcomes helpful hints as to making a better marriage relationship and home life for her family. She will be one of the wise who grabs a pen and starts taking notes. In over six decades of marriage, most of it spent as a pastor's wife in a thriving pastorate, I've learned through experience and observation some noteworthy things. There are generally three phases to marriage.

*Phase I.* **Courtship.** The bride is won by the adoration and pursuit of her beloved. He is fervent and so focused on her she cannot resist being swept into his arms and down the aisle to the altar. Such happiness and expectation she feels are almost overwhelming.

*Phase II.* **Discovery.** The honeymoon is all she dreamed it could be. She is the prize he has won and is now the center of his attention. A little cloud of bliss hangs overhead. Then reluctantly, they have to go home and start life. The cloud of bliss snags on the front door and dissipates. Soon, discovery sets in. *He is not perfect!* Furthermore, he realizes she isn't either. Reality dawns, and adjustments must be made. To her dismay, the *courtship* has almost disappeared! *Be advised that courtship is the bridge over which a man travels to get his prize.* When he gets her secured on *his side,* he burns the bridge! He loves her dearly, but he doesn't have the interest or time to keep up the "courting" since she is his wife. That doesn't make sense to a man; they are logical. That's a startling fact to a new bride.

*Phase III.* **Acceptance.** Usually, the new married couple try to subtly change each other to suit their expectations, *but it doesn't work!* So, the thing to do to insure a happy home is to accept your mate *as is.* Experiencing life together will develop maturity and strengthen the bond of love, making a happy environment in the home.

Delight:   Ephesians 5:25   Ephesians 5:22-23

Edna Holmes

# June 23

*"...for a man's life consisteth not in the
abundance of the things which he possesseth."*
Luke 12:15

    We know of a man who won the lottery, a sum of millions of dollars. Up to that time in his life he had an average happy family. But that money changed everything! It affected the wife more; she developed a superior attitude and began to display it among all their circle of family, friends, and acquaintances. In time, the husband was known to say he wished he had never won the lottery. His family was much happier before they came into possession of that wealth.

    When common men inherit a vast fortune, it is not unusual that they abuse the blessing of it. One of the best safeguards in that happening is to see what God says about wealth and let His word soak into the mind. Unless the focus stays on the Lord, the lust of the flesh and eyes is just too overpowering to resist the temptations that follow the sudden possession of riches.

    *"And when thy herds and thy flocks multiply, and thy silver and gold is multiplied, and all that thou hast is multiplied; Then thine heart be lifted up, and thou forget the Lord thy God."* De.8:13-14.

    Sudden riches may seem like good fortune, but if it has an adverse effect, it could be a tragedy instead for a family. To forget God is the worst thing that can happen in life. The happiest people on earth, *whether rich or poor,* are those who love God and trust in Him in everything. There is no difference in their status to God. The requirements for personal salvation, and the promised blessings for a life of obedience to Him, are the same. Let us be wise and not hoard anything of what we possess. *"For we brought nothing into the world, and it is certain we can carry nothing out."* I Tim.6:7.

Delight:    Proverbs 23:5    I Timothy 6:9

## June 24

*"Sing unto him a new song..."*
Psalms 33:3

Not referring to performers, singing denotes happiness or contentment for the most part. When you hear others going about their work or other daily activities humming or singing, you just know there is joy in their hearts. That attitude being displayed through song, gladdens others that hear it.

*I remember in growing up on the days that I heard my mother humming or singing while she tended the household, it signaled to me that she was especially happy that day, and it gladdened my heart too. Children feel more secure in their element when they sense that their parents are happy and content.*

We praise God with our singing. It is a powerful tool for worship and also to express the gratitude of our hearts for God's salvation and blessings. We should be singing a lot, just to benefit our own hearts and others who hear. God gave music to the whole of mankind as a special gift from their Creator. How grateful the world should be! Yes, some have twisted it up, and made it into a repulsive form of entertainment; we have to keep the God honoring music going strong and being heard. There's a powerful reason. Everything God says is true; everything He does is beneficial for us.

*"For the word of the Lord is right: and all his works are done in truth."* Psalm 33:4-5. *"...the earth is full of the goodness of the Lord."*

A great benefit of singing is defeating the devil in spiritual warfare. When he troubles your thoughts, sing out about the Lord and His salvation. Sing about His name. Sing *Holy, Holy, Holy!* Make a new habit of humming or singing your favorite songs around your home and family. It will benefit yourself, and everyone who hears.

Delight:   Psalm 95:1   Psalm 92:1-2

Edna Holmes

# June 25

*"What manner of man is this, that even
the winds and the sea obey him!"*
Matthew 8:27

He created the winds and sea! The disciples still did not realize who Jesus really was. "What manner of man..." indicated they had not moved into the "Son of God" bracket yet in their understanding. Jesus could have looked up at the stars and rearranged them in the universe had He desired to do so. *That's who He was!* Though they had seen Him do some mighty miracles already, they still couldn't grasp it. They thought the boat could sink in the storm...*with Jesus on board.* The disciples did not know instantly all about Jesus at first after He called them. They learned just like we do except Jesus spoke His word to them in person, while we read His written words from the Bible. They were in the early stages of spiritual growth, and as they stayed close with Jesus, they would come to have confidence and strong faith in Him. They had to learn to *pay attention and listen to His Words.* They also had to *observe* the things Jesus *did.*

That's the way we learn too, abiding with the Lord and feeding our hearts and minds on His Word day by day. Praying, until we are comfortable praying, is the way to strengthen our faith and resolve to be true and loyal to our Lord. We must also observe the works of the Lord, as he takes care of the church, and born-again believers who look to Him for everything.

Do we really know who Jesus is? We won't know it all on this earth, but God does give us little glimpses in His Word. I love it when He reveals a verse to me in more depth than I'd ever realized. He doesn't give us these gems every day. But when he does, we grow a *spiritual inch* because that truth becomes a part of us and makes a difference. Ponder on it! How much do I know about Jesus?

Delight:   John 4:25-26   Colossians 2:9

## June 26

*"Love not the world, neither the things that are in the world."*
I John 2:15

The Lord emphatically tells us to avoid the world, that part of humanity which excludes God. They mock God and disdain Christ. God said in I John 2:16, *"For all that is in the world, the lust of the flesh, and the lust of the eyes, and the pride of life, is not of the Father, but is of the world."* That's what is out there, and the Lord tells us to stay away from it! *It will stunt our growth.*

Long ago in my early childhood, coffee was an "adult drink." Children were told that it would stunt their growth, and so we were not allowed to drink it. All my siblings and I reached full growth; *we didn't drink the coffee*!

For real, the love for the world will *stunt your growth, your spiritual growth.* The reason is, the world *hates Christ!* Jesus Himself said so and warns us.

*"If the world hate you, ye know that it hated me before it hated you."* John 15:18. The Lord also said why it hates us. *"If ye were of the world, the world would love its own..."* V.19. The world has no interest in a Christian unless he is willing to conform to their ways. But the pleasures of sin are a short duration, then misery of heart will set in, *if one is truly a born-again Christian.*

Friendship with the world will stunt your growth and ruin your testimony. Remember the prodigal son ran into the open arms of the world, spent all his fortune among them and when he was destitute and hungry, they deserted him. He came to his senses and went home to his father, who forgave him and welcomed him home. What a picture of God's amazing grace! Stay out of the world to stay healthy and growing in the things of the Lord.

Delight:   I John 2:17   Colossians 3:2

Edna Holmes

# June 27

*"God is our refuge and strength,
a very present help in trouble."*
Psalm 46:1

The more of the world that Christians take into their thought processes, the less "real" or relevant God seems to be. While we would emphatically deny that, our actions betray us. We act less and less as though God is right there with us in our daily lives, and more like the world is making sense. *"Get real!"* the world says. That's why, in order to protect our spiritual soundness and well-being, we must focus on the reality of God.

We should pray every day as we read the Word of God that He would enlighten our minds to its meaning. Ask the Holy Spirit of God Who lives in you to reveal Christ to you from the scriptures. Use the part you read each day in some way, even if it's to recall it in the course of your day to keep your mind thinking right. Talk to God as though He is walking along with you all day. Actually, He is with you and reading your thoughts like words! Think of the wonder of your Savior, and His love for you. God is there! And He is more real than the world with all its pretense and gaudiness that tries to attract.

At times when my husband and I have watched something on TV, and endured the commercials between scenes, it occurred to us that *nothing much is real!* Almost everything is computer generated to create the bizarre characters and scenes in advertising. The world is all glitz and glamour, yet it is an unreal stage with fake characters.

In every situation of our lives, we should consider God is in the midst of things and it is a most comforting thought that *He is the Sovereign of the universe and all creation; He can handle it.* Our part is to talk to Him about it and stay out of the way as He works out things for our good. "Tis so Sweet to Trust in Jesus..."

Delight:    Psalm 37:4    Psalm 27:1

Delighting in the Lord

# June 28

*"Neither is there salvation in any other..."*
Acts 4:12

From this chapter in Acts, God gives a mountain of truth about His salvation given through the person of the Lord Jesus Christ. The world views this mountain of eternal truth and says it's not important, that it's just a molehill. So many souls have been deceived by this fatal lie which is propped up in the world by many other lies. The truth is as Peter preached it that day when he healed the lame beggar at the gate of the temple, and he and John were arrested and beaten.; he said, *"...for there is none other name under heaven given among men, whereby we must be saved."* Acts 4:12. You could search all through earth, the universe, heaven, and all eternity; you would never find another savior. Jesus is our Salvation! Selah.

God's truth about His Word is another mountain that the world tries to shrink into a molehill, or less, more like a grain of sand.
How the world has worked feverishly to render the Word of God as no more important than any book! They have watered it down with many other versions, translated in such a way as to make Jesus a mere man and not the Son of God. Now, several generations have been influenced by such lies. We have a whole new mission field right here in this country. Some folks have never heard the true gospel of Jesus Christ! That is the consequences of making a mere molehill out of the mountain of God's precious Word. Only the truth will set men free from the shackles of sin. Re: John 8:32. Jesus said,
*"...for if ye believe not that I am he, ye shall die in your sins."* Blessed are those who believe! Heaven will be sweet, *and real,* and we shall live *forever* there with God.

Delight:   John 8:47   Ephesians 1:7

Edna Holmes

# June 29

*"My sheep hear my voice, and I know them, and they follow me..."*
John 10:27

There are many who at one time or other struggle with doubts about their personal salvation. We hear such things as, "I can't remember what I said", or, "Did I use the right words to be saved?" It is usually a helpful thing to point them to the *works of God* factor. Jesus said, *"...believe the works: that ye may know, and believe, that the Father is in me, and I in him."*

Anyone who is saved has a change in his heart which shows up in his life. Friends might say, "He has had a change of heart!" *That is the works of God.* If one is a rational person, he will surely know if his heart has been touched and changed. It is the overload of the world's entertainment and philosophy being channeled into our lives that begins to make God's truth seem unreal to us. Christians can get shaken on eternal security if they neglect the Bible and also fellowship with other believers.

When we were married many decades ago, I was very young and nervous standing there at the altar while the pastor led us through the wedding vows. Later, it seemed like a dream. But no matter *how I felt, or what I said* at the time, which I can't remember, I was legally bound to my husband as his wife. The *works of marriage* followed! Over sixty years of time together, raising a family, serving the Lord four decades in the pastorate, helping each other in our older years through 'sickness and health', I could not for a minute doubt that I was married that day long ago. The works prove it!

Besides, Jesus has a golden promise for every seeking lost person who comes to Him. *"...and him that cometh to me I will in no wise cast out."* John 6:37

Delight:   II Timothy 2:19   John 5:24

# June 30

*"...for if ye believe not that I am he,*
*ye shall die in your sins."*
John 8:24

Very few, in that day, actually believed on Him. Jesus told them plainly that they had to believe He was the Messiah, *the anointed one,* sent from God to be the sacrifice for sin. We today, having the written Word, are amazed that Jesus was not readily accepted and believed. The people then were living with Him in time, as he traveled the hot dusty roads from place to place preaching the gospel to them. He looked like any ordinary man. So, the Lord did things that only God could do. "Who is this?" they said. "No one can do these miracles except God be with him." The multitudes followed Him about because they wanted to see miracles!

But He didn't come just to perform miracles; the Bible says He came to *"seek and to save that which was lost."* Re: Luke 19:10. Jesus said again why He came. *"I am come that they might have life, and they might have it more abundantly."* John 10:10. And the most precious verse of all as to why Jesus came is John 3:16. *For God so loved the world, that he gave his only begotten Son, that whosoever believeth in him should not perish, but have everlasting life."* Many scholars have tried to plumb the depths of that little word "so", but no one can aptly describe it. How can you explain the love of God?

Our thoughts on love are shallow at best. We use the term loosely. God cannot be in that category when we express our love for Him. He said we are to love Him with all our hearts, our souls, and with all our strength. Re: Luke 10:27. It is with awe and reverence that we say, *"I love You"* to God. He sees the depths of our hearts; He knows.

Delight:   John 14:23   Ephesians 6:24

Edna Holmes

# July 1

*"In the beginning God created the heaven
and the earth."* Genesis 1:1

    In this first verse in the Bible, we have the most profound information known to man. God was there *"in the beginning."* <u>He didn't have a beginning, He always was</u>. He is the Creator and the universe came into being by His Word. To think that somehow it happened by chance and evolved from chaos into order is the most foolish thought a man could have. Knowing God is our Creator and is in control of the universe that He made, is a most comforting thought to a Christian.

    *An excellent project for a family is to memorize Genesis, chapter one. To begin, read the chapter, emphasize what was brought forth on each day. Thoroughly acquaint your children or grandchildren with the order in which God created earth and living things on it. Then lead them in committing it to memory. Make a game of it! Do it according to the days, first, second, third, etc. Genesis 1 is the seed plot of the Bible, and to keep it in your heart by memory will be a guard for your mind. Children and grandchildren will stay established in the faith later in life with the facts of creation firmly fixed in their minds.*

    Today there is an all-out assault against the truth of Creation. Evolution is taught as fact, not theory. Parents are home-schooling or sending their children to Christian schools where Bible principles and truth are taught; they don't want their children brainwashed with the theory of evolution. There are broken-hearted parents who sent their children to college for a good education; instead, they come out with a different mindset about God, not believing the Bible anymore. May God give us a fresh zeal for the scriptures.

Delight:   Isaiah 40:28   Nehemiah 9:6

## July 2

*"The Lord knoweth the thoughts of man that they are vanity.* Psalm 94:11

    Most people do not have a real grasp of who God is. That He is omniscient, omnipresent, and omnipotent escapes their minds. *He knows everything; He is present everywhere; and He has all power;* it is impossible to elude God. He *knows* the conglomeration of thoughts that run through our minds continually, and the intentions behind them. How could we ever doubt the majesty and power of our God?

    Isaiah 55:8-9 *"For my thoughts are not your thoughts, neither are your ways my ways, saith the Lord. For as the heavens are higher than the earth, so are my ways higher than your ways, and my thoughts than your thoughts."* That should be a warning to consult God with our ideas and plans which we think are so good and workable, *before* we jump into a project. Otherwise we are wasting time and effort. The Lord *will not* bless things that are not His will, and men are not going to slip behind His back and push something through anyway and crow about "success."

    I always cringe when I hear someone refer to Jesus as "the man upstairs." Many people have that attitude about Him. Heaven is not *upstairs*, and Jesus is not a *mere man*. He is the eternal Son of God, and He took on a body of flesh to redeem sinners from eternal death, the penalty for sin. Those who have such a shallow opinion of Jesus, certainly don't *know Him.* Only God's Word and prayer is going to touch lost people. We cannot change a person's attitude, but God can! He is Omnipotent; Omnipresent; Omniscient. ALL POWERFUL, ALWAYS PRESENT, AND ALL KNOWING. Selah!

Delight:     Jeremiah 29:11     Romans 11:33-36

Edna Holmes

# July 3

*"The righteous shall flourish like a palm tree…"*
Psalm 92:12

Trees are an amazing creation of God, with each one distinctly designed to furnish needful benefits for planet Earth and mankind inhabiting it. One, especially, is the Palm tree. The first Psalm must be describing the Palm tree as the contrast to the blessed man who delights in the Lord. *"And he shall be like a tree planted by the rivers of water, that bringeth forth his fruit in his season; his leaf also shall not wither; and whatsoever he doeth shall prosper."* Psa. 1:3

The Palm tree is an evergreen, beautiful in appearance and produces dates, a very rich, delicious fruit. The branches and the leaves are useful to make many things in the tropical regions where the palm tree thrives. It lives to a very old age.

God compares it to the godly man. He bears fruit all his earthly life. Being faithful to God makes one of more value on earth than we could ever put into words. Do what you can to honor the Lord Who loves you and has given you eternal life. Your life will always affect someone as they watch you live and remember that every little thing you are doing counts, and sometimes, in the oddest places.

*When Grapevine got a Nursing Home facility, we had services there, as churches in town began to do. Most of the residents had Alzheimer's disease, yet they would sing the church songs with enthusiasm. I volunteered to play the piano for them one hour a week and let them sing hymns to their hearts' content. One day as we got into full swing with our music, a man was agitated by another and "cussed a blue streak!" I heard others saying "Shhh," the preacher's wife is here! The old fellow looked at me pitifully, and said "Sing 'Mazing Grace?" I said, "We need it." Amazing grace! our dearest treasure.*

Delight:    Psalm 1    Jeremiah 17:7-8

Delighting in the Lord

# July 4

*"And ye shall know the truth, and the truth shall make you free."* John 8:32

July is thought of as freedom month because of the Declaration of Independence enacted in 1776. After a hard-fought war, America gained freedom from British domination. That's why we see and hear the fireworks displays around the country. Our daughter, Jeanne, was born on July 4th and so it seemed to her in growing up that the whole country celebrated her birthday!

The truth of God's Word frees us in so many ways we can't count them. Initially, it frees us from the condemnation of sin when we receive God's unspeakable Gift of salvation, our Savior, Jesus Christ. Then thereafter, as we learn and grow by the Word of God, we are freed from anxieties and fears all through life as we learn the Truth; it gives us freedom from such debilitating things.

If we keep our focus on Jesus, and center our thoughts on who He is, it will drive out anything hindering our peace of mind.

*On the night before my husband's open-heart surgery, I was stricken with fear, that he might have a fatal heart attack before the surgeon could get to those five blocked arteries. Then I remembered the verse in Isaiah 26:3, "Thou wilt keep him in perfect peace, whose mind is stayed on thee: because he trusteth in thee." I ran that verse like a ticker tape through my mind until I dropped off into peaceful sleep. Many were praying, and the surgery was a huge success.*

Remember the Word of God has untold power to minister to every need. Stay in it! Cherish it! It is your life.

Delight:   Psalm 119:165, 130

Edna Holmes

# July 5

*"My heart is fixed, O God, my heart is fixed:*
*I will sing and give praise."* Psalm 57:7

Each individual life can be likened to a closet, as well as our hearts being likened to a garden. When our hearts are firmly fixed on God there will be an obvious difference in the order of our lives. The things which should be kept *inside* the closet and maintained with care affects the whole of our lives.

First is **God's Will**. *"I delight to do thy will, O my God: yea thy law is within my heart."* Psalm 40:8. To be obedient to God at all times will keep the closet of our lives in the best order.

The second element is to **keep our hearts** as in Proverbs 4:23. *"Keep thy heart with all diligence; for out of it are the issues of life."* In a well-kept heart, the Fruit of the Spirit is being cultivated to grow. The gardener is the Holy Spirit, the presence of Christ in us.

**Thoughts.** Philippians 4:8 is the clearest instructions in God's Word as to how we should think to keep the closet of our life perfect on the inside. *"…whatsoever things are true, whatsoever things are honest, whatsoever things are just, whatsoever things are pure, whatsoever things are lovely, whatsoever things are of good report; if there be any virtue, and if there be any praise, think on these things."* (emphasis mine) Can anyone read that verse and not feel some conviction? Our thoughts are prone to be scrambled, jumping from one thing to another even as we try to concentrate on reading God's Word or praying. I read a testimony of a great preacher in earlier times. He said he *"tried to pray for 30 minutes or so before he could really pray."* It's that way for most of us. But keep praying!

Delight:   Proverbs 16:4   James 4:14-15

## July 6

*"There is a way that seemeth right unto a man, but the end thereof are the ways of death."* Proverbs 16:25

Continuing on the subject of keeping the closet (our life) in order, there are things kept *inside* which make a happy productive life for the glory of God. But there are things to be kept *outside* of our hearts to be spiritually healthy and fruitful for the Lord.

Things to be kept *out* of the closet is **your own will**. Our text verse is emphatic. Man wants to "do it my way" and he reaps a bitter harvest when he spends his life doing *his will* instead of being obedient to God's will. That attitude should be kept *out* of the closet. *Don't hang that up in your life and keep it! Obedience is happiness for you.*

Another thing to shun is a **judgmental attitude**. Once I was taught a lesson, which I've never forgotten. *Our church had a Gideon representative speak to us, and during a question time, I asked if anyone ever stole those Bibles the Gideons put out in hotels. I felt very self-righteous because I'd never done that, and would never, ever, do such a despicable thing! At my next Ladies retreat in another state, I did just that! I absentmindedly picked up the Gideon Bible and put it in with my books and took it home. I was horrified when I discovered the theft and sent it back with an explanation. I know, for a while, they thought I'd stolen it. I was humbled.*

The Bible says you will be judged if you judge. The wheel of judgment rolls backwards. Back off! God is the Judge, the only one qualified. Our opinion should be mute about the "fruit inspection" aspect also. Our eyes and ears are unreliable agents, though we may swear otherwise. Trust what God says. Don't judge! Selah.

Delight:    Matthew 7: 1-2    II Corinthians 5:10

Edna Holmes

# July 7

*"I have been young, and now am old; yet have I not
seen the righteous forsaken, nor his seed begging bread."*
Psalm 37:25

One detriment to our happiness, yet something that so many Christians store in the closet of their life, is **worry**. God promises to take care of His children, and without fail, He does. *But we worry.* That should definitely be kept on the outside and thrust as far from us as possible. Worry is a waste of emotional energy, which also drains our mental and physical strength. The culprit is our **unbelief**.

Look at our text verse. King David said he was old then, but from the time of his childhood till then, he had *never* seen the children of God forsaken, or destitute of food. Christians don't have to beg; the Lord will see that their needs are met; not *wants,* but needs!

Matthew chapter 6 is the most wonderful reassurance that we, as children of God, will certainly be taken care of by our heavenly Father. Read it, and let your heart bask in His love and delight in His promises to you. Our unbelief of what God says is the basis for much of the miseries in life. Jesus rebukes us in His Word for our unbelief.

*"But seek ye first the kingdom of God and his righteousness; and all these things shall be added unto you." Matt. 6:33.* That is, surrender all of you to the Lord, and everything you will ever need will be provided for you. If we could only wrap our minds around that truth and never be tempted away from it! It takes the worry out of our lives and replaces it with lasting peace.

The Word of God, Prayer, and a submissive attitude to God is and shall always be the key to keeping order in your life.

Delight:   Matthew 7:24-27

# July 8

*"O give thanks unto the Lord; for he is good: for his mercy endureth forever."* Psalm 136:1

    A lady in our pastorate, in an exciting part of her spiritual growth, discovered Psalm 136. At the end of *every single* verse are the words: *for his mercy endureth forever.* That new Christian was thrilled every time she read them, though it sounded redundant to many others. Her enthusiasm was catching, so one day I sat down and prayerfully read Psalm 136. It reminded me of a story in Luke.

    It was as when Jesus walked with the two believers on the Emmaus road after His death and resurrection, and He expounded the scriptures to them. They didn't know who He was at first, but Jesus opened their eyes, and they recognized Him! Later, *"And they said one to another, Did not our heart burn within us, while he talked by the way, and while he opened to us the scriptures?"* Luke 24:32. In reading about their hearts burning, I felt such an affect in slowly reading and meditating on Psalm 136. The blessing is in all the Word of God if we linger over it until our hearts "burn". It is God-breathed; it's for the saved children of God; it's God's promises to us. Why don't we savor it as we read as we would good physical food?

    The devil tempts us with countless distractions until he finds one that will work; in that way he keeps us from taking in the Word "until our *hearts burn with in us.*" At those times you digest the scriptures, and don't forget it. Those verses will become anchors for your soul. No wonder the devil tries to keep us distracted at our devotional time when we are trying to read the Bible.

Delight:     119:49-50     John 15:1-5

Edna Holmes

# July 9

*"And they shall be mine, saith the Lord of hosts, in that day when I make up my jewels..."* Malachi 3:17

The Lord regards His children as "jewels". His love for us and attention to us is always fervent. Yet, though we are saved by His grace through faith in the Lord Jesus Christ, we are imperfect and will sin in spite of ourselves! We have a very special promise in God's Word which provides cleansing for sin and restores fellowship with the Lord when it is broken. We desperately need it, for we sin.

*"If we confess our sins, he is faithful and just to forgive our sins, and to cleanse us from all unrighteousness."* I John 1:9

*We were pen-pals while my husband was in Japan and he sent nice gifts for my birthday and for Christmas. He was very grateful for getting a letter or more every single day except Sunday. He was envied by the soldiers on the base who got little or no mail, especially from a girl! Once he sent me a beautiful wristwatch. I was in the field working when the package was brought to me. I took the watch out to put it on, and promptly dropped it in the soft fresh-plowed dirt! Then it wouldn't run, and all my crying didn't jump-start it. My father took it to town and the jeweler opened it up, found a tiny speck of dirt which had clogged the jewels inside, removed it, and the beautiful watch then worked perfectly.*

Like dirt, a little speck of sin will clog God's jewels. Sin will stop our 'working', serving the Lord. It will stop our fellowship with God, and we will lose power and desire to be a witness for the Lord. Only a "grain of sin" will clog the well of living water in us from fully flowing to bless others. Good news: when we confess our sins, He forgives!

Delight:   Deuteronomy 7:9   Psalm 66:18-20

Delighting in the Lord

# July 10

*"And Jesus knowing their thoughts said, wherefore think ye evil in your hearts."* Matthew 9:4

Jesus was speaking to the religious leaders of that day who constantly followed Jesus about to find fault with Him. How very foolish and void of any spiritual understanding. Religious, but lost!

We put it in a milder way, but we too have vain, evil thoughts because we attribute God's blessings poured into our lives to some of our own doing, instead of giving God the praise and glory. He has plainly told us in Psalm 68:19, *"Blessed be the Lord, who daily loadeth us with benefits, even the God of our salvation. Selah."*

We forget that truth, and figure in circumstances and chance. This is typical: *A man was late for a very important business meeting and when he got to the place the parking lot was full! There was not one parking spot available. Desperate, the man sent up a pleading prayer asking God to let him find a parking place immediately because he just couldn't miss that meeting. He circled around to the other row and right in front of him was an empty spot! He said, "Never mind Lord, I found one."* (L.A. notes)

That is an insult to God after He answered the man's desperate prayer and gave him that parking place. The man was beside himself and in a panic! Absolutely powerless. Jesus would say today as He did in His days on Earth, *"wherefore think ye evil in your hearts?"* Our faith is shallow if we do not believe that Jesus blesses us on every turn and "loads us with benefits" every single day. We should thank Him and praise Him for His goodness and mercy showered on us.

Delight: Psalm 72:17-19, Psalm 103:1-22, Ephesians 1:3

Edna Holmes

# July 11

*"I have not hid thy righteousness within my heart; I have declared thy faithfulness and thy salvation..."* Psalm 40:10

When God imparts the gift of salvation to the repentant sinner, He makes him "righteous." The blood of Jesus freely shed on Calvary's cross has the power to put righteousness in our hearts at the moment we believe and trust in Jesus. That righteousness cannot be hidden; it signifies the presence of the Holy Spirit.

Some things are easy to hide. For instance, it is easy to hide physically from a baby. All you have to do is cover your face with your hands and the baby thinks you have disappeared, because it just focuses on what it can see close up. When you jerk your hands away, the baby 'finds' you and usually giggles and laughs. But mature adults are not so easily fooled. They 'know' who you really are and will recognize the Godly attributes in your life...you can't hide them if they are really there. If you are born again, the Holy Spirit will be obvious to others and He will never leave you, since He seals you for eternity.

Some may wonder how that is so when Christians can be cold and indifferent at times. You can know who is "righteous" and who is not by the way they respond to the Word of God. Wayward Children of God are convicted of their sins sooner or later, and the unsaved are not. God's righteousness cannot be hidden. *"God is Light, and in Him is no darkness at all"*. I John 1:5. Putting it as simply as it could be, God in us will shine forth! Our words in talking, the songs we sing or listen to, reading our Bibles and talking about what God says, our connection to the church and other Christians, will all be evidence in our lives that Someone is abiding in us that shines!

Delight: Acts 20:20-21, 1 Thessalonians 1:8

(Note: My publisher, who is my younger brother, Max Holt, contributed the illustration to this devotional.)

Delighting in the Lord

# July 12

*"...Gather up the fragments that remain,
that nothing be lost.* John 6:12

    Our Lord is the creator and ruler over the whole universe. He is rich beyond our ability to compute, yet he was careful to make use of the fragments of food, crumbs, which the people carelessly left behind on the ground after they had eaten all they could hold. Jesus told the disciples, "Gather them up...that nothing be lost." It must be grievous to the Lord the way we waste the bounty of all things He so generously bestows on us. Precious time is the greatest waste of all. We complain of not having "enough time" while we blithely waste enough to accomplish many things that are routinely neglected. We should "Gather up the fragments" of each day's time and put them to good use in tending unfinished chores. If we carry over work to the next day...and the next, we never quite get through, and we get discouraged. Gather up the fragments!

    Many Christians in the pew feel that because they can't do *great things*, they can't do anything at all. A lot of talent of various kinds, hidden from view, is wasted. I remember a good example of this. *In our church we had two pews full of older ladies, widows, who always sat together. Some were sad at times saying no one "needed" them anymore, yet they were such a blessing to our church family simply by their faithfulness in attendance. One year I assigned the whole lot of them to be responsible for the ladies' Christmas banquet. I appointed one, a retired business lady, who could lead the group in their project. For several weeks they were too busy to be sad about anything and we had a beautiful banquet! It was as though we went to "grandma's house" for Christmas. They used "fragments" with great results.*

Delight: Nehemiah 8:10

Edna Holmes

# July 13

*"I Nebuchadnezzar was at rest in mine house, and flourishing in my palace..."* Daniel 4:4

In the modern age, it would be said that the king "had it made in the shade." Whoever originated that saying must have been a farmer. *Back a few decades ago farm work was done by hand in the field. The blissful moments of the day were in the shade at the end of a row; the workers could rest a moment, take off hats, or bonnets, and get a cool drink of water. For that few moments, you felt at ease and blessed beyond measure.*

Nebuchadnezzar was lifted up with pride, praised himself and gave himself glory instead of God. I'm always thrilled when I read how God taught the king a lesson he never forgot; after that the king made a dangerous declaration. *"The king spake, and said, 'Is not this great Babylon, that I have built for the house of the kingdom by the might of my power, and for the honour of my majesty?'* God's reply is chilling. *"While the word was in the king's mouth, there fell a voice from heaven, saying, O king Nebuchadnezzar, to thee it is spoken; The kingdom is departed from thee. And they shall drive thee from men, and thy dwelling shall be with the beasts of the field..." Quote from Daniel 4: 30-31.* Read the whole chapter for the complete story and understanding of how this haughty king came to believe in God.

The king obviously went insane and lived with the beasts for a lengthy duration, enough so that he finally *looked up and acknowledged Almighty God in heaven as the one to be praised and worshipped.* He was saved! His pride in himself was shattered to the core, and he came out a happy man praising God.

Delight:   Proverbs 16:18   Proverbs 11:2

## July 14

*"Pride goeth before destruction, and a haughty spirit before a fall."* Proverbs 16:18

The haughty king of Babylon was full of pride, so full in fact that he cast himself forth as a kind of god and at one point in time, he had the people worship him! We know now how God Almighty, the only true God, the Creator, brought him down.

Pride is on God's hate list. It's one of the three things in the world from which all other sins come. *"For all that is in the world, the lust of the flesh, and the lust of the eyes, and the pride of life, is not of the Father, but is of the world."* I John 2:16. Pride causes so much misery in the world, for mankind. It deters sinners from humbling themselves, like little children and trusting in Christ for salvation. We don't like to admit dependence upon God, but we are, not only for salvation, but everything else. Christ is our life!

*I remember so well my struggle with pride when the Holy Spirit brought me to the point of salvation. I'd been a church member since I was nine years old! Then in my mid-twenties I wrestled with the thoughts of "what people will think" to "I'm not so awful bad" and in the back of my mind tried to bargain with God somehow where I wouldn't have to confess before the world that I'd never been saved at all. It is one thing to **profess** and another thing to actually **possess** Christ.*

*God does not bargain! God's Son died the most humiliating death, suffered beyond description, and all for love of lost sinners. To think God would compromise a little, and we could get into heaven with our pride intact! Ten thousand times NO!*

If that is your struggle, surrender! Stomp your pride and go to Jesus and be saved. You will rejoice throughout eternity with God.

Delight:    Romans 10: 9-10,13

Edna Holmes

# July 15

*"My heart is fixed, O God, my heart is fixed:
I will sing and give praise.* Psalm 57:7

It is good if your heart is indeed fixed on God. If the Lord is the object of love and worship in our hearts, we can say our hearts are fixed on Him. That does not take away from your love and attention you have for others you love; actually, it enhances it. God makes the days productive for those who put Him first. You will lack for nothing, and at the end of the day, you will say, "Why don't I continually do this, pray and fix my heart anew each day on God?!" There is such blessing in it. However, the devil, knowing that, continually tempts us to be distracted from our resolve to do this. When we do slip off the track of obedience, we should stop right in the middle of our messed-up day and start over. *"Lord I've failed to keep my heart fixed on You...forgive me...help me to get back on track."* Don't we all know that God loves us so much, He will hear and answer such a prayer gladly? Certainly, He will. Just as the prodigal son's father took him back with rejoicing, so our Heavenly Father will do for us.

Our son, Louis A. Holmes, wrote several little choruses in years past that were used by his church in the worship service. One that I especially like sprang out of Psalm 57:7.

*My heart is fixed on you; My heart is fixed on you...*
*I will sing and I will give praise, For my heart is fixed on you.*

The tune to this chorus is very beautiful, and if I sing it, the music stays with me running pleasantly through my mind all day.

Singing God-honoring songs and hymns is a big help in keeping our hearts fixed on Him. *Wake up verses* are helps. That morning reading is vital. Fix your heart/mind on the Lord and stay with it!

Delight:    Psalm 37:4

## July 16

*"...behold, now is the accepted time; behold now is the day of salvation."* II Corinthians 6:2

    The old and very familiar acronym, ASAP, is known worldwide. Short for "As Soon As Possible", it appears on cards and notices and is indispensable in society today. My happy, smiling friends from church showed me another meaning you could put to these familiar letters: "Always Stop And Pray." That would be a good reminder on a card with a neat little 'praying hands' sticker added with it going to a Christian friend. And isn't that a very good message in the acronym?

    In every turn of the road in our day, there's always a need to speak to God in prayer. Common daily prayers are often little arrow prayers, *"Help Lord!",* when a situation suddenly arises. *"Always Stop And Pray"* is excellent advice.

    That reminds me of our text verse warning sinners of the urgency of salvation. We are all headed for the grave, sooner or later, unless the Lord comes for us in the rapture first. Satan will try and delude every sinner to keep him from knowing he is utterly lost unless he believes on the Lord Jesus Christ ASAP! Jesus paid the horrific price, His own life, to redeem us from the curse of sin, and the kingdom of darkness controlled by Satan. *"Who hath delivered us from the power of darkness, and hath translated us into the kingdom of his dear son: In whom we have redemption through his blood, even the forgiveness of sins."* Colossians 1: 13-14

    Use these two little helpful acronyms, in witnessing to the lost: "You need to trust Jesus for salvation, As Soon As Possible!" And in encouraging other Christians: *"Always Stop And Pray!"*

Delight:   Luke 19:10   I Timothy 2:4

Edna Holmes

# July 17

*"But let him that glorieth glory in this, that he understandeth and knoweth me…"* Jeremiah 9:24

No knowledge on earth is worth knowing compared to *understanding and knowing God* personally. That knowledge is conveyed to us through a personal relationship with the Lord Jesus Christ. Jesus came down, to redeem us and reveal God to us.

All other things we must know, to live, are graciously given to us by God, inherent in the laws of nature provided for man. That hardly seems reality today in our high-tech world that's changing rapidly where people are becoming more godless in their thinking. But God knows every age that has passed over the earth, *He designed them!*

God has an eternal purpose in place and the universe and mankind slowly moves toward the fulfillment of it. Can we imagine the end of all things as God folds up time and puts it away, and every human being from Adam to the last one born on earth realizes that God is real; He meant what He said, every word is fulfilled, and now we have reality of eternity facing us immediately? No time left for repentance; It's all over. The saints will be praising God! Those who disdained Him will be separated from Him forever in eternity...*suffering.*

Our God is not surprised or having anxiety problems as time goes on. He is long-suffering and unwilling that any should perish. Ref: II Peter 3:9. Our merciful God has given men over-time so that more may be saved. His love for mankind is unfathomable. And He proved it when *His Son died in shame and agony for us at Calvary.*

Read God's Word; it is all about Him! Wondrous knowledge!

Delight:   1 Samuel 15:22

## July 18

*"How shall we escape, if we neglect so great salvation..."*
Hebrews 2:3

Surely, all believers know the answer to that question. There is *no escape* if God's great salvation is rejected. No hope, in time or eternity. Only God, Himself, knows the gravity of going out into eternity without Christ. The human mind cannot grasp it. The love of God for mankind sent Jesus down to walk among mortals, feel their pain and sorrows caused by the curse of sin, and become the sacrifice to take away that sin curse. He *had to take on Himself a human body so that He could die!* For that was the remedy for sin, *death*. "For the wages of sin is death..." Romans 6:23

*Decades ago, a young boy was called from a TV audience to answer a question. With a correct answer, the boy would receive numerous gifts, one being a bicycle. THE QUESTION: "In thirty seconds, or less, what is the greatest thing in the world?" Without any hesitation the boy said, "God's salvation." The announcer was stunned, but soon gained his composure and said, "Son, I believe you are right, the greatest thing in the world is God's salvation."*

How would we answer that question? In that era of earlier television days, people were not as cowed down about their faith. Now it would take real courage to answer correctly as the little boy did, and it would be rejected altogether. Nevertheless, the world needs to hear the truth in high places broadcast all over the earth.

Delight: Hebrews 13:6

Edna Holmes

# July 19

*"...so great salvation..."* Hebrews 2:3

Can we say more of God's great salvation? It is such a thrilling subject; we should all spend more time meditating on the one thing that is the greatest in the world. Why is it so wonderfully great? The first part of the answer is because GOD THOUGHT OF IT. It is stated in Ephesians 1:4, *"According as he hath chosen us in him before the foundation of the world, that we should be holy and without blame before him in love."* To be in Christ, is to be eternally saved. It was planned for us in eternity, before God created the earth! God's ways are past finding out. We can only bask in His love and thank Him for His wonderful grace that saved us.

*Before the stars twinkled in the night,*
*Before the moon shined upon the ocean,*
*Before the sun gave a ray of light,*
*Before the universe was spoken into existence,*
*God thought of man's salvation.*

It was God who CONCEIVED, PLANNED, PURPOSED, AND EXECUTED this wonderful salvation. We do not know why He loved us so, nor shall we ever this side of heaven. John 3:16 is our clearest explanation of it with the little word 'so' being the golden key.

*"For God so loved the world, that he gave his only begotten Son, that whosoever believeth in him should not perish, but have everlasting life."* With these thoughts, renew the joy of your salvation. Then spread the *GOOD NEWS* around!

Delight:   John 3:17   John 3:36

Delighting in the Lord

## July 20

*"My soul, wait thou only upon God, for my expectation is from him."* Psalm 62:5

    This verse was shared with me by a friend, as it had become special to her. My heart was in need of encouragement when I soaked in the sweetness of this word from the Lord. Doesn't He always meet our needs?

    When we learn that nothing on earth can satisfy the expectations of our hearts, we cease to be disappointed in vainly looking for what cannot be produced by earthly means. God has the answers; He has the means; He faithfully works all things together for our good, and freely gives us the desires of our hearts if we delight in Him. He tells us in Isaiah 2:22 *"Cease ye from man, whose breath is in his nostrils: for wherein is he to be accounted of?"* Stop looking to man for your expectations; he will fail you!

    How does the Lord do that for us? First, He has given us the tools in hand to take care of our hearts' expectations. **The Word of God**, the Bible, is the Christian's greatest treasure on earth. If all you ever read were the Gospels, following along with Jesus on His earthly ministry, you would be held up by His power, His love, and learn how to live and be happy on earth. But God gave us so much more of His Word to thrive on. It will point us to God Who meets our expectations.

    Then the Lord gave us the ***privilege of prayer***. Let there be no pretense in prayer! God will not receive it. Be open and honest in all your communication, for He knows your heart. The greatest wonder is that He does listen to us praying our rambling, shallow prayers to our Heavenly Father…and answers them! Meeting our expectations.

Delight:    Proverbs 24:14

Edna Holmes

# July 21

*"And this he said to prove him: for he himself
knew what he would do."* John 6:6

Jesus never asked a question to learn something He didn't already know. God does not need information from His creatures. He *proves* or tests us with questions provoking us to think and exercise faith. In this case of Jesus preparing to feed the vast multitude the bread and fishes, His disciples were to learn a little more about the deity of Christ. That he was God living in a fleshly body had not taken permanent roots in their thinking. otherwise, Philip would not have questioned how so many could be fed with so little! Though Jesus was allowing Himself to be confined in an earthly body, He could not cease to be Who he was…the Sovereign Lord over all the earth.

Though He took the meager amount of food and multiplied it thousands of times over, the scraps of food left after the crowd was fed were important to Jesus as well. Being wasteful is a detriment to the well-being of humanity. Jesus was teaching them to be frugal! Yes, the Lord had everything at His disposal, but He wasted nothing just because it was nothing for Him to multiply food anytime! Not just food, there are many things we waste unnecessarily.

The worst is time. I could accomplish everything I need to in a day, if only I didn't get distracted and waste the time. One help along that line is keeping a list, marking each thing off as it is completed. I do very well, following that plan. We should not waste any of the bounty that God gives us in each day. He gave us a pattern when He had the disciples gather up the fragments that remained.

Delight:   John 6:12-13

Delighting in the Lord

# July 22

*"For my yoke is easy, and my burden is light."*
Matthew 11:29-30

In this portion of scripture, Jesus also said "Take my yoke upon you, and learn of me." The object is that we *learn of Him* and not that we are *pulling and working.* In an era past, when farms were all worked by hand instead of machinery, you could easily see by observing the farmer plowing with animals the yoke factor that the Lord was teaching about.

*When I was a young child, our farm had no modern machinery for plowing the fields and gathering in the crops. Mules and horses were used with plows and wagons. Two mules were hitched up to a plow; each had to pull his part and a whip was used to make sure the animals pulled together. The plow lines running from the harness around the mules were slipped over the shoulders, and the one plowing was actually yoked up with the team of mules, though he didn't pull any weight at all. Many times, I've looked across the field at the wisps of dust stirred by the mules, the birds following the plow, and hear the voice of the plowmen and the crack of the whip. My father and brother came in from the fields very tired from following behind the plow, but they never pulled it themselves. That was not their part in the work of plowing.* (Treasures...E.H.)

Jesus is the One who accomplishes His work on earth. He uses those who love him and want to serve Him by allowing them to "yoke" up with Him. We learn and grow as we serve alongside of Him, but the Lord's work can only be done in His power alone. He has told us emphatically in John 15:5 *"...for without me ye can do nothing."*

Delight: Matthew 7:24-27, John 9:33

Edna Holmes

# July 23

*"...her ways are moveable, that thou canst not know them."*
Proverbs 5:6

Proverbs is a plain guide to life and all the various ups and downs of its motions. We cringe as it warns us about *"the strange woman"* and all her wickedness in ruining lives. It carries a direct meaning, and an applicable one which is equally powerful, for our present time.

The world has innumerable ways of deceiving Christians and leading them astray. And it is doubly true that should we get wise to the fact we are being drawn away from faithfulness to God, the world changes her tactics. She is "moveable" and changes into a different mode of operation. The deceiver can shift easily into whatever mode will keep his victim ignorant of his real motives.

*Some decades ago, Christians stayed away from the movie theaters. They did not want their children and family to see the blatant portrayal of sin and become desensitized to it. What did Hollywood do to fix that problem and attract that segment of society? They began to show Disney movies, and even some "Christian" movies occasionally. But they also showed advertisements of the violent, vulgar features coming soon! A friend of my daughter took her three little children, during the afternoon, to see a Disney movie. During a break, the advertisements suddenly appeared on the screen, showing a violent rape! The young mother gathered up her children and left that place immediately.*

Liquor has finally made its way into the grocery stores! Yes, the world is "moveable" and can change to whatever mode it must to make sin appear acceptable and harmless. Don't be deceived.

Delight: Proverbs 7:10-21

## July 24

*"Seeing thou hatest instruction, and castest
my words behind thee."* Psalm 50:17

In reproving His people, God reminds them how far they had slipped away from honoring Him. Though they were strictly warned by Moses right before they went in to possess the promised land, the people so soon forgot the loving care God took in providing all they needed in that forty years of wandering in the wilderness, and forgot the warning not to have anything to do with the inhabitants of the land or their gods. The natives worshipped idols and were pagans to the core. They would lead the Israelites astray and in time they certainly did cause the downfall of a God-blessed nation. Israel disobeyed God; eventually, in ages to come, the nation was scattered to the wind all over the world!

Read the whole Psalm and you get a glimmer of how deeply we get mired down into the muck of this sinful world system. God's people are basically the same. It comes on gradually. We may consider ourselves superior in a way since we aren't doing any of the really bad sins, then we become judgmental, and that's our downfall. We start doing the same things. We forget our old nature lurks inside of us waiting for an opportunity to get out and "have some fun. "The things we used to disdain to talk about, we calmly watch on TV which is piped into the house, sometimes in several rooms! Are we no longer horrified by gross sins which ruin society and nations? No! We have gotten used to them by exposure.

Delight: Ephesians 5:15-21

Edna Holmes

# July 25

*"Fear God, and keep his commandments:  
for this is the whole duty of man."* Ecclesiastes 12:13

God made it very simple and easy for men to live on the earth and be happy and content. They have one duty, *the whole duty,* which every single soul can accomplish perfectly: *"Fear God, and keep his commandments."* With that, God takes care of every need and problem which arises. Obedience to Him is the golden key.

To fear God is to have a loving reverence and awe of Him which causes us to obey Him. The Lord delights in His children, and desires to have their love and attention. Remember how you felt when your children were small? Parents delight in the love and attention of their offspring. Multiply that many times over and it's a fair comparison of God's desire toward His children. Yet, we often neglect God, taking meager time to communicate with Him in prayer and fellowship with Him. We have many things we are more concerned with than the *whole duty* which God instructs us to observe.

The modern world has become a jungle of hi-tech devices which so occupies humanity, and keeps their brains jumbled that people can hardly think on their own anymore. The latest phones have taken over society. You hardly see a single person without a phone in hand. Babies, two years old, can work a phone! It is mind-boggling to the older generation of us who are living in the midst of this modern craziness. We do benefit from having phones to stay in contact with our children and grandchildren with calls and texts. But to go with it in hand continually is a hindrance in daily business. Let us remember the "whole duty" factor and take care of that for health and happiness.

Delight:   Colossians 3:2   Titus 3:8

## July 26

*"And because iniquity shall abound, the love of many shall wax cold."* Matthew 24:12

What has the abounding of iniquity got to do with the love of God's people toward Him growing cold? As we discussed the influence of sin in the world on us, gradually drawing us off the path of faithfulness, so we know our vulnerability in such an openly wicked world. It's human nature to become what we look at, long enough for it to affect us, and we begin to emulate what we see.

With sin abounding all around us in this world, it is difficult for us to keep our minds from getting entangled with the enticement of it unless we are *steadfastly* pursuing the Word of God and staying in close fellowship with the Lord. When we cool off in our love for the Lord, we start taking off the armor of God which protects us. But for the grace of the Lord Jesus Christ, we would be swallowed up in no time by the world. Its enticement is so strong.

As a Singles Pastor, my younger brother, Max Holt, used a good illustration while teaching singles who were contemplating marriage. He had a girl stand on a chair, illustrating the Christian life. He then chose a 'larger' guy, representing the 'world,' who would hold her hand. He then would tell the girl to lift the guy up onto the chair with her. The girls were never able to lift the 'worldly' guys into Christianity. But the guy could easily drag the girl down into the 'world.' His point was that Christians should only marry Christians. Being unequally yoked from the beginning of a marriage is a spiritually dangerous place to be.

Many *strong in faith* Christians have been dragged under by the force of the current of sin when they went too far in showing friendship to the world.

Delight: Revelation 2:1-5

(Note: My publisher, who is my younger brother, Max Holt, contributed the illustration to this devotional.)

Edna Holmes

# July 27

*"And Jesus knowing their thoughts said, Wherefore think ye evil in your hearts?"* Matthew 9:4

It is hard to keep this truth current in our minds. *Jesus knows what we are thinking...all the time!* That should be a strong deterrent to allowing sinful thoughts to get a hold on our minds. We waste precious time and emotional energy dealing with thoughts. The location of spiritual warfare is in our minds. Don't let your thoughts progress until you have a battle to fight.

The mind is the most powerful part of us, and that's why we are exhorted to use it wisely and think as God has instructed us to do in Philippians *4:8. "...whatsoever things are true, whatsoever things are honest, whatsoever things are just, whatsoever things are pure, whatsoever things are lovely, whatsoever things are of good report; if there be any virtue, and if there be any praise, think on these things.* That has straightened out my wayward thoughts many times when I'd get off to a bad start for the day. I put the verse on a card and posted it on my bookcase in front of my eyes to remind myself what's right and what's not about my thinking. The Lord gave us minds to think with....*for His honor and glory!* When we fall short, the Word is there to correct us. God's grace is there to forgive us.

Thoughts, not kept in subjection to the Word, can cause much heartache and trouble. People who imagine evil, often project their opinions to others and decide they are thinking evil thoughts also toward them. Be aware you must keep your thoughts plum with the Word of God. Memorize that key verse. *"The roots of happiness are found within the soil of a healthy thought life."* (Pastor's notes)

Delight:    II Corinthians 10:4-5    Proverbs 16:3

## July 28

*"We have seen strange things today..."*
Luke 5:26

Every day of Jesus' earthly life held many happenings which were amazing to the people. Wouldn't we have gasped with astonishment at seeing and hearing Jesus speak the word, and many hopeless cases were healed immediately! Don't you think you would have been convinced Jesus was God in a fleshly body if you had seen Him call Lazarus out of the grave, being tightly bound up in the traditional grave clothes? Some people there did believe on Jesus, but some did not! They went to the religious leaders and reported what had happened, so they could plot against the Lord. They wanted Him dead and started scheming as to how to kill Him.

Surely, when Jesus took a boy's lunch of five little pieces of bread, called loaves, and two small fishes and fed over five thousand people on that hillside, people being there seeing it told it far and wide what *strange* things they had seen that day. In the three short years of Jesus' ministry to the people before He died for our sins, He did so many "strange" things that astonished the people, that the world couldn't hold the books, should everything have been recorded.

*"And there are also many other things which Jesus did, the which if they should be written every one, I suppose that even the world itself could not contain the books that should be written. A-men."* John 21:25

Jesus did more than we can imagine; now He intercedes for us, keeping us secure. But the most amazing thing that Jesus does is save lost souls! We can be a part of His work by being a witness for Him. Partners with Christ! Think on that.

Delight:    Romans 3:23-24    Ephesians 2:8-10

Edna Holmes

# July 29

*"...I beseech you as strangers and pilgrims,  
abstain from fleshly lust that war against the soul..."*  
I Peter 2:11

On this earth Christians are indeed strangers and pilgrims. We are citizens of heaven by the grace of God and our Savior Jesus Christ. But right now, we have to live on earth, and journey through as pilgrims and strangers.

The world considers us a "peculiar" people just as the Bible says that we are. Peculiar and strange, we actually like *to read the Bible.* The unsaved do not; they can't understand it. We like to attend church services to worship and praise God. The lost people do not and can't understand why Christians want to go faithfully. There is nothing there for them! The world system mocks at Christians who give their tithes and offerings to God, through His church. They are totally blinded to their ignorance of the truth and the necessity of being born again into the family of God. We can't imagine the horror when someday at the judgment their eyes will be opened to see and understand they have *missed out on eternal life.* Will that be the time for the "weeping and wailing and gnashing of teeth?"

It behooves us to consider the plight of lost men and pray for and witness to them while there is still time. As the saying goes, *"take it with a grain of salt"* when you are mocked, railed on, laughed at, or criticized for witnessing for Christ. Let it make no difference one way or the other, but joyfully look for a prospect to witness to every day. Pray for opportunity. When a lost one is saved, it will be one of the happiest days of your life! There is nothing like the joy of winning a soul or having a part in it. That is why Jesus came, to save the lost.

Delight:   Psalm 145:18-19   Psalm 126:6

Delighting in the Lord

# July 30

*"But he was wounded for our transgressions, he was bruised for our iniquities..."* Isaiah 53:5

Jesus was *wounded and bruised*! That He would take that hurt for us and ultimately surrender His life for our salvation is beyond all human comprehension. His suffering was God's Love on display that awful day at Calvary. Just think of how he was wounded:

<u>In His feet</u>, for wherever we have walked in the paths of sin, there is still forgiveness for us.

<u>In his hands</u> as the nails gouged holes to put Him on that tree. Whatever we have done sinning with our hands, we have forgiveness in the Lord Jesus Christ.

<u>In His head</u>, and the needle-sharp thorns dug into his head as the soldiers beat the crown down on His head. Oh, the agony!
All the sinful thoughts and imaginations of our minds...forgiven.

<u>In His side</u> as the soldier thrust the spear into Jesus' side with the cruelty of a mind that relished wounding the Lord already dead on the cross. Yet Jesus was wounded for *our transgressions*. Whatever has dwelled in our hearts, He paid for that sin and we can go free! Never let Jesus' suffering slip very far from your mind. We need to remember the high price He paid for our salvation. No one else in the universe or heaven could have done it. It had to be God Himself in the Person of Jesus Christ. The Perfect Lamb of God.

It was so important, God had John the Baptist born for the specific purpose of pointing out Jesus and naming Him as "The Lamb of God" and baptizing Him. Think on that wonder!

Delight:    John 1:29:34    John 1:6-9

Edna Holmes

# July 31

*"Looking unto Jesus the author and finisher of our faith..."*
Hebrews 12:2

Why aren't we looking to Jesus as this verse directs us? So much of what we do, even as we serve Him, has a lot of ourselves mixed in our efforts. Our plans, thoughts, pride, feelings etc.

When Jesus is everything to us, the Author, which signifies the originator, or creator of our salvation, we should gaze heavenward continually by faith for guidance. The Finisher of our faith means Jesus will finish, or complete, what he originated in the first place in saving us. It's all done! Do we think we are helping Him in any way with the awful task of taking us to heaven? Spurgeon once said, *"We will never find happiness by looking at our prayers, our actions, or our feelings. It is what Jesus is, not what we are that gives rest to the soul."*

*When my youngest brother was in the last few weeks of his battle with cancer, I visited with him and the conversation turned more towards the Lord and heaven. My brother had trusted the Lord at an early age, but he lacked the initial teaching that gives children assurance of salvation. The last time we talked, he mentioned that his life had not been what it should have been, meaning that that might affect something. I told him that it was Jesus' life, not his own life that would get him into heaven. He said he had trusted in Jesus. After that he seemed to have a settled peace, and when he was asked later where he was going...he said "Heaven."*

Jesus is the Author, and Finisher of our faith. Never forget it. He created the original plan, then worked it Himself. Blessed Savior!

Delight:   Hebrews 1:1-3    Colossians 1:20-22

## August 1

*"Wherefore be ye not unwise, but understanding what the will of the Lord is."* Ephesians 5:17

There are questions often asked about the scriptures. We have helped new Christians, and others who want to learn.

People often ponder about the "will of God" factor. What exactly is it? The will of God is the Word of God; those who read and obey it are doing God's will. In specific everyday matters, the Word of God gives insight while He also uses daily happenings and incidents to guide one along toward His will for a particular thing. I was always vague on the thing about God's Will, until I understood one day that it is *doing what the Word of God says, and we know it covers everything from earth to heaven in our lives. Just obey what God says.* THAT'S GOD'S WILL FOR US!

God knows from the beginning what He intends to do with each one of His children. We tend to think that the unsaved are off of God's chart, and He is not aware of them. But, in fact, God tells us the duty of certain of His angels is looking after those who will be saved! *"Are they not all ministering spirits, sent forth to minister for them who shall be heirs of salvation?"* Hebrews 1:14

*Looking back over our life, we can see how God used the circumstances to eventually bring us to salvation and the ministry we have been engaged in since the day my husband was saved! The Lord changed his heart so completely, and he was chosen for fulltime work for God long before we were aware of it ourselves.* God's purpose and plans are never defeated! It shall all come to pass.

Delight:    John 5:30    Ephesians 6:6-7

# August 2

*"...for in the day that thou eatest thereof thou shalt surely die."* Genesis 2:17

Many Bible learners have been baffled by this portion of the scriptures, especially those new in the faith. They have said, "God said that Adam and Eve would surely die; but they didn't...they kept living." To that we have to explain that man is made up of three components, body, soul, and spirit. The body relates to the environment and is World-conscious. The soul relates to others, and is the seat of mind, emotions and will and self-consciousness.

The spirit of man is the part that relates to God. It is the Spiritual and God-consciousness of man. That is the part of Adam and Eve that ceased to be, or died, when they sinned. Sin immediately infected them, and they were cut off from God by that darkened spirit. They died spiritually! Spiritual death was passed upon all men since all came through Adam. The spirit of man remains dark until they experience the New Birth through faith in the Christ. By that we have been, *"...delivered...from the power of darkness, and hath translated us into the kingdom of his dear Son."* Colossians 1:13

Men can be living a good clean life, and still have a darkened spirit. They may be faithful church members, and still have a darkened spirit. Jesus said *"Ye must be born again"* and when He said *must,* you must! There is no other way to get an enlightened spirit. It is as the newborn baby comes out of the womb into the light. All are dead in trespasses and sins and in spiritual darkness until they are enlightened by that New Birth into God's Family. There is cause for rejoicing at that blessed event. Pray for lost souls to be saved.

Delight:   John 3:1-7    John 10:27-30

# August 3

*"And be not drunk with wine, wherein is excess;
but be filled with the Spirit."* Ephesians 5:18

Another puzzling part of the scriptures to those new in the faith is this part teaching being *filled with the Spirit.* Regardless of how one may feel about the *unknown tongues factor,* it is not mentioned in these verses in Ephesians, and it states outright exactly what you will be "speaking". *"Speaking to yourselves in psalms and hymns and spiritual songs, singing and making melody in your heart to the Lord; Giving thanks always for all things unto God and the Father in the name of the Lord Jesus Christ."* Eph. 5:19

The way the drunkard is controlled by alcoholic drink, is the illustration God used to emphasize how Christians are to be held in control by His Holy Spirit abiding in us. If we are, we can know it by reading what the Lord tells us in these verses.

*What will we do and say?* First, we will feed the Word of God into our own hearts. Sometimes I read it aloud to myself, just to hear it spoken, laying it more heavily on my heart and mind. Next, we will sing! Yes, whether we are talented singers or not, we won't care. We desire to praise the Lord in song. Last, we will let thanksgiving to the Lord flow out of our hearts, sometimes listing our blessings in a diary or notebook...reminding ourselves how very blessed we are as children of God! Remember Psalm 68:19. *"Blessed be the Lord, who daily loadeth us with benefits, even the God of our salvation. Selah"* Selah means, *'Pause and think on that."* Nothing is so sweet and soothing to the soul as recalling and basking in the blessings of God He's poured into our lives. He loves us THAT much! PTL!

Delight:     Psalm 67:5-6     Psalm 70:8

Edna Holmes

# August 4

*"But I fear, lest by any means...your minds should be corrupted from the simplicity that is in Christ." II Cor.11:3.*

In the early churches, it didn't take long for Satan to stir up adversaries to get into these fledgling congregations and spread false doctrine to destroy their faith in Christ. Thus, we often read of Paul admonishing them to hold fast to sound doctrine, *teaching.* The false teachers were always trying to add something to salvation, as though Jesus did not complete the plan of salvation. They would say that it couldn't possibly be as simple as the Apostles preached it to be.

Things that are simple have often times been made that way by others or someone who has worked through the complicated part aforetime. Christ, by His great work of redemption, made salvation obtainable and simple so mankind could be saved. Otherwise, no one would have "made it to heaven", by the *skin of their teeth,* or any other way. We shall never know the depths of the Lord's suffering unless God chooses to reveal it in heaven.

But with His fathomless love for us and His suffering, He did make salvation's plan ultra-simple for the human race. The religious zealots of that day just couldn't accept Jesus getting the glory and praise for what He alone accomplished. They wanted to add something on.

Christians today sometimes try to take some of the honor and glory to themselves when they accomplish a good work for the Lord in the church. Men want praise! But Jesus said in John 15:5, *"Without me ye can do nothing."* God enables us to do whatever we do. To God be the glory, great things He has done; it is all Him!

Delight:   John 5:44   Hebrews 1:1-3

## August 5

*"In all things shewing thyself a pattern of good works..."*
Titus 2:7

Once I was asked to speak to a large Sunday School class on the subject: The Way of Happiness for Christian Women. I love teaching women the Word of God. It's the only thing which will make a lasting difference in their lives.

First, I urged them to establish a concrete testimony of personal salvation. Until you know who you are and what you are in Christ, there will be a hint of worry about it, taking away your joy of the Lord. If that is your case, even though you have assuredly ask Jesus to save you, then read the little assurance book, I John, every day until the joy of belonging registers in your heart.

Second, I urged them to spend time daily with Jesus. Have fellowship with Him. It is vital as it keeps us focused on the right things and equips us for life and its situations. We have patterns in great men and women of faith who have gone before us.

Enhance your prayer life by praying in conjunction with reading your Bible. You will be prompted at times to stop and pray. In addition, in reading and praying, we will often see answers to prayer and solutions to problems with which we've been coping.

Keep a notebook to record what you glean from the Lord.

You can only love deeply those you know personally in a close relationship, their particular character and disposition. To know Jesus that way is the way of happiness for us on earth. *"As ye have received Christ Jesus the Lord, so walk ye in Him."* Colossians 2:6.

Delight:   Psalm 37:4   Psalm 68:19

Edna Holmes

# August 6

*"These things have I written unto you that believe on the name of the Son of God; that ye may know that ye have eternal life…"*
I John 5:13

The Epistle of 1 John is the assurance book. Older mature Christians may counsel a new Christian to read it through each day for a week in order to settle salvation assurance once and for all time in the heart. There is FACTS, FAITH, and FEELING in that order.

*FACTS is the foundation, the truth, which is the Word of God.* Our salvation is based on the fact that Jesus paid the price of sin, which is *death*, to redeem us. On the third day after He died and was buried, He rose from the grave, triumphant over death, hell and the grave! That gives us the blessed hope which nothing can take away from us.

FAITH is belief in the facts. We imagine faith rather like a fog which can have us "socked in", that is, *strong in faith,* or it can disappear under circumstances as a literal fog under bright sunshine. Remember, faith is believing God's Word and totally trusting in Him.

FEELING is the resulting joy, which registers when we have believed the facts and understood that we are really saved.

FACTS is the TRUTH, THE WORD OF GOD.

FAITH is believing the facts of the Word of God.

FEELING is the resulting joy of salvation by trusting Christ.

If we invert that order such as expecting *feelings* before trusting in the Lord, we will be foolish. Always, our belief must be based on the facts of the truth in God's Word, or we will have nothing.

Delight:   Romans 10: 9-10, 13    I John 5:11-13

## August 7

*"...ye are of more value than many sparrows."*
Luke 12:7

The meticulous attention in detail that God gives to His children is beyond our comprehension. Can you imagine that all the hairs on your head are numbered? God said it.

*"But even the hairs of your head are all numbered. Fear not therefore: ye are of more value than many sparrows."* That is our text verse in full, and we know our Lord never embellished when He spoke of things. He didn't amplify or diminish the facts. Because He is God, God does know everything, everywhere, all the time, and so He knows the amount of hair, the number, on everyone's head! This chapter of Luke is a gold mine of preaching by our Lord. No wonder the crowds followed Him and were astonished at His sayings.

*"I was born on this day long ago. I was the only one of ten children born outside of Texas. It was during the depression years; life was hard for everyone. Finally, we migrated back to familiar territory. I grew up with a strong sense of insecurity, and when in God's perfect timing, I was saved, I couldn't grasp it at first as I read about what we have in Christ. It was feasible to me that others might have those benefits, but me? It has been a lifetime enjoyment, learning how the Lord loves me and takes care of me as His child."*

The world is full of fearful, insecure people. We should take opportunities to sow the Good News of salvation. <u>Jesus saves!</u> Witness by sending cards with verses; keep simple gospel tracts to give out as the Lord directs you. And He will! While you can, do *something* to win others. Time is running out for all of us.

Delight:    Psalm 91:4    Psalm 40:5

Edna Holmes

# August 8

*"For thou, Lord, art good, and ready to forgive; and plenteous in mercy unto all them that call upon thee."* Psalm 86:5

God can forgive us for our daily sins because Jesus has already paid for them through His death, *the supreme sacrifice*. He saved us initially at the time of salvation and provided the cleansing from sin which besets us continually, and will continue, as long as we are in this body of flesh. How the Lord can love us so is more than we can understand. We could not do without His continual flow of grace and forgiveness channeled into our lives.

We also need to forgive others and seek forgiveness when we have offended a brother or sister and know of it. Unless we do, it will certainly impede spiritual growth in our lives, and we will be miserable in spite of everything we do to cover it up.

*I soon learned the detriment of having an unforgiving spirit as I began to pursue growing in knowledge of the Bible and things of the Lord after I was saved. I barely made any progress and could hear the still, small voice of the Lord speaking to my heart about my attitude. You see, I had a big basket of "unforgiven" hidden away in my heart, and I was definitely NOT going to forgive those people who I had determined were unforgiveable. I even had some folks in my basket that were dead! God convinced me through strong conviction that the basket had to go. I finally surrendered to the Lord, and took the basket to my place of prayer, got on my knees, and took every soul stored in my basket out and forgave them, according to the grace of God granted to me as I obeyed. With the heavy burden lifted, my life took a fresh start in spiritual growth as I studied God's Word.*

Forgiveness must be practiced daily, if need be. Don't allow bitterness to accumulate in your heart. Forgive!

Delight    Psalm 51:1-2    Psalm 103: 4,5

Delighting in the Lord

# August 9

*"Then took they up stones to cast at him..."* John 8:59

There are times when certain parts of the Word of God send chills up my spine as I read them. This is one of those verses. We do have an advantage, because, in our time *we know Who He is.* We who are saved and have the Word of God which reveals our Savior to us are the most blessed people on earth because we can *know Him personally. The religious, but lost, Jews of that day did not.* They would not believe on Him, so were so blind in heart and mind, they intended to kill Jesus with rocks from the ground! Reading it, I marvel at the love and tolerance our Lord had for those blind religious people, filled with hatred for Him, the Savior of the world. I instinctively want to yell, *"Stop!! You can't do that! That's God your Creator!"*

If they had flung a rock at the Lord, it would have fallen to the ground before making a mark on Jesus. I've no doubt of that. But the Lord chose to make Himself invisible to them, and went out *through the midst of them, and so passed by.* That's how Jesus "hid" Himself. He didn't jump behind a pillar of the temple or any such tactics like a mere human would have to do to hide.

Have we, in any way, ever *stoned the Lord?* I'm sure your answer is an emphatic *"NO!"* But the sad truth is we do! We hurt Him with stones. One is *indifference.* We get distracted from devotion to Him and cease to pursue His Word and prayer. The heart-breaking stone, which hurts the Lord so much is our indifference. Examine your heart thoroughly today by Psalm 139:23-24.

Delight:    Psalm 31:23    II Thessalonians 3:5

Edna Holmes

# August 10

*"...we are his people, and the sheep of his pasture."*
Psalm 100:3

The Lord calls His children *sheep.* He also said in the other part of the text verse: *"Know ye that the Lord he is God: it is he that made us, and not we ourselves...". We can learn so much about ourselves and our utter dependence on God by believing Him and learning about the sheep and its traits.*

Sheep can't take care of themselves! They are doomed if they don't have a shepherd to lead them along, guide them through difficult places, protect them from predators, point out the feeding places, and safe watering holes. We are also totally dependent on our Shepherd, the Lord Jesus Christ. Men want to take credit for their own destiny, but how pitifully lacking is their ability to do so. They cannot make a particle of air they depend on every minute of their lives! They cannot make a drop of water! They cannot make it rain out of the clouds to water the crops of food or other plant life which also sustains earth life in some way. *Helpless mankind!*

In recent years, a song has become popular to sing at funerals: *"I Did It My Way".* It must be obedience to God, our Shepherd, or we will fail to have a satisfying, fulfilling life on earth no matter how hard we try and "do it my way."

Totally dependent as the sheep are by nature, they are a most valuable animal. They furnish wool, plus other by-products useful to mankind from their fleece. We will elaborate on our value as sheep on the next page.

Delight:   Psalm 95: 6-7   John 10:27

## August 11

*"My sheep hear my voice, and I know them, and they follow me."* John 10:27

Jesus claims ownership of His sheep, and He declares that the sheep *know their owner!* He owns us, His sheep, by purchase. With His own blood through death on the cruel cross, Jesus redeemed us and put us out in His pasture of blessings to spend our life on this earth. He made us valuable to earth by our blessed association with Him.

We are lights in the world. Jesus is THE LIGHT of the world, and we are to reflect that light. Jesus said in Matt. 5:14 *"Ye are the light of the world."* Here is the reason for the Lord leaving us down here after He saved us, making us His sheep. Phil. 2:15 *"That ye may be blameless and harmless, the sons of God, without rebuke, in the midst of a crooked and perverse nation, among whom ye shine as lights in the world."* The more we stay close to Jesus in fellowship, the more brightly we will shine for Him!

Besides being lights in the world, Jesus said we are SALT; salt in the spiritual sense. We understand it is a very significant thing, because we know the actual element of salt is used for making food palatable. It *seasons* what we eat. Christians are likened to that invaluable commodity. Salt preserves, seasons, is healing, and has so many other helpful uses. Using the salt factor, Christ illustrates how the whole earth is blessed by Christians. However, Jesus said we must be careful not to lose our "savor." That's our freshness. We keep to the very best stage of salt life by abiding in Christ. What a privilege to be a Christian!

Delight:   Mark 9:50   John 10:28-30

Edna Holmes

# August 12

*"And unto one he gave five talents, to another two,
and to another one…"* Matthew 25:15

This is the parable of the master giving his servants talents, expecting them to invest them wisely. These talents were money. The servants did with the gifts from their master much like people would do today. Some were diligent to invest to the fullest, some, a little less enthusiastic, and the last one hid the talent and didn't put himself out to bother with it at all.

It is clear. The Lord finished the work that His Father in heaven gave Him to do. He went back to heaven and left His servants, the Christians, with various talents and gifts to be used in His service. We should improve on and develop the talents Jesus gives. Many accept the basic talent but do not develop it. I understand this well, for all my family have musical talent, or the "play by ear" factor in our background. My father was a county fiddler who never had lessons but could play so well you would never guess he couldn't read music. People who have that capability oftentimes leave off developing their skills to a higher, more useful level.

*A man working in our church building one day saw the beautiful grand piano. No one but my husband being there, he sat down and played a fair rendition of a semi classical tune, all by ear. That was it though…just one piece over and over. Obviously, the man could have been a fine musician with the basic gift God gave to him, but he hadn't learned to read music.* What have you done with the "talent" God has given to you? *Improve it by using it and honoring the Lord.*

Delight:    I Corinthians 6:19-20

# August 13

*"The ear that heareth the reproof of life
abideth among the wise."* Proverbs 15:31

Blessed is the Christian who *hears* God as He speaks. If one has that habit of hearing the Lord, it is because he has *practiced hearing as he reads scripture.* Write down precious things God reveals through His Word at every opportunity. God will number you among the 'wise'. Those are ones whose ears are tuned to hear what delights their hearts, a personal word from their Savior.

*One year, our family gathered at the home of our granddaughter and her husband to celebrate the first birthday of their baby boy, Zed. After a few hours, the baby was put down for a nap in the nursery upstairs, and the womenfolk all congregated in the kitchen helping prepare the meal. It was noisy with many voices going at once. Suddenly, our granddaughter stopped what she was doing and bounded up the stairs! Soon she came back down with her baby in arms ready to resume her work. I was taken with the fact that in all the racket, she was the only one that heard the baby! But then, she is the baby's mother, and her ear was tuned to hear the baby's voice.*

The noise and clamor of the world is relentless in its pursuit of our attention and time. Do we tune it out, and listen attentively for the Lord's voice and message to us from His Word? We must put our mind to it and pray for power to withstand the noise of the world. The Lord doesn't raise a clamor; He speaks in a still small voice in the inner core of our hearts. *Enable us to hear you, Blessed Lord.*

Delight:    Psalms 119:130    Hebrews 2:1

Edna Holmes

# August 14

*"And let it be, when thou hearest the sound of a going in the tops of the mulberry trees, that thou shalt bestir thyself..."*
II Samuel 5:24

This verse is more or less buried in the Old Testament, but once you discover it, it makes an impression. David enquired of the Lord as to the time of going after their enemies, the Philistines, in battle. The Lord told him to wait until there was "the sound of going" in the top of the mulberry trees. That's when the Lord came down to lead the battle and the host of Philistines were destroyed. The wind stirring the trees signified the Holy Spirit of God had arrived!

Every time I sit under trees and hear the swish of the wind stirring the top branches, I think of this verse. The Holy Spirit, who indwells us, is always with us but most Christians do not ask Him for advice, instructions, answers to our problems or any such thing. We don't want to wait until the "sound of going" is heard; we just forge ahead unprepared in our hearts for God to work. We should meet God early before we start the day's activities, and ask as the apostle Paul did when he met Jesus on the Damascus road; "Lord what wilt thou have me to do?" If we consult with the Lord and follow His orders, we are surprised at what is accomplished. The Lord makes the way smoother, opens up doors that are shut tight, makes tough chores easier, and much more. Our present-day society expects "instant if not before" service about everything. There is no waiting for "the sound of going" for the Lord to work. So, they lose out on the best of life.

Delight:   Isaiah 40:31   Psalm 25:5

Delighting in the Lord

# August 15

*"...he causeth his wind to blow, and the waters flow."*
Psalm 147:18

We have heard the expression, "they are in the doldrums." There were many such sayings a generation ago that had a special meaning to them because they harked back to real. When one had the "doldrums" he was listless and unable to call up the energy to get his normal day's work done. His "power" was gone.

*The Doldrums, in actuality, were a part of the ocean near the equator where sailing vessels were caught in a great calm with no wind to fill the sails so the ships could continue on their journey. They were helpless to move until the wind came again, rippling the waters and filling the great sails with the "power" the wind furnished to speed the ships on their ways. The waiting time could be weeks, even months! But they absolutely lay helpless in the water until the winds came to the rescue.*

And so, the doldrums can be a listless time where the power is gone from our lives. Sin causes that dilemma. We may not know exactly what got us off track, but God does. So, we do as I John 1:9 tells us, *"If we confess our sins, he is faithful and just to forgive us our sins, and to cleanse us from all unrighteousness."* The Lord made it simple. Go back at the place where you sailed into the doldrums and ask God to reveal the cause so you can get right with Him, and avoid the sin that trapped you in the "doldrums." The winds of blessing and power will flow again into your life. Amazing...amazing grace.

Delight:    Proverbs 28:13    Isaiah 55:7

Edna Holmes

# August 16

*"The fool hath said in his heart, There is no God.
Corrupt are they..."* Psalm 53:1

We would say, "How on earth could anyone say such a foolish thing"? It's because the lost are *DEAD* in trespasses and sins and don't have any spiritual understanding of the Word of God. They are easily deceived by false teachers. We who are saved understand the Word of God because He the Spirit of God reveals the truth of it. He is *Christ in us*. No matter how a man may be noted for his literary work as a poet, philosopher, writer, historian or such; if he does not know God, he is ignorant of what matters in life. He is lost.

Such a one was Voltaire, the greatest of the French writers in the seventeenth century. He fought against Christ, mocking God's people and denouncing the Word of God. He claimed that in a few years, from his time, the Bible, the Word of God would be eradicated. Instead, the building used by him and his associates in a few years after his demise, was used by the Bible Society which worked to print and distribute Bibles! In recent years I heard our Pastor in preaching, tell us that in an auction long ago, a ninety-two-volume set of Voltaire's books sold for four dollars! *Four dollars!* At the same time, an ancient manuscript of the Bible sold for $500,000! Voltaire's generation passed on, and they who listened to him are realizing the foolishness of his teaching. He influenced many which are now experiencing a place of darkness and misery in hell without Christ.

Thank God for your salvation today. He is worthy to be praised.

Delight:    Proverbs 12:23    Ecclesiastes 10:3

# August 17

*"...and they are they which testify of me."*
John 5:39

Jesus had told the scribes and Pharisees to, *"search the scriptures, for in them ye think ye have eternal life: and they are they which testify of me."* The Lord's appeal was always to the scriptures. He quoted the Old Testament constantly. Those men did search but they already had their minds made up, so they saw it in a different way. Christ is concealed in the OT and revealed in the NT. When we are saved, it is then that we begin to recognize the Lord on every page. To search the scriptures is the greatest thing you can do for your heart.

The entire book of Psalms is the favorite of countless Christians. *I read that Billy Graham's wife, now passed on to heaven, lost her eyesight to the point where she could hardly see to read her Bible. She had her aide type the book of Psalms in huge, huge print so she could read it as she was lying in bed, an invalid at that time. She had many, many notebooks holding those precious pages of the Psalms she pored over every day.* What a wise, happy lady Ruth Graham was because she delighted in *"searching the scriptures"*. When something comes into your life which takes your time and attention from reading, searching the scriptures, and you lose interest; beware that it is a trap to pull you away from closeness with the Lord.

Since the Lord has told us to "search the scriptures", He is not going to pour Bible knowledge into our minds while we are asleep with the Bible on the nightstand near our heads. He said, "Search!" Get you a simple plan and work it every day. God is serious about His Word; and life goes infinitely better for us if we are too. Selah.

Delight:    Psalm 119:89    II Timothy 3:16

Edna Holmes

# August 18

*"I have not hid thy righteousness within my heart; I have declared thy faithfulness and thy salvation..."* Psalm 40:10

It is difficult, if not impossible, to hide God's righteousness which He imparts to those saved through faith in Jesus. It will show up, even in ultra timid folks who want to remain anonymous in the crowd. The *new life* from God in us can't be hidden. It will eventually break free from restraint and make itself known in the life of the believer. God's is thorough. *He changes us completely so that we are a new person on the inside. This new "you" begins to be more assertive as you learn and grow from the Word of God. People can see a change has come over you.*

Remember Nicodemus came to Jesus in the night; we all assume his motive was to not be seen with Jesus! But we know he heard Jesus' direct message to him which was the *must part* of being *Born Again*. "Marvel not that I said unto thee, Ye must be born again." John 3:7 Somewhere between that time and the crucifixion of Jesus, something life-changing happened to Nicodemus.

We wouldn't know that if it had not been recorded how he came and helped take Jesus' body from the cross and bury him in a grand style for that day, in a rich man's tomb, with costly spices and grave clothes wrapped around His body. Apparently, Nicodemus couldn't conceal his love for Jesus any longer; he boldly came and helped Joseph of Arimathea take care of the burial. It was dangerous and costly. Have you let your faith in Christ be known openly since you have become a Christian? Do it today to honor your Lord.

Delight:    Psalm 31:19    Psalm 34:8

Delighting in the Lord

# August 19

*"He that hideth hatred with lying lips, and he that uttereth a slander, is a fool."* Proverbs 10:18

Christians may have little sins hidden in their lives. Since we don't always come clean with God every day, and keep our sins confessed "up to date", sins get stored in our hearts and put a spiritual drag on our lives. It's those little sins, most respectable, that we keep like pet snakes because we don't consider them to be harmful. Beware! Sin is *always* harmful. Little sins grow up just like pet snakes, and at first opportunity, will put a deadly poisonous bite on you. Many times, we determine to get rid of every hindering thing in our Christian life, but when cleaning time comes in our prayer corner with God, we decide to keep one or two…they are so enjoyable, and harmless of course. Mistake! And so, sin keeps a hold on us, and the devil uses it to defeat us.

**Tolerance for gossip** is a popular pet sin. It *does not gossip, but it will listen!* It does not gossip, *but it is sympathetic.* It does not gossip, *but it likes to keep up with rumors.* Tolerance encourages the sin of gossiping because of all the above traits of its character.

What is *gossip* anyway? Some years ago, I read a definition by Shelly Esser. Gossip is "having certain perceptions and opinions of someone that you tell *unnecessarily* to others." That stamps "guilty" on most of our foreheads. We need to pray for control of our tongues so when the urge comes to speak when we should remain silent, we can refrain from it. Admit to friends when you sense a "gossip session" is coming, that God has convicted you of talking unnecessarily about people.

Delight:    Proverbs 11:13    Psalm 19:14

Edna Holmes

# August 20

*"I will only, without doing anything else,
go through on my feet."* Numbers 20:19

The Israelites, on their journey toward the promised land, had to go by Edom, the country belonging to Esau's descendants. Israel asked for permission to cut through instead of going the long way around making a greater hardship on the people. They said they would not even drink the water, unless they paid for it. Still, the king of Edom flatly refused to allow the people to walk through their country with the threat of going to war with them.

Then Israel, in a last attempt to get permission, told Edom that *"I will only, without doing anything else, go through on my feet."* But Edom threatened again, so Israel plodded on, and took the long arduous journey around the land of the Edomites. Many years later, Edom would pay dearly for their cruel treatment of God's people.

In our journey on earth, heading for heaven, our eternal home, we are to diligently *go through on our feet.* The Lord's work requires going faithfully at a steady pace, and to stay on our feet! If we sit or lie down or dawdle in any fashion in serving our Lord, the devil will make us comfortable. He doesn't want us to *stay on our feet ready to respond to any command from our Lord.*

How do we stay on our *spiritual* feet? I'd say we should start each day with the Lord. Feast heartily on His Word to give us spiritual stamina and strength. Pray the Lord to lead us in a plain path because of the enemy who would entice us off the path, to sit down and wile away time! Let us go through *on our feet!* Keep moving.

Delight:   I Corinthians 15:57-58   II Corinthians 4:16-18

Delighting in the Lord

# August 21

*"Thou wilt keep him in perfect peace whose mind is stayed on thee: because he trusteth in thee."* Isaiah 26:3

Do we actually *believe* God when He told us that amazing truth in His Word? No matter what's going on, all the tangled affairs of our lives which can reach tragic proportions, perfect peace can keep our minds at rest if we keep Jesus front and center in our thoughts. Because we *TRUST* in Him. That means we are putting it in the hands of Jesus to take care of it all. In that way, the peace will come and abide in our minds. Someone has aptly said: "Apart from Him, the minds of the redeemed will find no rest." We foolishly try to make it happen in other ways with our own efforts or looking to other good, but lesser, sources. But we have to get back to the "bottom line" truth. It is Jesus; it will always be Jesus; He gave us life; it has to be Jesus. Are we keeping our minds on Him? If your peace of mind flits in and out and you want it settled; get your mind focused on Jesus and keep it there.

I've tried this verse and found it to be exactly as it is stated. I was so terrified before my husband's open-heart surgery; afraid he would die. I was beside myself. Then this verse in Isaiah came to mind. I snatched it to my heart and began running it like a tickertape around and round in my mind in the night until I fell asleep. That Word from God kept me sane; and praise be to the Lord, it all turned out well. My husband has been preaching the Word for over a decade since his main heart problem was fixed.

God's Word is the most powerful thing on earth. Use it for everything you need to keep a sound mind and joy of heart. It is there for all of us, to keep us "in the way" as we journey through this life.

Delight:   Hebrews 4:12   Psalm 116:1-2

Edna Holmes

# August 22

*"Because that by reason of him many of the Jews went away, and believed on Jesus."* John 12:11

Jesus had raised Lazarus from the dead. Now the chief priests were wanting to kill Him! Not only did they want to kill Jesus, they wanted to put Lazarus to death too. Why? Because of him being dead and brought back to life by the Lord, more people were believing on Jesus and the religious Jews did not want that. They had their religious system in place, and they intended to keep it that way! Jesus was interfering with it, preaching the truth about God and the way of salvation. He came to *"seek and to save that which was lost".* Luke 19:10 The Jews were walking around in their spiritual blindness, dead in trespasses and sins. They didn't recognize their Messiah when He did come to redeem His people from Satan's hold on them. They rejected Him altogether and sought to get rid of Him.

There is a plain contrast here. The world hates Christ and rejects Him, more and more as the generations are passing one after the other. They try to hinder the Lord's work and have targeted the Christians for persecution in any way they can do it for the same reason they wanted to do away with Lazarus. *Because of him other people got saved. Jesus raised Christians today from the dead, for we were all "dead in trespasses and sins" till Jesus saved us. Now the world hates us too and wants to stop Christians from causing others to be saved as well.* But they cannot. *"Greater is He that is in you, than he that is in the world."* I John 4:4. The Lord said it. Believe it!

Delight:     Proverbs 14:12     II Corinthians 10:3-5

Delighting in the Lord

# August 23

*"For sin, taking occasion by the commandment, deceived me, and by it slew me."* Romans 7:11

The Bible tell us that *"All unrighteousness is sin..."* so we may all understand plainly that if it's not right...it's sin! If we do anything contrary to God's Word...it's sin! Finally, we learn that we can only live the Christian life totally depending on our Savior, Jesus Christ. *Jesus paid it all, all to Him we owe.*

For all the instruction in His Word, warning us of sin, we are still very vulnerable to sin's deception. We are not *afraid* of it; therefore, the devil has an advantage. He makes sin appealing so that when the Christians get close, he springs the trap! Sin *always* has consequences, whether it's a little insignificant sin, in our minds, or a big horrendous offense which leaves a deep scar of suffering. God forgives sin; but consequences follow. God does not cancel them.

*"A horrible torture during the middle ages was that of a cell, which, at the prisoner's first entrance presented an air of comfort and ease; but after he was confined a few days, he observed the dimensions of his cell beginning to shrink. Once the discovery was made, the fact became more appalling every day. Slowly but terribly the sides drew closer and the unhappy victim was crushed to death. And such is the deception of sin."* (modified) From: Treasures to Keep

*"Be not deceived; God is not mocked: for whatsoever a man soweth, that shall he also reap."* Galatians 6:7. We can *never, never* get away with sinning. Clear every day with prayer before you lay down to sleep at night.

Delight:   Psalm 107:17   I John 1:9

Edna Holmes

# August 24

*"Looking unto Jesus the author and finisher of our faith; who for the joy that was set before him endured..."* Heb. 12:2

We know that the strength we need for victorious living and the spiritual warfare we are engaged in daily, *is not in us!* There is only one place to look as our text verse spells it out. We must be *"looking unto Jesus the author and finisher of our faith..."* Jesus paid in full the terrible price it took to redeem us from the curse of sin. As Children of God, there is power in store for us to draw on for every need of our lives.

Jesus suffered such agony and shame in dying on the cross. His body was human flesh, just like yours and mine. He suffered every moment as He was tortured to death to pay for our sins, and when it was done, He said, *"It is finished."* and dismissed His spirit from that broken body.

*He did it for love. John 3:16. He showed us the "so" of His love.*

*He did it for the joy that was set before Him. (Souls saved.)*

We would do well to keep the fact of the crucifixion of Jesus fresh in our minds. Love and gratitude will stay fresh in our hearts. *I have a Christian friend who loves the Lord so much and her heart is tender. Every time she reads the account of Jesus' crucifixion, she cries all the way through it. She is so thankful for her personal salvation.*

We should not let our hearts get callused to that old familiar story of "the Author and Finisher of our faith..."and how He suffered to purchase our salvation. What He bled and died for, He in turn offers as a Gift to we who believe on Him. Can we fathom such love? Surely, we can be true and faithful to Him in everything. Blessed by His name!

Delight:   Revelation 5:12    Philippians 2:9

## August 25

*"Put on the whole armour of God, that ye may be able to stand against the wiles of the devil."* Ephesians 6:11

The wiles of the devil are commonly known as his tricks he uses to trap Christians when he has them off guard and vulnerable. Unless we are close to the Lord in fellowship; we can be fooled very easily. He used his wiles on Eve in the Garden of Eden and she was a perfect woman, *freshly made!* We simply forget that the devil is out to get us; he wants everyone of us to fall into some sinful practice, and to dishonor the name of Christ. And we are vulnerable. After we have patched up little cracks and holes in the fence guard around our hearts, we relax because it's perfectly safe, in our minds. We forget about the devil who is "seeking whom he may devour", and he works on breaking through our defenses. He often succeeds.

*A few years ago, I went into the kitchen, and noticed at the far end something unfamiliar on the floor. I walked closer and bent down to retrieve what looked like a big thick shoelace from a work boot, or such. Multicolored. Then it moved! It raised up at one end and looked at me. A SNAKE! It was about eighteen inches long. It frightened me so that I couldn't even scream. I just stood in the door pointing at it and gasping out the word 'snake.' My husband came running and soon the snake was deceased and thrown out of our house. We never thought anything could get into the house through the small crack at the corner of our outside door. But the snake found a way.*

Keep your love for the Lord fervent, obey Him and He will safeguard your life. The Holy Spirit gives us those subtle warnings; at times when I've listened trouble was avoided. When I wasn't sensitive to His voice; we were beset with unnecessary problems. Be aware that Satan is your enemy. Pray daily for God's wisdom and protection.

Delight:    Ephesians 6:12    I Peter 5:8

Edna Holmes

# August 26

*"...who did sin, this man, or his parents,  
that he was born blind?"* John 9:2

This is a foolish question the disciples asked Jesus about the blind man. How could the man sin *before he was even born?* But that is the typical attitude toward human misfortunes. Who is guilty? Jesus answered "Neither." The rest of the Lord's answer is quite amazing: *"...but that the works of God should be made manifest in him." v.3 When* we see someone living with a handicap from birth, we wonder, Why? Just remember that you are looking at the *underside* of the tapestry; eternity will reveal the purpose of it all when earth time is over, and heaven becomes reality to us.

*I have a niece born with spina bifida. I was there when the doctors performed surgery on that tiny newborn. We all cried and wondered if Dana would live, with hardly a chance; but God knew. The doctors predicted perhaps 16 years. Dana is fifty years old now, and very much alive. She has lived her whole life in a wheelchair, but you wouldn't know by her attitude. She exhibits wit and charm many healthy folks don't have. She has many interests and that keeps her happy in spite of her severe disability. Her biological mother is deceased, but her stepmother has loved and tended Dana as her own. Recently, Dana received a beautiful gift from her, two bracelets, one with the inscription: "You were given this life because you were strong enough to live it." The other said, "She thought she could, so she did." Actually, it's by God's design that Dana has lived so long. He had a plan, and she has, by His grace, carried it out. We can only wonder at how many lives she has unknowingly inspired on life's journey.*

*"Trust in the Lord with all thine heart; and lean not unto thine own understanding. In all thy ways acknowledge him, and he shall direct thy paths."* Proverbs 3:5-6. If you don't understand what God is doing, then just trust Him! You will understand by and by.

Delight:     Proverbs 31:19     Isaiah 26:3

Delighting in the Lord

# August 27

*"Examine yourselves, whether ye be in the faith; prove your own selves..."* II Corinthians 13:5

We would be stronger and more assured of our relationship with Jesus, if we only kept as close to Him in fellowship as God warns us to be in His Word. Somehow, we get careless and cool off in our dedication. Soon, we are miserable and feel like, at times, we have lost it all. "Where is God?" Our text verse tells us we can give our own test, and it will prove what our status really is. The saved have some distinct spiritual marks put there by the Lord Jesus Christ.

Examination: *Do I desire the Word of God?* That means wanting to read it, and hear it taught and preached. If you answered 'yes' from your heart, that is enough to prove you have been born again into God's family. Unsaved people do not desire God's Word, and they cannot understand it because they are dead spiritually. That's a fact that people forget.

*Do I love the church and fellowship with other Christians?* We are all in the same family and God is our Father. There should be a longing to be at church every Sunday. It's the Lord's day for us to worship and remember Him.

*Do I have conviction of sin when I do something wrong?* If you are a child of God, you certainly will. You won't have peace of mind until you confess your sin and ask for forgiveness.

This is just three questions to make us pause and examine ourselves to see if we are indeed saved, and on our way to heaven. God CANNOT lie. What His Word promises, He will do! Not by feelings, but by faith in God and His Word.

Delight:   Ephesians 2:8   John 5:24

Edna Holmes

# August 28

*"Behold how great a matter a little fire kindleth."*
James 3:5

Recently we have seen that fact demonstrated before our very eyes as wildfires have sprung up in several states this summer, burning many acres and destroying homes in its wake. *Someone carelessly tosses a match or cigarette into the grass; immediately a fire starts which spreads…going wild…doing serious damage.*

The detriment of the tongue happens in a similar fashion. Someone tosses out gossip, and it immediately explodes into a *wildfire of poisonous words, misinformation, and slander which leaves a trail of destruction. In some cases, when public apologizes have been made and things made as right as possible in the aftermath of the devastation, still the victim will be left with a pile of ashes, once a good reputation and testimony, now marred beyond recognition. The Bible always gives the best advice: "But let your communication, Yea, yea; Nay, nay: for whatsoever is more than these cometh of evil."* Matthew 5:37.

That sounds impossible doesn't it? I do believe the Lord is teaching us that long *wordy* conversations can turn into the detrimental sort. We "let our hair down", so to speak; we get too familiar in the conversation, and *things* can be said that should never have been spoken. The tongue is the most dangerous member of our bodies. Let's believe what the Word of God says and put a guard on it by prayer and reading the book of James, the third chapter, often.

Delight:     James 3:6     James 6:5-8

## August 29

*"...With men this is impossible; but with God all things are possible."* Matthew 19:26

When we realize that God can do anything He wants to do, we feel much more secure in our relationship with Him. God is the One in charge of earth and its inhabitants. Most certainly nothing can thwart God's plans and purpose. Let us pose a hard question: Can God stop a speeding train with a swarm of flies? We know of one instance where God did indeed do just that.

*Many years ago, a great passenger train, the Grand Trunk flyer in Canada was stopped abruptly on the tracks. Investigating the cause, they found that about twenty miles out that morning, running full speed, the train ran into a "sea" of peculiar flies; millions of them, perhaps billions, but the train was going fast it was hard to estimate. The cars became quite dark as the train ploughed through the mass of insects, and the train came to a sudden stop. The engine was full of flies! The little things were ground into a mass in the driving rod. They were in everything on the engine. I'm sure when officials were asked, "What stopped that train", the answer was a great surprise. "Flies!"*

A few flies could not have stopped that train. But a swarm of an unspeakable number did! What could happen if all the Christians in our nation banded together to pray for our country? There is a promise. *"If my people, which are called by my name, shall humble themselves, and pray, and seek my face, and turn from their wicked ways; then will I hear from heaven, and will forgive their sin, and will heal their land."* II Chronicles 7:14

Christians, pray daily for this nation. It desperately needs it.

Delight:   Matthew 7:7-8   Romans 14:12

Edna Holmes

# August 30

*"The words of a man's mouth are as deep waters..."*
Proverbs 18:4

In deep waters, you can't see the bottom; you don't know what's down there. Words that are spoken oftentimes conceal what's underneath the surface in conversation. Some who have suffered peculiar sorrows in life have very deep waters underneath their words. However, the Bible tells us that *"...but a man of understanding will draw it out."* Proverbs 20:5. A mature Christian that has abundance of wisdom from the Lord is a very valuable counselor with whom you can share your heart. However, Jesus is our best Counselor; He loves us and delights in us. If you feel a sadness inside, or a vague longing for relief which you don't understand, take time to stop and talk to Him. Jesus can open up your heart and both of you look in and sort things out. It is not just empty phrases when we say, "Jesus is everything to us..." "...He is our life" "He is our best Friend." Remember the good old song by Elisha A. Hoffman...

"I must tell Jesus all of my trials; I cannot bear these burdens alone.
In my distress He kindly will help me. He ever loves and cares for His own.
I must tell Jesus! I must tell Jesus! I cannot bear my burdens alone.
I must tell Jesus! I must tell Jesus! Jesus can help me, Jesus alone."

Since Jesus is our Counselor, we can open our hearts and confess all our woes, fears, regrets, and emotional hang-ups that hinders us from the fullness of life God promised in the Lord Jesus Christ. He listens; He loves us; He won't tell others; and He has power to help us! What a wonderful Savior and friend.

Delight:   Isaiah 41:10   Psalm 36:7

Delighting in the Lord

# August 31

*"...but there is one kind of flesh of men, another flesh of beasts, another of fishes, and another of birds."* I Cor. 15:39

This verse does away with the theory of evolution; that we all evolved from the same life form in the beginning. Foolish men now reject the Word of God which tells plainly how God created the earth and everything in and on it in that awesome week of creation.
*"And God made the beast of the earth after his kind, and cattle after their kind, and every thing that creepeth upon the earth after his kind: and God saw that it was good."* Genesis 1:25

The animals can only communicate with those of their own kind. By instinct they are defensive when other animals come into their territory, which will be designated in some fashion. Man can tame the animals, and train them to respond to their commands. But they cannot communicate with them as humans to humans.

*Our children were given a little squirrel when they were young. It was raised from a baby by humans, who loved animals and took good care of it. It had a nice cage and seemed happy with the kids handling it by feeding it little tidbits of food. It all went well until one day, for some reason, the cage was taken outside, and that little animal was exposed to its natural habitat. It never was the same again. We finally had to take it outside and let it go. The minute its feet hit the ground it was running toward its own kind!*

It is the same in the spiritual world. Man cannot naturally communicate with God. He has to be changed by the new birth and become a child of God. Christians have their own language and ways that the world does not understand. *After his kind!*

Delight:   I John 3:1    I Corinthians 2:14

Edna Holmes

# September 1

*"And the house, when it was in building, was built of stone made ready before it was brought thither."* I Kings 6:7

Solomon's temple was the most awesome sight on earth in its time. It was lavishly beautiful and costly, beyond description. King David amassed the wealth and materials to build the Temple, and had a purposed plan, but he was not allowed by God to build it. Solomon, his son, was chosen to build the temple.

The unique detail about the construction was that there was *no building noise* on the site. Unheard of! But God's plan was that *"...there was neither hammer nor axe nor any tool of iron heard in the house, while it was in building."* All the hammering, chiseling, and smoothing of the stones to certain dimensions was done away from the temple site. The stones were then brought, already prepared, to be added to the building.

All the Bible is "God-breathed" and in it, we find untold treasures. When I saw the double meaning of this amazing account of preparing the stones of the temple beforehand, my heart was thrilled. It speaks to me the wonder of God's preparation of our hearts before we are brought to Christ and added to Him. No one hears or sees the work of the Holy Spirit of God as He stirs the sinner's heart to salvation, but when that "stone" is cut and ready, it becomes a part of God's building, the church.

I Peter 2:5 *"Ye also, as lively stones, are built up a spiritual house, an holy priesthood, to offer up spiritual sacrifices, acceptable to God by Jesus Christ."*

God's Holy Spirit also uses the hammers, axes, and chisels of the Word of God to keep His lively stones cleaned and polished.

Delight:   Psalm 65:4   Jeremiah 23:29

Delighting in the Lord

## September 2

*"Everyone that is of the truth heareth my voice."* John 18:37

Without exception, those who are born again, children of God, will hear when the Spirit of God, in them, speaks to their hearts. They may be in a backslidden condition and not obey, but conviction of sin will register when they do hear the voice of God through any means by which He speaks.

One of the sure marks of a Christian is he will have conviction of sin. A "doubting" Christian would be helped if he would remember the identifying marks of a Christian and do a checkup often. Every single time we sin, that is, actually do something we shouldn't do, or think a thought that is not according to Philippians 4:8, God will correct us. He is never looking the other way, busy, or disinterested. He looks after His children every minute as though each one is the only one He has. And remember, sin in our lives will *always* be spoken against by the Holy Spirit; by that you can be assured that you are safe and secure in the family of God.

*Once, when flying home from a Ladies' Retreat in another state, I was grazing through John Ch. 15 and thinking on the great success of the retreat where I'd just spoken. My thoughts soon turned prideful. Just as I was warming up to the idea of the success of the meeting having to do with my speaking, the Lord gave me a powerful rebuke! It seemed that the Lord put His finger under John Ch. 15:5, the last line: "...for without me ye can do nothing." And He held my attention there for several minutes! I shall never forget that rebuke. I feel compelled to share that before I speak to a ladies' group now.*

Delight:    Philippians 4:8    Proverbs 3:12

Edna Holmes

# September 3

*"The fruit of the righteous is a tree of life;  
and he that winneth souls is wise."* Proverbs 11:30

Personal soul-winning produces more joy in your heart than any other part of the Lord's work. Even if your part is very limited, to know that souls are being saved because of whatever effort you are putting forth, brings great joy to your own soul. Besides the Word of God, prayer is the greatest tool in bringing the lost to Christ. You can do that even if you are lying flat on your back, helpless.

When we served in the pastorate, we had many missionaries come by and our family had the privilege of getting personally acquainted with these courageous servants of the Lord. I loved to hear their accounts of the ministry on the mission field, especially their most unusual soul-willing experiences.

One missionary from Honduras, said a Chinese family settled there. He could not communicate with them at all and had none other who could help him. He sent for a Chinese Bible and gave it to this family. After a year, they came to him and said they had read the entire Bible, and they were now ready to take Jesus as their Savior. The Word of God, faithfully shared by a soul-winner, did it!

*The most unusual one I've found in my enquiries about salvation and soul-winning experiences is a lady who was saved during childbirth! She realized her need of the Savior and during the throes of childbirth pain, just as the baby was born, she asked the Lord to save her.*

This would be an interesting hobby to pursue. It makes one more aware of soul-winning and the opportunities that may occur any time and the joy of engaging in that good work. Try it!

Delight:   Psalm 126:5-6   John 4:36

## September 4

*"...the place whereon thou standest is holy ground."*
Exodus 3:5

When Moses turned aside to come near the burning bush and the presence of God, God did not say "relax Moses, it's ok." Instead, He emphatically reminded Moses of who He was, and instructed him to not come any closer without taking his shoes off, for Moses was standing near to God, and on holy ground.

*"And he said, Draw not nigh hither: put off thy shoes from off thy feet, for the place whereon thou standest is holy ground."* Exodus 3:5

Do we learn anything when we read this account of God and Moses' meeting there on the backside of the desert? We have brought up a generation that think lightly of the house of God, the church, and God Himself for that matter. Our generation has gradually slipped away from awe and respect of God, much to our detriment. God spoke those words to Moses, and He emphasized it again to the children of Israel when at Mt. Sinai the Lord came down on the mountain. He is our Creator and Holy God. He does not welcome disrespect in the house of God, the inappropriate way some dress before the Lord in His house and the disrespectful way they worship Him. People rationalize it with the "Well, it's a different time; you don't have to dress up for church." It is apparent that "dressing down" has affected behavior.

We can see the way earth's kings and queens are treated. No one is allowed an audience unless he is invited, dressed appropriately, and follows the rules of protocol. And yet, many Christians treat God as though they are equal to Him. There's little respect, which is a sad, fearful thing. Remember Who He is! Tell someone else.

Delight:   Isaiah 43:10-11   Romans 11:33

Edna Holmes

# September 5

*"Death and life are in the power of the tongue: and they that love it shall eat the fruit thereof."* Proverbs 18:21

This verse ties in with James 3:6 which describes the tongue in graphic detail. *"And the tongue is a fire, a world of iniquity: so is the tongue among our members, that it defileth the whole body, and setteth on fire the course of nature; and is set on fire of hell."* Every Christian should dedicate their tongues to the Lord regularly and ask Him to put a guard on it to remind us when we use it in a wrong way. It can create so much misery. Just think of the *"death and life"* factor in the power of the tongue. Many people have had all encouragement and hope killed out of them by the thoughtless, insensitive remarks of others. Some folks aren't hearing what they are really saying, but others are, the victims of a cruel heartless tongue. And a lifetime negative memory is imprinted on their hearts.

In my growing up years, such words were spoken to me that have affected my whole life. Yes, after salvation, things do become new; initially, and long-term as we learn and grow in the knowledge of the Lord. But what is imprinted on the brain in formative years stays there...affecting us if we turn back and dwell on it.

We have the responsibility and privilege of using our tongues for the glory of God and encouragement of His children. Read the Bible to someone who can't see to read anymore; tell your testimony often; invite people to church every week; witness to someone; tell your family and others that you love them; sing when the church sings and your tongue will be a blessing to all who hear it.

Delight:    Colossians 4:6    James 3:2

## September 6

*"...let us lay aside every weight, and the sin which so easily beset us..."* Hebrews 12:1

Besetting sins come and stay. We get comfortable with our sins. A moment of conviction in reading the Bible or a revival with hard preaching may loosen sin's hold and we seek to get rid of it with a repentant prayer, but soon we began to miss it; it can move back in.

*"I was reminded of the hold that besetting sins have on us when I visited my daughter's family in another state. My granddaughter, at the time, was about three years old. She had allowed Jeanne and I to clean out some of her things and especially some worn out stuffed toys. Many were piled in a net strung up in a corner. I spied an old worn out doll; I thought I'd get rid of that and she would never miss it. I put it on a pile of 'discards' out back in the laundry room. She found it! I heard a little commotion, and here came the most solemn procession you could ever see. She came through the house slowly dragging a baby blanket by one corner; it spread out behind her with the doll laid on it. She looked sad. When she reached her room, she carefully picked up the doll, tossed it up on the heap and said emphatically, "Now, you stay there!"*

Besetting sins, such as being habitually late for church, is a detrimental habit, a bad example, and discouraging. Not being fully *prepared* for duties causes stress and poor performance. Such are besetting sins which Christians are hesitant to "throw away". Habits can hold us like chains, but God can break them. His Word is power. *"He that covereth his sins shall not prosper: but whoso confesseth and forsaketh them shall have mercy."* Proverbs 28:13

Many besetting sins are in the "respectable" bracket. But they do as much harm as the big "awful" sins Christians fall into. Whatever hinders us from serving the Lord well should be dealt with.

Delight:     Proverbs 16:6     Ecclesiastes 8:11

Edna Holmes

# September 7

*"So the people of Nineveh believed God."* Jonah 3:5

We should never doubt that God can save the worst of sinners. Nineveh was the capitol of Assyria, the most wicked, cruel people in the world at that time. Every nation feared to be taken by them because of their cruelty to captives.

Jonah was honestly expecting God would rain down His wrath on Nineveh, he hoped it in fact, because he pouted when God spared them. However, Jonah reluctantly preached God's message to them and the entire city repented of their sins! You would have thought Jonah would have been revived too with such a tremendous outpouring of the power of God on his preaching. Not so! Jonah thought those people were too wicked for God's mercy, and he wanted to see a spectacular judgment fall on the city.

Are we guilty of prejudging others? Do we harbor the notion that God can't change certain ones, that their case is just too hard? Well we should look in the Bible at what the Word of God is likened to.

*"Is not my word as a fire? saith the Lord; and like a hammer that breaketh the rock in pieces?"* Jeremiah 23:29

Fire! A hammer! Who can stand against these weapons of God Almighty? His Word holds the power that is unimaginable. Our understanding of it is puny at best. It changes lives forever. Has it changed yours yet? Check up and make sure you have trusted in the Savior Jesus Christ only, and not some other element thrown in, like good works. Jesus is the way, the ONLY way to heaven. Trust Him!

Delight:     Hebrews 4:12     Romans 1:16

## September 8

*"The lot is cast into the lap; but the whole disposing thereof is of the Lord."* Proverbs 16 33

We would call this the like practice of the "heads or tails" call on a coin before some sports event, which side will start first. The *lot* was used to settle issues and was a trusted means of deciding matters of business. The Bible scholars say it is not known exactly *how* it was done; but the Bible says that the outcome of it was of the Lord. *He ultimately made the lot come out to fulfill His divine purpose.*

*That is a comforting thing to know. Once in our pastorate a lady, recently widowed, needed to find employment. So, she put her application in at a place where she was qualified to work and asked us to help her pray for that job, for she needed it very much. This verse surfaced in our Bible Study time, and we dwelled on it awhile. It brought a peace in all our hearts, knowing God was in control, and if that job was good for this lady, she would get it! Soon, she did indeed go to work there, and we rejoiced with her.*

Are we really believing God's Word? Do we believe what the Bible says about God knowing the number of hairs on our heads? Do we believe Him in what He says about prayer? If we would *only believe* Him, we should not worry another moment. God is the One who is in control at all times. Yes, bad things happen because sin is rampant in the world, and sin always brings misery and torment for the human race. But God holds the reins; Satan can only go so far. God didn't make robots, he made humans with fine brains and the free will to make choices.

The choices we make determine the quality of our lives in every way. Ask wisdom of God every day for choices you will ultimately make. That will be some of your most beneficial praying.

Delight:   Joshua 24:15    Luke 10:42

Edna Holmes

# September 9

*"I am the good shepherd, and know my sheep, and am known of mine."* John 10:14

Notice that the Lord said He *knows* His sheep, and His sheep *know* Him! Jesus is God; He knows everything about us, every thought and imagination of the heart; He knows our *birthdate,* and our *death date!* He knows our past, and our future. There is *nothing* our Lord does not know about us. *And He allows us to know Him!*

We know Him as Savior, but we learn about Him on a broader scale if we pursue the Word of God. We can't know it all in a single lifetime, but *we know Him!* When something strange comes to us as being from the Lord, we can detect it because of our close association with Him.

*We have done many funerals during our ministry. I played the piano usually. I'd take a large stack of appropriate hymns to use from before and after the service. At one funeral in a country church, the people lingered and lingered at the casket and I played soft background music until I'd repeated all the music twice; so, I made up some tunes and played them in the traditional style of hymns. My husband immediately recognized "strange" music. He had listened to me for decades. Afterwards he said, "Stop making up songs!" I thought no one would notice, <u>but he did</u>.*

We are safe following after Jesus. But in spiritual warfare, the devil often entices us to wander off the trail. The Lord gives us extra protection. *"There hath no temptation taken you but such as is common to man: but God is faithful, who will not suffer you to be tempted above that ye are able; but will with the temptation also make a way to escape..."* I Cor.10:13 There will be inner warnings by the Holy Spirit indwelling us. Be sensitive to the still small voice speaking in your conscience. It will save you from a multitude of troubles in life.

Delight:   I Corinthians 10:13    John 10:27-30

## September 10

*"...he formed it to be inhabited..."* Isaiah 45:18

The earth came fully equipped for the human race that God created. People deny that with the theory of evolution, which they say took many billions of years. The truth is in God's Word. In six regular days, God created the earth, plant life, animal life, and finally man. *"It is a sign between me and the children of Israel for ever: for in six days the Lord made heaven and earth, and on the seventh day he rested, and was refreshed."* Exodus 31:17

Embedded in the earth and space is all humanity needs to be satisfied and sustained. Think of that! The earth was made by God to be the habitation of the souls He made. And Almighty God thought of everything, *which includes air and water*! The audacity of those who believe it just "happened" and proclaim evolution as a fact, is appalling. The entire verse of our text says: *"For thus saith the Lord that created the heavens; God himself that formed the earth and made it; he hath established it, he created it not in vain, he formed it to be inhabited: I am the LORD; and there is none else."*

Soon after this wonderfully commodious earth was presented to Adam and Eve, they listened to the Satan's lies and plunged the whole human race into sin. Now Satan had control and God did the most amazing thing in human existence; He gave Jesus His only begotten Son, to pay the sin debt for lost sinners. Our Lord did that, and in His death, burial, and resurrection He took the keys of death and hell away from Satan! Our victorious Savior!

Do you know your Creator, as your Savior? He loves you.

Delight:   Exodus 31:16   Revelation 1:18   John 1:1-3

Edna Holmes

# September 11

*"God is our refuge and strength, a very
present help in time of trouble."* Psalm 46:1

An infamous date America should always remember is September 11, 2001. Our enemies struck suddenly, destroying key skyscrapers in New York City, killing over three thousand, and injuring many, many more. They hi-jacked passenger planes, loaded with people, and flew headlong into the World Trade Center. They flew a plane into the Pentagon, wreaking havoc on that place. Another plane would have struck the White House but was deterred by brave men on board who faced the hi-jackers and forced the plane down before it reached Washington. Some people on board had phones and called loved ones since they knew they were about to die. The country was ordered into a "lock down" mode and almost immediately GOD became the most spoken word of the day as people sought out churches and other places to pray. It was a horror that turned our lives upside down for that year and showed us clearly the nature of man.

Very few want God close to them in worship and fellowship as a way of life; but ALL want God near when trouble comes, especially of that magnitude. The grace of God becomes more *amazing* when you think on that truth. How could He love us so? Jude 21 tells us: *"Keep yourselves in the love of God, looking for the mercy of our Lord Jesus Christ unto eternal life."*

How can we do that? First, bathe your mind in the Word of God daily. Note something that touched you. Pray; you will be ready for a better day with God's blessing.

Delight:   Ephesians   5:2   Deuteronomy 6:5

Delighting in the Lord

# September 12

*"He that goeth about as a talebearer revealeth secrets..."* Proverbs 20:19

Someone has said *"flattery will get you everywhere"*. It will for sure get one into the confidence of another whom he "flatters", and so secrets may be revealed in an unguarded moment. The one who has disarmed another with flattery goes his way with "secrets" he may use to compare, reveal, and in a subtle way disarm another in the same manner. There is a warning in the rest of our text verse: *"...therefore meddle not with him that flattereth with his lips."*

Man is basically a vain creature, and easy prey to the flattering tongue. In my young teen years, a favorite thing to do was to "trade compliments". We told what someone had said complimentary about the other. It seldom happened that a compliment was freshly said so we could repeat it; we often had to make up something so each of us would have a compliment! How we all love flattery! That's why it is a good tool for Satan to use.

In this evil time, famous people are reaping the bitter results of flattery which led to secrets which led to blackmail and the ruin and devastation of individuals and families. The world is a wicked and miserable place to embrace, yet unsaved people prefer that and do not want God in their lives. Many view Christians with disdain, yet we have the benefits and blessings of God poured over us every day. Those who are associated with Christians are blessed. Remember Jacob's father-in-law confessed that fact. Re: Genesis 30:27. The "mixed multitude" that trailed along with the Israelites when they left Egypt did so because they were blessed being with God's people.

Talebearers have this indictment: *"...and he that uttereth a slander, is a fool."* In today's world, that is a "silly, stupid person."

Delight:   Proverbs 11:13   James 3:5

Edna Holmes

# September 13

*"...he that hath begun a good work in you will perform it until the day of Jesus Christ..."* Philippians 1:6

Are we really hearing God as He speaks to us through His Word? Here is another key verse to give us assurance of God's salvation. What Jesus starts; He finishes! And if you realized you were changed inside on the day you came to Christ for salvation, then His *good work* was started, and will continue till the day you die! We all have our setbacks in learning and growing in the Lord, but His good work never stalls on the road of life. It goes steadily forward even as tests and trials examine us to check on our personal spiritual progress, to find out if we are learning anything.

Christians can be stubborn, self-righteous people. They judge and never give thought to the fact that God said not to. Some of us have to be tested over and over till we finally get it!

*I received a rebuke from the Lord a few decades ago which I never forgot. It was a humbling experience. The issue with men wearing earrings was up front. It was in vogue for them to wear only one, and on whichever side it was worn signified something. One day in a store, I was browsing when a young man came in wearing only one earring! My judgmental wheel started turning, and when he went out, I went to check out and voiced my dismay at such behavior of these men that wear earrings for whatever reasons. The clerk looked a little amused, and when I was through, she said, "Why are YOU wearing just one earring?" I was stunned and embarrassed. Sure enough, I was missing an earring! I'd lost one and knew immediately why. I stopped my earring judgment and have never been inclined to start again. GOD IS THE JUDGE! Leave it to Him.*

The Bible is our textbook for spiritual growth. We must read it, underline key verses that have taught us, and BELIEVE it!

Delight:    Philippians 1:9-10    Psalm 138:8

## September 14

*"The lips of the righteous know what is acceptable: but the mouth of the wicked speak forwardness."* Proverbs 10:32

Only the Christians who have listened and learned from God's Word will be able to obey Him in the matter of controlling his impulsiveness to speak. The impulse is so strong at times to put in our "two cents worth" of wisdom, knowledge, expertise, and plain out brilliance to an ongoing conversation. Actually, that indicates that we have a problem. *"He that hath no rule over his own spirit is like a city that is broken down, and without walls."* Proverbs 25:28

A lot of our woes come from this one detriment in our lives. That is the inability to control our impulses. "On an impulse" we have often done something. Now, there are issues ebbing and flowing from that solitary action through time which we can never go back and change. The same is true of our words. We impulsively speak without thinking it through first. God's Word is infinitely true. *"Whoso keepeth his mouth and his tongue keepeth his soul from troubles."* Proverbs 21:23.

Discernment is another godly quality which comes from staying close in God's Word. Discernment is its own unique element and is invaluable to Christians. It saves much heartache as we practice and use its amazing power. It comes from wisdom, which comes from God. *"If any of you lack wisdom, let him ask of God, that giveth to all men liberally, and upbraideth not; and it shall be given him."* James 1:5. God will not berate us for not asking sooner for wisdom. He will freely answer our prayer for wisdom and grant it. True wisdom is waiting on God when you aren't sure of what His will is about a matter. He works "all things together"
and His timing is perfect; His ways are perfect; listen to Him.

Delight:   James 3:17-18   Proverbs 30:5

Edna Holmes

# September 15

*"That in every thing we are enriched by him, in all utterance, and in all knowledge."* 1Corinthians 1:5

When something is *enriched*, additional nutrients have been added to enhance its value, health-wise. Our verse says that we are enriched by Christ! If you meditate on that verse in undistracted thought, your heart will know fresh delight.

It is the Lord Himself that is our enrichment. From the moment of our salvation in Him, His enrichment program began. His presence in us by His Holy Spirit makes us children of God! Heaven's our home though we haven't moved in yet. How much richer can we be?

The Lord opens our understanding to the Word of God. Through it He channels the enrichment of the life of Christ in us into all facets of our lives. Did your talk, *utterances,* change when Christ came into your heart? He naturally comes into our conversations.

A *natural* man, one without Christ, can't understand the Word, because he has not the Holy Spirit in him. *"But the natural man receiveth not the things of the Spirit of God: for they are foolishness unto him: neither can he know them because they are spiritually discerned"* I Corinthians 2:14

We can communicate only with our own kind, having the same like-spirit in us. *Once at the parsonage, I heard the noise of something or someone rattling our trash can in back of the house. I went to a bedroom window and spied the culprit. A possum was desperately trying to climb up and over into our trash can close by the window. I raised the window and yelled but it ignored me completely. We didn't have the same spirit to communicate.* Christians understand the things of God only after He puts His Spirit in us at the new birth, making us His kind! Blessed salvation!

Delight:   Romans 8:16   Romans 8:9

Delighting in the Lord

# September 16

*"For ye know the grace of our Lord Jesus Christ, that, though he was rich, yet for your sakes he became poor…"* II Cor.8:9

In a purportedly true story, a young wealthy man wanted to get a wife who would love him for himself without his immense wealth being a factor in the picture. He made arrangements and moved to the far side of the city into the poorer section of town and promptly got a job in a factory. He met and fell in love with a young woman who worked there. He courted her until their love was mutual, and they got married. After the honeymoon, he drove her to the place he had gotten for them to live. He stopped in front of a magnificent mansion. His bride protested that they couldn't afford it! Inside, she was speechless at the beauty and grandeur of the place. The man turned to his bride and said, "All this belongs to me; welcome home darling."

Now this only faintly compares to what our Lord did for us for His riches are beyond our comprehension, and so is His love. How could he love us so? Even while we were sinners, He died for us! Never has one come from such riches and glory, to such poverty and shame as our Lord Jesus Christ. It was all because of lost humanity that He loved and determined to redeem from the curse of sin. Jesus, the eternal Son of God is the only one who could pay the horrific price for our salvation. And He did…for love!

Should not we demonstrate our love for Him and show gratitude for all He does for us every day. He "daily loads us with benefits" as Psalm 68:19 tells us. That's not just a 'few' but a whole load! Try writing down a few of the daily blessings you receive from the Lord each day and see how it increases your awareness and gratitude. Get a spiral notebook; write "Blessings" on the front, and it will become a source of joy as you fill it up recording the blessings.

Delight:     Psalm 68:19     Psalm 117: 1-2

Edna Holmes

# September 17

*"For whosoever shall call upon the name
of the Lord shall be saved."* Romans 10:13

This verse is not a blanket "formula" for salvation. One who takes Jesus lightly in unbelief could not take the promise as a pass into heaven. It's not automatic! The Bible tells us in the next verse:

*"How then shall they call on him in whom they have not believed? and how shall they believe in him of whom they have not heard? and how shall they hear without a preacher?"* Romans 10: 14

The last command Jesus gave to the church before He ascended into heaven after His resurrection was to "go into all the world and preach the gospel". Lost humanity inhabiting this planet must hear the gospel, *good news,* and have their hearts stirred to believe it by the Holy Spirit *before* they can "call upon the name of the Lord" for salvation. Preachers, missionaries, who are called by God to preach in foreign lands, and our own land, must be sent so that all may hear of the Savior, Jesus Christ. Every healthy church has an active Missions Program, however small or large, engaged in helping to support missionaries as they go in our stead to spread the gospel message all over the world. My husband and I have been in many countries and seen the results of such faithful labor.

*In New Guinea, a primitive land near Australia, we saw the results of the power of the gospel to save "whosoever will believe". We were there for the celebration of the Christians getting Bibles the missionaries had translated into their language. Our church and others had funded the project of printing them. The people received those Bibles as though we had given them diamonds. They carefully fitted paper over them to keep the covers clean. My heart was touched as I viewed this fervent love for the Word of God. These Christians had heard the Word, believed on Jesus, and "called upon the name of the Lord".*

Delight:    Romans 10:9-10    John 5:24

Delighting in the Lord

# September 18

*"...that I may dwell in the house of the Lord all the days of my life, to behold the beauty of the Lord..." Psalm 27:4*

Beauty is defined as *"the quality attributed to whatever pleases or satisfies the senses or mind as by behavior or attitude."* Additionally, it means attractive features.

There are many amazing features about the Lord Jesus Christ; but we only learn of Him through searching the scriptures, and personal experience. <u>We have forgiveness of sin!</u> *"If we confess our sins, he is faithful and just to forgive us our sins, and to cleanse us from all unrighteousness." I John 1:9* What a merciful provision from our loving, beautiful Savior. He didn't leave us to fend for ourselves after saving us. He sends help!

<u>He will never leave us or forsake us.</u> This is a promise that is most comforting when Christians really grasp it. Re: Hebrews 13:5

When our granddaughter was in college, studying to be a nurse, they took the class to a Nursing Home to experience that area of medical care and intermingle with the patients. Our granddaughter approached a little lady wandering down the hallway, took her hand and walked with her. She asked the lady's name, and she said, "I don't know my name...I forgot." After a pause, she looked up at Crystal and said brightly, "But I know Jesus loves me!" Then she asked, "Do you know Jesus loves you?" Our granddaughter enjoyed telling her she did know Jesus loved her. That is an amazing testimony of the truth of God's Word. Everyone was gone from that Alzheimer's patient's memory...even her own name...but not Jesus. The beauty of the Lord is His love and faithfulness to His children who have trusted in Him.

Take a day in your quiet time to just praise the Lord. He is worthy of all honor and praise from our hearts. If you love Him; tell Him!

Delight:    Psalm 31: 23    Ephesians 3:17-19

Edna Holmes

# September 19

*"...for whom a man is overcome, of the same is he brought into bondage."* II Peter 2:19

    Christians can be in bondage in any area of life. One common form of bondage is with our thoughts. Uncontrolled, thoughts in a certain line of thinking will bring a Christian into bondage very hard to break. If your thoughts do not line up to the standard God has put in His Word for us, then it is imperative that you pray for deliverance from those thoughts. Put verses on a card in large print so it can be easily read and post it in several key places, so you see it often. Every word that we speak is a thought before it is verbalized. They rule our lives! When our thoughts are negative, it has a toxic effect on our minds and bodies.

    I have a vivid imagination, and I can jump on a fantasy and build it into a stronghold in no time. A fantasy is fiction, and much like the plot of a novel that's being written. As I entertain such thoughts, it becomes a stronghold in my mind. Soon I'm trapped with my foolishness because I want to think on it all the time. It wastes valuable time and my energy when I could be doing the things I should be doing. But I have to start again with feeding much on the scriptures, repeating aloud what God says until God pulls down the stronghold my thoughts have made. My favorite verse for help on thoughts is Philippians 4:8. Use it like the tool that it is. When a fantasy thought lands in your mind, say aloud at once, "Is it true?" Then say the answer "NO!" Then go down the list in that verse checking out the validity of each thought. God's Word will soothe and settle your mind and start your thoughts on the right track again.

Delight:    Psalm 119:59    Psalm 19:14

Delighting in the Lord

# September 20

*"...Take heed, and beware of coveteousness..."*
Luke 12:15

The synonym for covetousness is *greed.* It's a continual desire for more and more; while to covet, one wants what someone else has and may endeavor to get it. Sometimes it is a good spiritual exercise to examine ourselves in light of the Word of God and see if that sinful attitude is lurking in our hearts. I've done that in times past and found, to my surprise, that a spirit of greed did abide in my heart. God will show us what is showing up on the *outside* which we had tucked so far back in the recesses of our hearts, we were not really aware of it ourselves on the *inside.* It is sin wherever it is; confess and forsake it.

Think of the awful tragedy caused by Achan's greed as shown to us in the book of Joshua chapter seven. After Israel had won the battle at Jericho, they lost the next battle in a much smaller city with few people in it. Something terrible was wrong! God told Joshua there was "sin in the camp" and for him to get it out! It was found that Achan had taken spoils he had coveted and hid them in his tent. Now Jericho was wholly dedicated to God; spoils belonged to God! So Achan and all of his family, and possessions were disposed of in the valley of Achor: stoned to death and burnt with fire. It was a horrible end to an entire family, all because Achan did not repent of his covetous, greedy heart before he acted on it.

In our present time, greediness shows up in common ways: our *wanting the biggest piece of pie! When greed is coupled with pride, we must have as much as our neighbors, and more!* When we sense that greed is raising its head, we should run to the Lord for divine help.

Delight:    Ecclesiastes 5:10    I Timothy 6:9

Edna Holmes

# September 21

*"For the love of money is the root of all evil."*
I Timothy 6:10

This is one of the most misquoted verses in the Bible. Look closely. It DOES NOT say *that money is the root of all evil.* It plainly says, *'the love of money is the root of all evil.'* When people love money and spend their lives trying to acquire it, it usually brings ruin to them and much sorrow to their families. "Greedy" describes them and it is evident at times just how far the truly greedy and covetous folks will go to make money.

*"A man and his family going to church one Sunday passed by his neighbor's ranch and noticed a pasture full of sheep lying on the ground. He thought they were asleep, but later it was learned that over a thousand sheep were dead. They were caught in a cold front that came through, and they froze to death. <u>Their owner had sheared them early because the price of wool was up</u>."*

The root of all evil—the love of money—manifest itself in the lust of the flesh, lust of the eyes, and the pride of life. Every sinful act that mankind commits has its source in one of these three categories.

*"For all that is in the world, the lust of the flesh, and the lust of the eyes, and the pride of life, is not of the Father, but is of the world."* I John 2:16

The "world" God is referring to is not the world of nature, or humanity, which God so loved He sent His Son down to redeem them. But it is the world *system* which operates without God. It is getting stronger in its opposition. Men are actively working to push God out of everything. God's grace and mercy are freely available today, but in the end, it will be only His wrath! Honor Him with your life now, and don't give the world any part of it.

Delight:   I John 5:19   Galatians 1:4

Delighting in the Lord

# September 22

*"If iniquity be in thine hand, put it far away, and let not wickedness dwell in thy tabernacles."* Job 11:14

Strangely, stumbling stones can roll into our lives and never make a sound. We are not aware of the subtle change in our attitude and thoughts. Self-confidence levels rise, enforced by a low-key pride. Our attitude may be that we are so helpful to other Christians and the Lord's work because we have experience and know so much. We can even skip our devotional time; we are so confident that our "self" is in good shape. When we begin to neglect drinking from the fountain of life every day, the Word of God, we are very soon in trouble! We need the Word *to be spiritually strong,* just as we need food for our bodies to be physically strong and healthy. The most of our spiritual battle every day is fighting the devil as he tries to keep us from the Bible, and prayer. Have a routine and put real effort into keeping it intact.

When you slip away from it, it is hard to stop the slide. For many years, I kept waiting for it to get easier; it didn't happen. I didn't understand early on how vital it was, and how the devil fights it. On top of giving us the Joy of the Lord to keep our hearts happy, the Word of God is *mentally healthy* for us. That fact should be a shot of encouragement to Bible readers. It makes one more mentally alert, and it is known that children do better in school when they have started the day with reading even a verse or two of God's Word. Parents; try it! See how the Lord will bless that effort, and you will have happier more secure children.

Delight:    Psalm 68:19    Romans 6:12-13

Edna Holmes

# September 23

*"And all the people that came together to that sight, beholding the things that were done, smote their breast…"* Luke 24:48

A scene usually explains itself. For example, when you come upon two cars on the highway smashed together, you know there's been a wreck. Scenes tell us something.

*In my parents' early years my dad worked on a ranch out West. They had only two little ones then. They lived behind the big ranch house which had a huge open-top water storage tank. A wooden ladder was propped on the side of the tank in the edge of their yard. Mama had asked that the two bottom rungs be taken off so the two little ones could not crawl up that ladder. Daddy neglected doing it. One day my mother looked out to see the baby, just walking, perched at the top of the ladder dabbling his hands in the brimming tank of water! Speaking softly to him, she eased up the ladder, got the baby in her arm, and eased back down. When Daddy came home from work, the scene he saw spoke volumes! He knew! The first two rungs of the ladder were a pile of chopped up pieces, with the axe lying on top! He picked up the wood and put the axe in the shed but didn't say another word about it.*

In reading about the crucifixion of Jesus, I can imagine what a stranger would think who walked upon that scene as Jesus was suffering the pain of torture beyond our grasp. He might wonder with great consternation what horrific crime it was that put Jesus on that cross. Well, we know why Jesus was there. *He became sin for us.* It was an amazing exchange! He took us, *dead in trespasses and sins,* and gave us His life in exchange. The wonder of it! We have His life in us by the Holy Spirit of God. *That why Romans 8:9 emphatically states* "…*Now if any man have not the Spirit of Christ, he is none of his.*" Think on it, to rekindle the love in your heart for the Lord.

Delight:    I Peter 2:24    I John 3:5

Delighting in the Lord

# September 24

*"Most men will proclaim every one his own goodness:*
*but a faithful man who can find?* Proverbs 20:6

One reason we can know for sure that the Bible is God's Word, and not the words of mere man, is because in it, sin is defined. Sin is called what it is, and man's sin is exposed. Though God used men through several ages in history to write down His Word for His people, not one word of it comes out of their hearts and intellect. It is God-Breathed and has not the taint of man in it. Man would cast himself in a better light concerning the fact of sin. He would not be known as a "sinner". He would most certainly have "proclaimed his own goodness."

Through spiritual growth, we eventually learn just how sinful we really are, and what it cost Jesus to redeem us from the curse and penalty of sin. He took it on Himself, the only perfect sacrifice that could "take away the sin of the world."

*I was very young in the faith when we took our first, and only, pastorate. I remember a man who was a new Christian and very humbled in his gratitude to God for his salvation. He always prayed in his prayer: "Thank you God for saving a wretch like me." For a long time, I pondered on that and my thoughts were: He may have been a wretch, but I was not a wretch! In time, I came to understand from reading God's Word that I was indeed a wretch! It became a part of my prayers too. 'Lord, thank You for saving a wretch like me.'*

The Word of God is so powerful, we need only sow it as the Good Seed that it is, and it will take care of stirring the hearts of men to come to Christ. It is our *life*. We must hug it to our hearts, feeding on it continually so that we stay strong in faith and have peace of mind in this troubled world.

Delight:   Hebrews 4:12   Mark 13:31

Edna Holmes

# September 25

*"He that walketh with wise men shall be wise: but a companion of fools shall be destroyed."* Proverbs 13:20

By spending time with the Lord morning and evening, if possible, we keep the proper perspective about our fellowship with those who are *citizens of "the world"*. Remember, the unsaved are on a different wavelength altogether than Christians, and it will definitely make a difference if you make yourself available to the temptations hidden in "friendship". Our flesh is naturally drawn to the world out there where they do seem to have the most fun. That's how many Christians think. But when they are dealing with the sorrows garnered from friendship with the world, it comes home to them...a little late. None of us fully realize the awful power of sin, and the control it can wield over us if we don't guard our hearts with the Word of God.

We are to reach out to all men in all kinds of ways which will not compromise our relationship with the Lord. If we linger in the world, as Lot did in Sodom, then discipline will surely touch our lives. Why? Because *God won't allow His own children to stay in the world for long.* Judgment came to the nation of Israel for turning from God and embracing the idols in the land of Canaan. Israel had everything a nation could desire; God had given it to them. They had seen the mighty miracles as they left Egypt. How could they forget the parting of the Red Sea, water flowing from a rock, their clothes and shoes not wearing out, and manna fresh from heaven every day? But they did. They forsook wisdom and turned to fools who drew them to their gods. Be discerning about making friends. If you feel wary, back off!

Delight:   James 3:13   Job 28:28

Delighting in the Lord

# September 26

*"And let us consider one another to provoke unto love and to good works..."* Hebrews 10:24

*There is a fascinating little book, written by Andy Andrews, titled The Butterfly Effect, which emphasizes the far-reaching effects of the movement of a butterfly's wings even to the other side of the globe! Comparisons are given of decisions made and deeds done in centuries past that effected the course of history, often by one person.*

That is the case in the history of the Lord's work. Every Christian can make a difference in the world, simply by being faithful in what the Lord has led him to do. People who faithfully give of their means to help send missionaries out all over the world, are indeed causing a far-reaching affect. What a glorious part of the Lord's work on earth in which to be involved!

My husband and I timidly stepped into that part of the ministry as baby Christians, knowing little about missions, and having never met a missionary in person. We began to give a very small amount each week through our church, to help send missionaries out to preach the gospel to the "regions beyond". Soon, unexpected blessings came into our lives regularly and we understood that God was pleased with the faith we were "trying out". Needless to say, we grew in faith and increased our giving a little each year. We have never lacked for the essential things needed in life. God has supplied for us.

The most powerful tool to use for the Lord's work is *prayer! Anyone can carry out that responsibility.* Let's give our best help to the Lord's work, especially missionaries, by praying for them first of all, and giving of our means as God moves our hearts to do so.

Delight:   Romans 8:26-27   Ephesians 6:18

Edna Holmes

# September 27

*"Thou preparest a table before me in the presence of mine enemies."* Psalm 23:5

The "world" is our enemy and it harbors many other enemies which hinders Christians daily in order to oppose God and make us fail and be discouraged in our service for Him. But the Lord loves His children and daily prepares us a table of blessings right before our enemies' eyes watching us in the world. We could say it's the "table of blessing" as described in Psalm 68:19. *"Blessed be the Lord, who daily loadeth us with benefits, even the God of our salvation. Selah."* People see that Christians are so blessed, and some begin to wonder why, which may ultimately lead to their own personal salvation.

*Our granddaughter, Crystal, got married in recent years, and it was a beautiful wedding with several of their friends being in the wedding party. One young man later came to Scott and said, "I know you are a Christian, but why is it life goes so good for you?" Scott told his friend that he puts God first in his life. Then he told him of God's salvation. The next week, the young man confessed Jesus as Savior and was saved! The witness had been the "table prepared in the presence of his enemies." His friends could obviously see that God favored Scott in a special way.*

People are watching as Christians are feasting from the table of blessings, and right before the world, their enemy. How loving and kind our Lord is to His children. He will "never leave us or forsake us" ever. May you have a renewed hunger for God's Word, which when read and obeyed creates such blessings in Christians' lives.

Delight:     Isaiah 30:23     Malachi 3:10

## September 28

*"And the Lord said unto him, What is that in thine hand? And he said, A rod."* Exodus 4:2

God did not accept Moses' excuses. God put him through several tests to show Moses the power, protection, and provision that God would bestow on him and Aaron as they took leadership of the people.

Many times, Christians fall into a gloomy state because they feel that they don't have special talent or ability or means with which to serve God. We must look around us with a willing heart and desire to do something for the Lord...then go forward with what God provides.

*"Faithful Is he that calleth you, who also will do it."* I Thess. 5:24

*When the auditorium was being constructed in our pastorate, we suffered several setbacks. Yet, we moved forward. When the contractor poured concrete for the foundation, the day turned rainy. The workers had to stay into the night working the concrete surface with long handled tools which pushed the water off the foundation. About midnight, my husband came in and asked if we had anything at all I could fix for the men to eat. They'd had no supper; they were hungry and wet and could not stop the work. I shot up an arrow prayer: "Lord show me what I can cook for them!" I looked in the nearly empty cabinet. It contained a can of corn and a can of spam! I quickly mixed a big batch of cornbread batter, diced the spam into it, added the can of corn, and mixed it up and cooked it like pancakes. I made fresh coffee and the preacher took a huge platter of hot corncakes out for the men who eagerly ate, holding food in one hand as they continued to work with the other. The foundation was saved.*

God often provides a need *with what we already have in hand. He did that for us when we had a very meager income and a growing family. My trust and praise for the Lord grew day by day. What is that in your hand?* Use it! God can do wonders with *anything*!

Delight:    Colossians 3:15    I Thessalonians 5:18

Edna Holmes

# September 29

*"For he performeth the thing that is appointed for me:
and many such things are with him." Job 23:14*

Many Christians have the mistaken notion that after they are saved, God turns them loose and they are sort of on their own to "live like a Christian". Not true! God has a plan for every one of His children and that is to conform him to the image of Christ!

The first thing of His will is to identify with Jesus after being saved. That is in baptism, just as the Lord identified with mankind on earth by having John the Baptist baptize Him. After baptism, we are to "desire the sincere milk of the Word of God" and grow thereby. All along the way the Lord is working in us, to enable us to accomplish the things that the Lord appointed for us to do. We are not counting on our own ability, but what God can do as we yield to His will.

*"The Lord will perfect that which concerneth me: thy mercy, O Lord, endureth for ever: forsake not the works of thine own hands."* Psalm 138:8

We forget the scope of God's power; His omniscience, His omnipotence, and His omnipresence which we can never full grasp. We just know that it is! He is at work in our lives in ways and means that we are not aware of. Rest assured He will do as His Word tells us; He will complete, *that is perfect,* us in every aspect of our lives. Though we may take one step forward and two backward, God moves steadily on in His completion work in us. He sometimes gives us a good "housecleaning" and that can be painful. He cleans out the clutter of little sins we've been hiding. He takes out covetousness and pride which He hates. He deals with our bitter spirit which will not forgive others. With repentance, we have revival in our souls!

Delight:    Psalm 139: 23-24    Psalm 143:8

## September 30

*"Keep thy heart with all diligence; for out of it are the issues of life."* Proverbs 4:23

This is one thing that the Lord instructed us to *keep.* That is our hearts. Of course, you know that can only be done by constantly perusing the Word of God and talking to God in prayer.

It would be the simplest thing to do if we did not have the spiritual warfare going on in us and around us continually *to hinder our pursuit of keeping our hearts.* We must determine every day of our lives that we love the Lord and guard our hearts, so the devil does not have the opportunity to sow evil seeds in them. Some of those can be a sinful attitude, bitterness, anger, pride, and other detrimental things. Keep those elements out! A healthy relationship with the Lord Jesus is our goal, and nothing else matters.

"The main thing about Christianity is not the work we do, but the relationship we maintain, and the atmosphere produced by that relationship. That is all God asked us to look after, and it is being continually assailed." *(Selected)*

The atmosphere produced by our close relationship with the Lord is wonderfully beneficial to us; it is as different as a furious storm of wind and rain, compared to a fair, sunny day. *"We are not citizens of this world trying to make our way to heaven; we are citizens of heaven trying to make our way through this world." (selected)* We need the sweet fellowship with the Lord to take in His joy and gain strength for the journey. It's easy for the devil to bump us off the track; we are so easily distracted from our dedication to God. Keep focused!

Delight:    Luke 24:32    I Corinthians 15:58

Edna Holmes

# October 1

*"I, even I, am the Lord; and beside me  
there is no savior."* Isaiah 43:11

The greatest asset a human being can have on this earth is a personal acquaintance with God. Nothing else matters in the realm of time or eternity. We know that our connection can only come through the Lord Jesus Christ, the eternal Son of God. He was in the beginning with God. *"All things were made by him; and without him was not anything made that was made."* John 1:3.

We cannot comprehend how far Jesus descended from out of eternity to put his feet on the dirt of this earth. Love that we also cannot fathom brought Him down.

*"For God so loved the world that* he gave his own begotten Son, that whosoever believeth in him should not perish, but have everlasting life. John 3:16

Jesus is the only way to God; He emphatically said so. *"Jesus saith unto him, I am the way, the truth, and the life: no man cometh unto the Father, but by me."* John 14:6 Can we fully grasp what Jesus said? People that are thinking they are going to make it to heaven by doing other things other than simply trusting Jesus for their salvation, are going to be separated forever from God in eternity. Wherever God is not, is darkness; eternity without Christ is forever to be darkness without a ray of light. Think on that, not to mention the suffering in hell, one kind of suffering being the memories people will have which will torment them forever and ever.

Tell someone, ever opportunity you have, that God loves them, and He sent Jesus to die for their sins to save them. We believe on the Lord Jesus to be saved. HE IS THE GIFT OF SALVATION.

Delight:    Romans 10:13    Acts 16: 30-32

## October 2

*"And Micaiah said, As the Lord liveth, even what my God saith, that will I speak."* II Chron. 18:13

The prophet of God, Micaiah, was known by his character. One outstanding characteristic was his truthfulness as he would tell exactly what God told him to tell; he would not change the message to please anybody…even the king. Read the entire chapter about when Jehoshaphat, king of Judah, came to see Ahab, king of Israel, and intending to go to battle together, they consulted the prophets. Micaiah was the only absolutely truthful prophet and would not say the lies that King Ahab wanted to hear. The prophet had character, which he maintained by his consistent obedience to God.

What does your character reveal about you? It is, for one thing, our reputation. It is our disposition. It's the pattern of behavior or personality found in a person. So, what kind of characters are we known by? When we mingle among people they observe and form an opinion; it's as natural as breathing. Good character is a great personal asset to everyone, especially Christians. If we hope to attract others to the saving knowledge of Christ, we must refrain from things in life that would tarnish our character.

*"Good character is more to be praised than outstanding talent. Most talents are, to some extent, a gift. Good character, by contrast, is not given to us. We have to build it, piece by piece---by thought, choice, courage and determination." (H.J.Browne)*

Look back in your own life; do you remember some people who had good characters, who influenced others, even you? And you never forgot them. Pray for a good character whereby you can bring honor to your Savior, the Lord Jesus Christ.

Delight:   Ecclesiastes 10:1   Galatians 5:22-23

Edna Holmes

# October 3

*"The prophet that hath a dream; and he that hath my word, let him speak my word faithfully."* Jeremiah 23:28

In the Old Testament times, God often communicated with His people in dreams, which also included the prophets. However, the prophets were given the Word from the Lord more directly. They were the *fore-tellers* of God's message to the people, and often possessed great power from the Lord. Can we forget Elijah, or Elisha who followed in his place? Marvelous miracles were done by them in God's power.

In this low period of time in Jeremiah's day of preaching to the people of coming judgment, the people didn't want to listen to it. The *false prophets* told the people about the dreams they had as though it was God's Word given to them. Then the Lord told them the value of His Word compared to mere dreams. *"Is not my word like as a fire? saith the Lord; and like a hammer that breaketh the rock in pieces?" V.29*

We understand fire! And the blow of a hammer smashes things to smithereens. God wants us to understand the power of His blessed Word. A most powerful description of the Word of God is Hebrews 4:12. *"For the word of God is quick, and powerful, and sharper than any two-edged sword, piercing even to the dividing asunder of soul and spirit, and of the joints and marrow, and is a discerner of the thoughts and intents of the heart."*

Dreams are worthless, as far as power in them to change men from sinners to saints. The Word does that! God rebuked the dreamers, which called themselves prophets. He would tell us today, *"Stick with the everlasting Word of God. Believe it and live by it."*

Delight:   John 1:1   John 1:14

# October 4

*"She openeth her mouth with wisdom; and in her tongue is the law of kindness."* Proverbs 31:26

    The Proverbs 31 woman, we bring out as an example and admire her though she is centuries old, but still very much alive in the Word of God. We all want to be classified like that superior lady. She certainly had to discipline herself to stay consistently on track with the Lord. Moving her to modern times, I'm sure that would translate to the very things Christian ladies do today take care of all the details of life and have precious time for fellowship and learning from the Lord. We have the Word of God complete and available to us, whereas that lady did not. But she got her wisdom and kindness from the same place! A godly woman is always beautiful inside and out. It comes from fellowship with the Lord.

    I like to gather helpful hints about practical ways which will help me stay on tract. I welcome them and insights from others who are in the good fight of faith as I am. And those helps may come from unexpected sources. Always be alert and receptive.

    BEAUTY BASKET...This may be just the thing that will work best for you. It could be an actual basket, or something that suits you to hold several things for personal devotional time. First is your Bible. Inside, put a *Thank You* card to remind you each day to give praise and thanks to the Lord. Also insert words of a hymn to sing, or read over, during your devotional time.

    Keep a *prayer list*. Make a new each month, adding names, and deleting where God has answered prayer. You are then ready to receive maximum benefits from fellowship with the Lord. Selah!

Delight:    Psalm 119:18    Colossians 3:16

Edna Holmes

# October 5

*"...but the Son of Man hath not where
to lay his head."* Matthew 8:20

I've had people to ask me about the title of Jesus as "the Son of Man" when He certainly was *not* the son of a man. He was the virgin born Son of God. Son of Man seems to be His favorite designation of Himself in His earthly ministry, and it is used over 80 times. In the book of Daniel, the prophesy of Jesus as the Son of Man, the Savior, is recorded in chapter 7:13-14.

*"I saw in the night visions, and, behold, one like the Son of man came with the clouds of heaven, and came to the Ancient of days, and they brought him near before him. And there was given him dominion, and glory, and a kingdom, that all people, nations, and languages, should serve him: his kingdom is an everlasting dominion, which shall not pass away, and his kingdom that shall not be destroyed."*

The title of the Son of Man emphasized His lowliness and humanity. *"And Jesus saith unto him, The foxes have holes, and the birds of the air have nests; but the Son of man hath not where to lay his head.* Matt. 8:20

It emphasized His suffering and death. *"For the Son of man is come to seek and to save that which was lost."* Luke 19:10

It emphasized His future reign as King. *"For as the lightning cometh out of the east, and shineth even unto the west; so shall also the coming of the Son of man be."* Matt. 24:27

The fact, that Jesus condescended to take the lowly title of the Son of man is beyond our comprehension. It took a birth, a VIRGIN birth, in order to identify with the human race. In contrast, when man becomes a Christian, identifying with God, it takes a New Birth through faith in the Lord Jesus Christ.

SON OF MAN is the name that links Jesus to the earth and His mission.
SON OF GOD is Jesus' divine name. Matt. 8:29
SON OF DAVID is his Jewish title. Matt. 9:27

Delight: Matthew 25:31, Mark 8:31

Delighting in the Lord

# October 6

*"Therefore seeing we also are compassed about with so great a cloud of witnesses..."* Hebrews 12:1

Some folks honestly believe that this verse indicates that all heaven is watching the Christians on earth run the race in serving the Lord, that people in heaven are the "witnesses." Heaven is in eternity, not in the realm of the universe God created to accommodate the earth, the dwelling place for God's prize creation: man. All earthly ties are severed when one passes from this life into the presence of God in heaven. There is only one focus in heaven; that is the Lord Jesus Christ, not the Christians on earth.

In every generation from the beginning, people of the world have been watching, observing the people of God. They are the great cloud of witnesses. The Apostle Paul said that *"Ye are our epistle written in our hearts, known and read of all men."* So, we live our Christian life under intense scrutiny. *The world of witnesses is not admiring us but it is looking for weaknesses and hoping we will fall out in the race! That is why we should get rid of "besetting" sins, which weights us down. Jesus said the world would hate us.* He also said they hated Him before they hated us. Re: John 15:18

Our text verse reads *'Wherefore seeing we also (as they were before us) are compassed about...'* We are not observed from above; we have these witnesses "about" us; we are completely surrounded by them! Yes, there is a great cloud, *multitude,* watching the race that Christians are running for the Lord. They delight in those that fall down, and don't get up to keep running. We must be faithful through our whole life and run a good race!

Delight:     Hebrews 12:2     II Corinthians 3:3

Edna Holmes

# October 7

*"For God so loved the world, he gave his only begotten Son…"* John 3:16

God has one Gift for us: Christ the Lord. All other gifts and spiritual insights which we desire or need, are in the first Gift.

Need more patience, tolerance, and longsuffering? Draw closer to Christ and He makes you more like He is, and He is all these things. Did you ever long to know what the Father is like, really like? Christ is the very image of God. Jesus told the disciples *"If you've seen me, you've seen the Father."* John 14:9. Think of that! That is a marvelous truth to mediate on. It will enrich your soul, put awe in your heart for the Lord that will last.

Would you like to know and understand more of the glory of God, where the Bible says in Psalm 104 that He is covered with light as with a garment? *"Bless the Lord, Oh my soul. O Lord my God, thou art very great; thou art clothed with honour and majesty. Who coverest thyself with light as a garment: who stretchest out the heavens like a curtain."* Psa. 104: 1-2

It is simple. Draw close to Jesus Christ to get a look at God. That will not be in any physical appearance. We don't know what Jesus actually looked like in His physical body. Artists, down through the centuries have painted pictures of Him leaning toward a soft feminine look. Long flowing hair, soft hands and any way they could to make it look more or less "sissy." But that was a false image. The Lord was physically strong enough to withstand the scourging of the Roman soldiers ordered by Pilate. Many men died under the whip. But Jesus lived to die on the cross, the cruelest, tortuous death a man could die, and He did for us. For us, lost sinners! Praise Him forever!

Delight:   Colossians 2:9-10   Colossians 2:6-7

## October 8

*"Thy word is a lamp unto my feet, and a light unto my path."* Psalm 119:105

Any light must have fuel to keep burning. I grew up with full knowledge of the importance of always having kerosene on hand to fuel the lamps we had for light. On a dark farm far away from power lines to bring electricity to our area, it was double dark on moonless nights. The kerosene lamps were brilliant lights to us in the house when it got dark at night. But they had to have fuel, a trimmed wick in good shape, and the globe kept clean when it clouded up. I'd write letters or get my homework at night and, at times, I had to stop and clean the lamp globe before I could finish my work. The globe atop the lamp displayed the light wonderfully, if it was kept clean.

We are lights for the Lord in this world. He said so in Matthew 5: 14-16. Our fuel to stay bright is the blessed Word of God. Without the Word fueling us daily, we will stay dim. The globe will be clouded, and others won't notice Jesus faintly showing in our lives.

When God saved us, He put the Holy Spirit in us. It is then that we became His lights in the world. Christians need to be bright lights for people who are lost in spiritual darkness. Some are indeed bright lights in this world; they stand out. Why is that? They stay close to Jesus in fellowship with Him, usually the first activity of their day.

Let us take seriously the fact that we have a divine purpose in this world. It holds responsibility. We are lights! Whatever you do, make sure you are shining brightly! The Lord Jesus is worthy.

Delight:    John 8:12    II Corinthians 4:6

Edna Holmes

# October 9

*"Now faith is the substance of things hoped for,
the evidence of things unseen."* Hebrews 11:1

The definition of *faith* is an elusive thing to many people. For myself, *faith* is simply believing God. If you believe in Jesus, and the Word of God as truth; you have real faith.

But there is a loftier way of defining the mystery of faith, and I love this one: *Faith perceives as real fact what is not revealed to the senses.* We can't see, hear, or touch all that we believe in and are assured of by God through the Gift of salvation, Jesus Christ. But we know it as surely as if we did. And that is faith.

When faith takes hold in us; an important change takes place. The Holy Spirit takes up His abode in our hearts; the Bible says that *"If any man have not the Spirit of God he is none of his."* Rom.8-9.

We could never plumb the depths of God's love and grace which did that for us. Through God's love, Jesus redeemed us through His death and resurrection. It was an exchanged life: Jesus took us when we came to Him to be saved, and He gave us His life in exchange! The Holy Spirit of God is the Lord Jesus Christ living in us. *"To whom God would make known what is the riches of the glory of this mystery among the Gentiles; which is Christ in you, the hope of glory."* Colossians 1:27. It is a most blessed moment when Christians read that verse and that truth lodges in their hearts in reality. *Christ in me....* It comes into full understanding then. *We could not "be a Christian" in any way if Christ did not give us His life and dwell in us. The only One we have to brag about is our Lord Jesus Christ; He did it all...and will do it to the end. Give Him the glory!*

Delight:     Ephesians 2:8     Galatians 6:14

Delighting in the Lord

# October 10

*"And be ye kind to one to another, tender hearted, forgiving one another..."* Ephesians 4:32

We are not capable of doing that by ourselves. We don't have it in us. But the Lord Jesus Christ does, and He is ever so willing to come to our aid, shed His love abroad in our hearts and taking the bitterness and hatred out. Hatred is defined as "strong dislike."

*Decades ago, there was an altercation between me and one of my seven brothers. I was visiting my daughter and her family in another state where this brother was an Associate pastor in their church. When we went in to church that Sunday morning, we met in the foyer and had some sharp words for one another, and I got as angry as a pastor's wife (as I was at the time) should never get! So, my attitude for the day was set. I vented my anger at lunch and into the afternoon. My children bore it patiently. In the afternoon, I got my Bible to read to see if I could get peace of mind. Suddenly, as I was reading Ephesians 4:31-32 the anger I felt just melted away, and peace came into my heart. It was over! I was so grateful to the Lord and then regretted the miserable way I'd behaved myself in front of my family. Angry, bitter people can be so obnoxious, and only God can fix it! His Word has the extraordinary power to clean our hearts. I made peace with my brother that night.*

There is an urgent reason for us to get rid of anger and bitterness that may try to take hold in our hearts. We will always need forgiveness of sin in our own lives, and the Lord adds a strong directive. *"But if ye forgive not men their trespasses, neither will your Father forgive your trespasses."* Matthew 6:1

Delight:   I John 1:9    Psalm 130:4

Edna Holmes

# October 11

*"While the bridegroom tarried, they all slumbered and slept."* Matthew 25:5

The Bridegroom of the church, our Lord Jesus Christ, is one day coming just as He said He would. He is coming for His bride! That seems like a fairy tale to the world, and many Christians seem to have forgotten that it is a fact. Jesus will come and get His bride.

We saw a beautiful illustration of this fact when our daughter, Jeanne, got married while we were still in the pastorate. My husband was especially touched, and the Lord gave him an idea as to how to honor the Lord during that blessed event.

*The first day of December that year was the most beautiful I've ever seen. Mild weather and bright sunshine seemed to give the day a special brilliance.*

*Jeanne was as beautiful as brides are with a glowing smile as her dad brought her down the aisle stopping her at my seat. She gave me a rose and lingered as her dad continued on to the platform where Jeff and the groomsmen were waiting. It was then that my husband spoke of the coming of the Lord, our Bridegroom who will someday come for the church, and how we should be ready. Then he turned to Jeff and said, "Jeff, your bride has made herself ready; go and bring her to the wedding." How eagerly he came down and escorted Jeanne to the place where they said their vows. There were tears, and several resounding 'amens' from other pastor friends that were in attendance.*

None of us want to be "slumbering and sleeping" when our Lord comes. Jesus paid such a price for the church, His bride. God tells us that our Bridegroom gave Himself for the church, made up of the *born-again* children of God. We are His precious bride!

Shouldn't we be diligent in making ourselves ready for His coming? Be true to Him here and now, and don't let anything lure you off the path of faithfulness. Praise Him! Love Him! He is coming.

Delight:    Ephesians 5:25-27    Philippians 1:9-10

# October 12

*"And he said unto Jesus, Lord, remember me when thou comest into thy kingdom."* Luke 23:42

At first the two thieves crucified with Jesus railed on Him like others around the cross. But as time and their agony wore on into hours, one of the thieves came to his senses. Surely, he had heard about Jesus, as all the people in Jerusalem and the surrounding area had. He began to rebuke the other thief, reminding him that they deserved the punishment they were getting, but Jesus did not! He realized in that moment *actually who Jesus was,* and he asked the Lord for salvation. What were his words? *"And he said unto Jesus, Lord, remember me when thou comest into thy kingdom."* And the Lord, in the midst of dying in agony, *"Verily I say unto thee, To-day shalt thou be with me in paradise." That was about the sixth hour, and there was darkness over all over the earth until the ninth hour.*

Think of it! The "saved" thief lived only three hours more on the cross, and he had not time for the works Christians do as result of their salvation. He wasn't *baptized!* Some people would say that it is necessary for salvation. That mocks the finished work of the Savior. Jesus is the Author and Finisher of salvation, and the many things we do in serving and worshipping Him on earth *has absolutely nothing to do with our personal salvation.* Those works are only evidence of the change that took place when Jesus saved us.

Think on the time that you were saved. Where were you? How long did it take for you to realize there was a difference in you? Rejoice in your personal salvation today.

Delight:     Zephaniah 3:17     Acts 4:12

Edna Holmes

# October 13

*"Ye are our epistle written in our hearts, known and read of all men."* II Corinthians 3:2

We have written much referencing the subject of Christians being epistles, letters, which the world reads every day. The lost are curious and skeptical of God's people that they observe with a critical eye. They *read us* faithfully, no doubt with more interest than many Christians have for the Word of God. It behooves us to keep our testimony in good shape to make sure the world is reading a good report in us continually.

God has wonderful ways. He *knew* that the unbelievers in this world would not read His Word, so He gave them something they could read and understand: the *born-again* Christians who remind them of Christ. The fruit of the Spirit showed in Jesus here on earth. Our character should strongly resemble that of Jesus. He is the most loving, kind person who ever lived on the earth. He was the ultimate pattern or "letter" for the world to read.

A sinless life was Jesus' testimony. Yet, the world hated Him. He was, and is now, a powerful reminder that men are lost sinners in need of a Savior. *"But the fruit of the Spirit is love, joy, peace, longsuffering, gentleness, goodness, faith, meekness, temperance: against such there is no law."* Galatians 5:22-23. In this verse, it lists what the Holy Spirit of God develops in us as we learn and grow spiritually. It's the only way we will be good letters for the world to read as they observe us. Do you really love anybody? Are you patient with others? Are you meek, or prideful? Is your faith strong and growing? We must examine ourselves; stand beside Jesus and look in the "spiritual mirror" and see if you are looking more like Him.

Delight:   Ephesians 3:16    I Thessalonians 5:5

## October 14

*"And both Jesus was called, and his disciples,  
to the marriage."* John 2:2

Jesus averted a disaster for the Bride and Groom at their wedding at Cana. To run out of wine at the wedding feast was a big humiliation in that day. Jesus told the servants to fill six huge water pots with water, then draw it out and take it to the governor of the feast. We don't know the mystery of just when the water became wine; it doesn't record Jesus saying anything. He didn't have to. The "winds and the waves" obeyed Him in a storm. The water obeyed Him at the wedding: it turned into wine! The ruler of the feast called the bridegroom and made an amazing statement, with a clue as to the custom of the day.

*"And saith unto him, every man at the beginning doth set forth good wine; and when men have well drunk, then that which is worse: but thou hast kept the good wine until now."* John 2:10

Grape juice was stored in concentrated form. For wine, they added water according to their taste and preference. The less water, the tastier the wine. In case of a special occasion like a wedding feast, they put out their best wine first, then as the supply of concentrate ran low, they added more water to stretch the supply of wine. Hence, the first served was the good wine, more tasteful, and the last was weaker. I'm sure the bride and groom never forgot the Lord's kindness to them in saving their day from great humiliation.

We are all empty vessels until the day Jesus fills us with the water of life, which is Himself, and we are saved. What a wonderful day of joy when Jesus comes into our lives and makes us His own.

Delight:     John 4:10     John 5:24

Edna Holmes

# October 15

*"He must increase, but I must decrease."* John 3:30

Think on this wonderful verse spoken by John the Baptist. It was an absolute necessity for John the Baptist, and it is or should be the main goal of our lives. John was in the world for one reason. He was to point out Jesus as the Lamb of God which takes away the sin of the world. Also, John was to baptize Jesus because the purpose of God had decreed it to be so. John obeyed God, and his earth time was over. God took him home!

As we grow in knowledge of the Word, and God's amazing grace, it will fill our hearts with a fervent desire for Jesus to increase, and ourselves to decrease. The pride that so easily comes into the heart is a destroyer of the awe and humility that should register in us every day of our lives. Our prayer each day should be that the Lord Jesus would daily increase so that others will see Him in our actions and conversation. Do you know any people that makes you think of the Lord when you are with them: their love and kindness toward others; their fervent desire in bringing lost souls to the Savior; the ease and comfort with which they talk about Jesus? Jesus is *increased* in them, while they, themselves, have decreased. The old nature retreats to the background as the presence of Jesus becomes more preeminent.

The Holy Spirit in our heart will inevitably warn us when thing creep into our lives that causes Jesus to *decrease*. It happens and the result is a vague unrest lingers in us. Confess and forsake sin! Ask Jesus to *increase* again in your life.

Delight:   II Corinthians 4:11   Romans 6:11

Delighting in the Lord

# October 16

*"How forcible are right words?"* Job 6:25

Not only *right* words, but *wrong* words are equally forcible and so impressionable to the ears that hear them. Many children are so influenced by forcible words, detrimental ones, that their lives are altered, and they grow in adulthood greatly hindered. Children, and grownups as well, are listening to what is being said when you may assume they are not. Children are great listeners, and they store the information that is inadvertently given out to them in adult talk, and always their thoughts are stored with those forcible words! As adults, when they hear the same words in unrelated cases, it brings back a grievous memory, and old thoughts become revitalized to bring back the hurt. That's what forcible words can do. Are we aware of the power that right and wrong forcible words can do? We should put prayer in the mix of our daily verbal communication for good reason.

*From the time I was a small child, certain of our relatives made my first name as ugly as possible with a deliberate mispronunciation of it. They turned Edna into Ed-Ner which distressed me to no end. I could not stop it. Asking or pleading only increased their fun. In time, we moved from that area and then I had opportunity to make peace with my opinion of my name I had grown to dislike very much. Negative words are very forcible and make deep impressions to overcome and reconcile.*

We can only speak right if we pray for the mind of Christ to be in us continually. Since out of the "abundance of the heart, the mouth speaketh" (Matt. 12:34) then we should maintain a heart like Jesus.

Delight:   Matthew 12:34   Psalm 51:10

Edna Holmes

# October 17

*"Whether therefore ye eat, or drink, or whatsoever ye do, do all to the glory of God."* I Corinthians 10:31

Many Christians misunderstand this verse; and in way it is a puzzle. How are we to "glorify God" in every little thing we do? We don't quite get what it means to glorify God. That is not jumping up and down and running in circles in a place of worship. It is simply behaving in everything we do in such a manner that it reflects our love and honor of God in our lives. When a Christian obeys God, serving Him joyfully, he glorifies God and His Son, Jesus Christ. That's a good witness in the world, and so glorifies our Savior and our Heavenly Father. Observing us, people may be *prompted* to think of God and inquire of Him. Remember, they are *reading us!*

In the context in which the Apostle Paul wrote this verse, he is teaching the church at Corinth about the freedom they have in Christ, and how to behave interacting with the weaker Christians in the church who did not yet understand what they had in salvation.

The Lord tells us simply how to glorify Him. In one Psalm in particular, it reads: *"Whoso offereth praise glorifieth me: and to him that ordereth his conversation aright will I shew the salvation of God."* Ps.50:23

In the Biblical sense, our *conversation* is the outward motions of our lives, not just verbal expression; are we living right, as well as talking right in this world? When we *praise God*, we are very much *glorifying Him.* Brag on the Lord! Tell what He has done for you and others. Talk about His wonderful Word, and what It does for you. Just try to explain how He loves us. Praise *glorifies Him!*

Delight:    Psalm 150    Psalm 145:3

Delighting in the Lord

# October 18

*"Let your light so shine before men, that they may see your good works..."* Matthew 5:16

We had a powerful theme one year in the pastorate as we planned our Missions Month. We had teaching and preaching about Missions at home and abroad. At that particular time, our theme for the year was "Life on a Mission."

Every Christian is to be on a mission for the Lord. He has told us what He expects us to be in this world. First, we are lights, simply because we *reflect the glorious light of Jesus, who is the Light of the world!* We must keep our sins confessed *up to date* to keep our light burning bright for the Lord. The world is in spiritual darkness; they desperately need the light of the gospel.

We are salt! It seasons and preserves a corrupt world. In Matthew 5:13, It tell us of the value of salt: *"Ye are the salt of the earth: but if the salt have lost his savour, wherewith shall it be salted? it is thenceforth good for nothing, but to be cast out, and to be trodden under foot of men."* People gathered salt on the shore of the Dead Sea and used other methods to extract salt from the sea. It is said that they poured sea water into holes in the rocks, and when the water evaporated, they gathered the salt out. After so much time, the salt could go "flat" or tasteless. People would throw it out on the pathways, and it was "trodden underfoot of men." Our goal should be to stay fresh and useful to the Lord by obedience to His Word. We are the salt of the earth!

We are also examples of the grace of God; we are witnesses of the love of God as we reach out in love and caring to bring souls to the Savior, Jesus Christ. Just know that every child of God is most important in God's program. Be faithful!

Delight:   II Corinthians 3:2   I John 3:2

Edna Holmes

# October 19

*"And no marvel; for Satan himself is transformed
into an angel of light."* II Cor. 11:14

Satan's hatred for Christians is as fervent as God's love for them, if there could be a comparison of God's love. He works without ceasing to cause Christians to sin, bringing shame on the name of Christ, our Savior. He can work his wiles easily on the human race. God's people are so gullible since the world has such appeal to the flesh; we just allow ourselves to be led into temptation until we are too far in to resist. The devil makes sin attractive and promises blissful results in our wrongdoing. If we could actually see him with the physical eye, we would flee in terror! He is the epitome of evil, and evil is ugly. That is a mild description. If we could only see the danger that sin poses in our lives.

*"Once when we were visiting friends in Oklahoma, they took us upon a mountain where their brother was the overseer of the area. Wild boars roamed freely, and this man had a boar's head trophy on the wall from one of these animals. It was huge, with two long tusks protruding from its mouth: an absolutely fearsome beast. If I'd lived there, I would never have gone out at night on that mountain. Just a look at the boar's head convinced me of the danger."*

From Treasures, by E.H.

The devil will always make sin appear good and beautiful to us to trick us into complying with the temptation to indulge the desire. To protect ourselves, we should pray each day for discernment. The Word of God gives us that, and the Holy Spirit gives us warning. *Listen* when He speaks to you in a 'still, small voice'. It is always that: a still small voice. God does not scream in our ears; but the devil does! Be aware and pray for discernment to always recognize the Lord.

Delight:   John 10:4    I Kings 19:12

Delighting in the Lord

# October 20

*"Better is little with the fear of the Lord than great treasure and trouble therewith."* Proverbs 15:16

From one of my husband's notebooks, a small piece of paper fell out which had the most interesting data on it. It suggests that everyone needs to keep life simple by doing a few things listed. I like helpful hints; you never know what you will read or hear about which will benefit you greatly.

The first item was "having something to do." I've heard the old saying from childhood: "an idle mind is the devil's workshop". We know that that is really true. If our minds are not busy with constructive thoughts which generate useful actions and good works, then we will be inviting the devil to stir up evil instead of good in our minds. Having something to do makes us wake up each day with a purpose. If I have a list of daily goals, my energy comes awake too, and I feel very good, mentally and physically. We need to definitely have *something to do!* It will keep us out of trouble, too.

"Having someone to Love!" And that must be, first of all, God! God and the Lord Jesus Christ will be our happiness to enjoy throughout eternity. Love them now, and you will be happy and content on this earth. With loving the Lord, you will love all others as God's love will be shed abroad in your heart. There is great contentment in having a heart full of love.

"Something to believe in." Yes! And that is the Word of God. The promises make all Christians rich beyond measure, if they will believe them and use them! They are ours as children of God. To be content, though we be not rich in goods, is great treasure.

Delight:   Proverbs 9:10   II Corinthians 8:9

Edna Holmes

# October 21

*"Better is little with fear of the Lord, than great treasure and trouble therewith."* Proverbs 15:16

Continuing the thought of how we can be content and keep life simple, let us look closely at our text verse. It speaks to me for I grew up in the country culture where life was very simple. Our family and everyone else we knew were in the *poor* bracket. My parents went through the 'dust bowl' days, and the great depression era. God-fearing folks always had enough to eat, and shelter for the family. They were the happy, contented ones. I've seen many now in my lifetime who had all their hearts desire but were miserable and bitter at life.

Again, our needs must be simple for us to be happy. One is our need to have *something to hope for*. Our hope is in Christ! Every day when we get out of bed, our minds should go to the wonderful hope we have in our blessed Savior. Repeat a 'wake up' verse and start your day. Sing! Jesus saved us, that's a fact; He supplies our needs; He hears our prayers; He is one day coming back for His bride, the church; all His promises to us are sure and Jesus will never fail. All that is a fact, so our hope should shine like a bright star in our lives.

Find something you can do for the Lord and do it consistently. There is satisfaction in simple service. *We had an elderly man in our congregation who stayed behind after Sunday services and cleaned out around the pews, straightened the hymn books, and got the auditorium ready for the next service. That simple task, faithfully done, was a huge blessing to our church. Ask God what YOU can do and see what turns up! God is so good.*

Delight:   Hebrews 13:5   I Timothy 6:6

Delighting in the Lord

# October 22

*"...unfeigned faith that is in thee, which dwelt first in thy grandmother Lois, and thy mother Eunice..."* I Tim.1:5

When you read the full text of 1 Tim. 1:5, we discover that the Apostle Paul reveals that the early training of Timothy by his mother and grandmother sowed the seeds of faith in his heart. He readily believed the gospel when he heard it as a young man. Mothers have the most influence in the world on their children, *if they start early enough before they are exposed to the world and its devices.*

In a quote about the Mother role, it is said that raising a child is the "process of taking a little life, seeing it pass through your life and disappear into adulthood with you as a pattern." That is especially true with daughters! Though a mother and daughter may not look alike physically, there are always obvious signs that the daughter is the off spring of her mother. The mannerisms, voice, posture, are all things that can pair the daughter with her mother. My mother is long time deceased, but sometimes the sound of my own voice so much reminds me of my mother; it seems for a moment she is there! Her good posture is a rich gift that she left me. When Mama passed on at age eighty, she still stood straight with no drooping shoulders.

Every little girl has something of her mother she is carrying through life, and the best legacy of all is faith in the Lord Jesus Christ. Nourish that faith! Teach them daily, more and more about Jesus. As mothers and grandmothers, think of the good we can do by being a good example before our children and grandchildren *as long as we live!* We will know the blessed results in eternity with the Lord.

Delight:   Colossians 2:6-7   Proverbs 3:5-6

Edna Holmes

# October 23

*"Examine yourselves, whether ye be in the faith; prove your own selves."* II Corinthians 13:5

*When I'm writing, my husband helps me in the household chores, so I can work without interruption. One morning I stripped the bed and left the dirty sheets and pillowcases piled on top and forgot to go back and put clean ones on and take the dirty ones to the laundry room. My kind husband came in later, saw the bed unmade and sheets there which he promptly put back on the bed! He thought they were the clean ones I'd put there. He sincerely thought they were clean because he couldn't tell the difference just looking at them.*

That made me think of the danger of *assuming one is saved without the new birth.* Many church members, who seem like good individuals, have not experienced *the* new birth, which changes the heart and life of everyone trusting in Jesus Christ. I know; I was one of those and I remember too well the emptiness in my heart as I went through the motions of being a good church member.

You cannot conjure salvation up by positive thinking; you can't work diligently in church and make it happen; you can't bargain with God and "get in." There is no way to settle the issue of you going to heaven for sure until you come to Jesus for salvation. God is impressed with one thing: the sacrifice that Jesus made to pay for our sins. There is nothing we could *ever do* that God would even glance at. Jesus is the way. His blood is precious, and that's what it takes. Those who come to Him with conviction in their hearts, and call on His name, *will be saved.* If you haven't been born again, admit it to Jesus, and ask Him to save you. Everyone, <u>without Christ</u>, will miss heaven.

Delight:    Romans 10:9-10,13    John 3:18

## October 24

*"For the wages of sin is death; but the gift of God is eternal life through Jesus Christ the Lord."* Rom.6:23

Once I had Romans chapter 6 memorized, and I loved to recite it every day to keep in practice, and also witness with it when we happened to be in public. In waiting rooms when opportunity presented itself and it was obvious nobody would be offended; I'd often recite it aloud while my husband checked it for mistakes. One lady was saved because of the Word she heard one day as I repeated that chapter. Afterwards I talked to her as she spoke to me first about it. Always remember, the power is in the Word which brings a soul to Christ; it is not in the messenger. Our responsibility is only to share it. God does what He wants to with it.

I often stress salvation and how to be sure you are saved, and some of the identifying marks of a Christian. I'm motivated by the fact of my own testimony when I went for many years ignorant of the fact that I did not know Christ at all! I had not been born again, and if someone had recognized my lost state and told me of the marks of a true Christian, perhaps I'd known sooner. Even faithful church members have distinct changes when they get saved.

The strongest indication of the new birth is a desire for the Word of God. I did not understand the Bible, and I read only what was necessary to function. With salvation, *it opened up for me.* I can't stress this enough. Do you love to take in the Word of God? Do you like to talk to the Lord...pray? How has your life changed since you trusted in the Lord for your soul's salvation? Write it down. Share it.

Delight:   John 3:16    I Peter 2:2-3

Edna Holmes

# October 25

*"As newborn babes, desire the sincere milk  
of the word, that ye may grow thereby."* I Peter 2:2

Beside the desire for reading and learning the Word of God, there are other plain marks which identify born again Christians. Another immediate change which takes place is an intense desire to be in the house of God when one hears the preaching and teaching of the Bible and enjoys the fellowship of other Christians. I was again amazed when my husband not only began reading the Bible every spare minute, but he would not miss attending church services for any reason. He loved the house of God and other Christians!

The conviction of sin in our lives is a sure sign of salvation in us. Before, sin did not bother us, but after being born again into God's family, a mighty change takes place inside. The Holy Spirit takes up His abode in our hearts, and He does not allow us to have peace when we sin against our Heavenly Father. He convicts us until we confess our sin and ask God to forgive us. Christians will sin, the Bible says so: *"If we say that we have no sin, we deceive ourselves, and the truth is not in us. If we confess our sins, he is faithful and just to forgive us our sins, and to cleanse us from all unrighteousness."* That comes from the book of I John 1:8-9, which is also a book of assurance of salvation. Doubters and worriers may settle their hearts by reading I John every day, prayerfully, for however long it takes.

There is a change, however small, in every Christian after they are saved. In time, those changes are strong and permanent.

Delight:    Proverbs 28:13    John 3:36

## October 26

*"Are they not all ministering spirits, sent forth to minister for them who shall be heirs of salvation?"* Heb.1:14

This verse speaks of the angels and their particular ministry on earth which God has designated for them. For one thing, they do minister to those *"...who shall be heirs of salvation."* We know also we are protected in many ways *before and after* we are saved. If God did not watch over us, you could be sure the devil would do away with all Christians. He is certainly powerful enough. Job was in his hands only by permission from God Almighty. He allowed Satan to test Job's faith in God to the limit, even to the loss of his health...but He said, "Save his life..." and so it was, Job did not die. God later gave Job twice as much in riches and honor and Job has ever after been an example of patience and great faith in God, even to this day.

God uses angels to do His bidding. You may remember incidents in your life when you were sure God kept you from tragedy.

*When I was ten years old, we were visiting one Sunday with relatives in the country. Someone sat my brother, eight, and I on the back of a horse to take a ride. We had no saddle, but just the bridle and reins to guide the horse. My brother held onto me, and we started off down the road when several horses ran to the fence and spooked our horse. He took off like a bullet running furiously down the road with me hanging on for dear life to the reins. The dirt road was extremely muddy and soon my brother fell off in the mud, as the horse kept plunging on. I don't know if I passed out, but when I became conscious that the horse was stopped, I was sitting in front of his feet in the mud, still holding the reins.*

Angels must have been there that day, or I could have been trampled under the hooves of that animal! In ways we will not understand this side of heaven, we are amazingly protected.

Delight:   Psalms 91:11   Hebrews 13:2

Edna Holmes

# October 27

*"Fear God, and keep his commandments:  
for this is the whole duty of man."* Ecclesiastes 12:13

God made it very simple and easy for men to live on the earth and be happy and content. They have one duty, *the whole duty,* which every single soul can accomplish perfectly: *"Fear God and keep his commandments."* With that, God takes care of every need and problem which arises. Obedience to Him is the golden key.

To fear God is to have a loving reverence and awe of Him which causes us to obey Him. The Lord delights in His children, and desires to have their love and attention. Remember how you felt when your children were small? Parents delight in the love and attention of their offspring. Multiply that many times over and it's a fair comparison of God's desire toward His children. Yet, we often neglect God, taking meager time to communicate with Him in prayer and fellowship with Him. We have many things we are more concerned with than the *whole duty* which God instructs us to observe.

The modern world has become a jungle of hi-tech devices which so occupies humanity, and keeps their brains jumbled that people can hardly think on their own anymore. The latest phones have taken over society. You hardly see a single person without a phone in hand. Babies, two years old, can work a phone! It is mind-boggling to the older generation of us who are living in the midst of this modern craziness. We do benefit from having phones to stay in contact with our children and grandchildren with calls and texts. But to go with it in hand continually is a hindrance in daily business. Let us remember the "whole duty" factor and take care of that for health and happiness.

Delight:   Colossians 3:2   Titus 3:8

## October 28

*"But God is the judge: he putteth down
one, and setteth up another."* Psalm 75:7

At times, as the years roll by, we may tremble with fear and dread when our nation changes leadership. We fear the future and what will happen when drastic changes take place. We have scriptures to go to which will calm our fears and assure us of Who is in charge; and that is Almighty God! It is the devil who gives us the "spirit of fear" to combat. Jesus told His disciples *'fear not'* and we do not have one thing to fear because we belong to the Lord. We are as secure as one could ever be from whatever comes because we belong to God, and He is in control of our destiny. The estimation of the nations on earth are *less than nothing* to the Lord.

*"All nations before him are as nothing; and they are counted to him less than nothing, and vanity."* Isaiah 40:17. The world system does not impress God one bit, but His children are His treasure! So, wherever we dwell on earth, God has His eye on us in loving watchfulness. *"I will lift up my eyes unto the hills, from whence cometh my help. My help cometh from the Lord, which make heaven and earth."* Psalm 121:1-2

*"Once, after a major earthquake had devastated a city, the rescuers discovered an elderly lady on the second floor of her house which was damaged. She was rocking and singing to the Lord. She said to her rescuers, "Isn't it wonderful how our God can shake this old earth?"* She certainly was viewing her circumstances with an eye of faith. Let us endeavor to do the same.

Delight:     Proverbs 3:5-6     Matthew 6:26

Edna Holmes

# October 29

*"And to know the love of Christ, which passeth knowledge..."* Ephesians 3:19

There are things which cannot be fully known. One of those is the *love of Christ.* We are not capable of understanding the kind of love which caused Jesus to come down, enter the world as a baby in a body of flesh, grow up and experience life on earth as the "Son of man." His body had the senses like everyone else. He got hungry and tired, needing sleep and rest. But He got very little rest on earth because the needs of the people drove him on, always with the cross of Calvary in His mind. He came to die!

On the way to that goal our Lord did so many miracles showing compassion and mercy on the people, they couldn't be numbered. John 21:25 tells us an amazing fact. *"And there are also many other things which Jesus did, the which, if they should be written every one, I suppose that even the world itself could not contain the books that should be written. Amen."* The four gospels only record a fraction of Jesus' ministry on earth. God has written what was written for men to understand the gospel which is the *good news* of salvation through Jesus Christ the Lord.

We bask in the love of our Savior, but our minds can never grasp it entirely; it remains a mystery. As I've said before, when I read the account of the crucifixion, the torture beforehand, and the unspeakable suffering on the cross, I thrill with relief when the Lord utters the words: *It is finished!* 'Blessed Savior, your suffering is over' is the prayer thought that resonates in my heart.

Ask the Lord to shed His love abroad in your heart today. It will help you to love others as He loves them. Serving will be easy.

Delight:   Psalm 18:1   Romans 5:5

## October 30

*"Who his own self bare our sins in his own body...
by his stripes ye are healed."* I Peter 2:24

On a recent visit to our family doctor, a Christian, he gave me a wonderful idea to illustrate how Jesus is indeed our substitute and actually took the judgment of sins that was ours to suffer. We take it too lightly. Even children need to have the message conveyed to them in such a simple way, they understand it better.

*"In speaking of the era of our growing up as children, the favorite correction my mother practiced on us was given with a good sturdy switch from one of our trees around the place. We were sent out to break one off a limb and bring it back for our "switching." Now if Jesus Himself came walking back with the guilty one carrying the big switch saying that He Himself would take the punishment deserved, and did endure a painful thrashing; that, merely illustrates in a small way the truth of what Jesus did for us all. We are the sinners; Jesus is the perfect, sinless Son of God; yet he loved us so much He did come to suffer and die, taking the judgement and punishment for our sins."* "And walk in love, as Christ also hath loved us, and hath given himself an offering and a sacrifice to God for a sweet smelling savour." Ephesians 5:2

That is why our thanksgiving and praise should be rendered to the Lord every day for His great love and sacrifice for us. He gave us life! Are we grateful? If you feel your heart not touched by that blessed truth, then repent quickly and ask God to give you a clean heart again; then rejoice in the love and grace He pours out in your life daily.

Delight:   John 15:13   I Peter 3:18   Psalm 68:19

Edna Holmes

# October 31

*"...they are gone far from me, and have walked after vanity, and are become vain?"* Jeremiah 2:5

Vanity is defined as "anything that is vain, futile, idle, and worthless." Obviously, that is life spent leaving God out of the picture very much of the time. Even for Christians, we slip off the track of fellowship with God and find ourselves entangled in some kind of diversion that is "vain, futile, and worthless." Vanity! It will drain the spiritual life out of you and ultimately leave you empty and unhappy. Even children can experience it.

*When I was twelve years old, my older sister took me to see Gone with The Wind in an afternoon showing of it at the theater. I was utterly enthralled with that movie! I was into it, fascinated with the splendor of beautiful mansions, and dresses, and breathtaking scenery and a lovely music theme playing throughout the movie. In that few hours, it was real to me. Then, it was over! The End. I felt such a let-down when the lights came on in the theater and real life emerged again. We left the theater, and the hot sun beating off the dirty sidewalk added to the emptiness I felt inside.* Vanity!

We should stick with the real and true on the earth. That is God, His Word, and His working in our hearts and life. What that involves should be the mainstream of our lives. We always feel betrayed, saddened, and disillusioned by the "lying vanities" which crop up and tempt us toward the world. *"They that observe lying vanities forsake their own mercy."* Jonah 2:8. Vanities beckon to us with promises of success and pleasure, but they are lying to us! Beware, and stick with what's true and real.

Delight:    Jonah 2:7-8    I Samuel 12:21-22

## November 1

*"That I may publish with the voice of thanksgiving, and tell of all thy wondrous works. Psalm 26:7*

One of the sure signs that thanksgiving is stirring in our hearts is what comes out of our mouths! We will talk about the Lord; we will tell about the wonderful things He has done and is doing for us. That practice will certainly keep a Christian happy and cheerful. I know firsthand how that counting my blessings and recording them on paper for therapy restored the joy of my salvation and lifted a blanket of depression off of me. I've told it and told it to anyone who might benefit from knowing. Those who believe it and try it find that it is absolutely a happy solution to the "spirit of heaviness" as spoken of in Isaiah 61:3. *"To appoint unto them that mourn in Zion, to give unto them beauty for ashes, the oil of joy for mourning, <u>the garment of praise for the spirit of heaviness;</u> that they might be called trees of righteousness, the planting of the Lord, that he might be glorified."*

A feeling of depression can sweep over us quickly, and the thing to do is dispel it before it takes hold on us for a long duration. Get rid of it! Keep a notebook and record some blessings from each day. We actually forget many things that the Lord does for us. Make a list and reflect on your blessings, and you will be surprised how many God has given to you. Fill your thoughts with them; thank God for them again and feel the joy well up in your heart. Make this month the absolute thanksgiving time in your life and involve your children in activities, making it "fun" to see how many personal blessings they can recall for themselves. Prompt them to express thanksgiving in their prayers at bedtime all during this month. Perhaps, good habits will start.

Delight:    Colossians 3:15    Psalm 50:14

Edna Holmes

# November 2

*"Him hath God exalted with his right hand to be  
a Prince and a Saviour..."* Acts 5:31

Peter is doing some powerful preaching in this chapter of Acts, and the religious crowd that hounded Jesus to the cross were not liking it. They rebuked the disciples saying they could not preach anymore in the name of Jesus, but Peter and the others told them they must obey God, not men.

Really, those ungodly, *religious,* hypocrites paid a great compliment to Peter and the others. What were they preaching? It was the gospel, the good news, of the death, burial, and resurrection of the Lord Jesus Christ. "You have filled Jerusalem with your doctrine," was their complaint. The truth was coming too close for comfort, and they certainly didn't want to hear it and be convicted of their sins. They were afraid already and no doubt trembled as their slaying of Jesus was coming back to haunt them.

Peter thundered *"The God of our fathers raised up Jesus, whom ye slew and hanged on a tree."* Further in the chapter, the Bible says they were *"cut to the heart" by that message.* No wonder! They could not have been guiltier in their sin. Perhaps some of that generation might have been saved later as the gospel spread all over the world at that time. When the power of the gospel is unleashed in any place, the results are always amazing.

*In the first ten years in our pastorate, we saw many people come to Christ. Almost every time we went out on visitation, my husband would lead some in the household to the Lord. I pacified children often, while my husband would witness to parents. The church was excited and happy as new people came into the fellowship by salvation and baptism. Pray for souls to be saved in your church. That's what brings revival and makes a happy congregation.*

Delight:   Acts 5:28   Acts 2:46-47

Delighting in the Lord

# November 3

*"Truly the light is sweet and a pleasant thing it is to behold the sun."* Ecclesiastes 11:7

The sun in the heavens is often used as an illustration of the Son of God. Its light nourishes the whole earth, which could not do without it. We know our Lord is nourishment and sustainer for the inhabitants of earth, saved and unsaved alike. It is the mercy and grace of God which makes it so. Taken personally, the Lord saves to the uttermost those that come trusting in Him and receiving the Gift of salvation: Jesus Christ.

Perhaps Solomon wrote our text verse as he was just emerging from a cold, hard winter. Haven't we all rejoiced to see more of the light and warmth of the sun in spring? Let it remind you of the Lord. In the winter of trials and troubles, the warmth and light experienced when our Savior draws near at our bidding is a pleasant thing. His light and enlightenment are sweet. Rarely do we call on Him soon enough; we let Him wait in the shadows while we try to figure out a way that we can solve the situation ourselves. In the deep-down core of every human being is an "independent streak", a nicer sounding term for rebellion. The only way to combat it is to stay close to the Lord in fellowship. Jesus has untold benefits for us which He pours out daily just because we are His children. *"Blessed be the Lord, who daily loadeth us with benefits, even the God of our salvation. Selah."* Psalm 68:19.

But Jesus has more for us when we earnestly pray. He tells us to "Ask, and it shall be given you..." in Matthew 7:7. Yes, there are conditions: we can't be harboring sin, or the Lord won't regard our prayers. A clean heart has boldness to ask of the Lord great things.

Delight:     Psalm 139: 23-24     Psalm 66:18

Edna Holmes

# November 4

*"...thou hast tried me, and shalt find
nothing..."* Psalm 17:3

Testing is going on in the life of a Christian continually. It may be a big unforgettable test of our integrity and honesty, or a small test which is often overlooked. Remember that God is conforming us to the image of His Son, Jesus, and testing for progress is frequently on God's agenda. The measure of progress requires testing to be verified. Am I getting stronger in faith and Christian character?

*In the first ten years of our marriage, we made a big thing of our wedding anniversary each year. We got our picture taken at a studio, and always planned an evening out for us on a special dinner date. One anniversary, (this was before God had called him to preach), my husband came by the bank on his way from work, being Friday, and cashed his check before hurrying home to get ready for our big date. Everything went wonderful, as it always did. We loved celebrating our wedding anniversary. On Monday, I got a call from the bank. A shaky young voice said "Mrs. Holmes, do you have your husband's check?" I replied, "No, he cashed it Friday evening when he came home from work." She said, "He cashed the stub." I went to check receipts in the drawer, and sure enough, there was the check on top where he had dropped it. I took it immediately to the bank, much to the relief of that frightened teller. She had not noticed the error when this excited, distracted customer put down the stub, the same size and resembled the check, instead of the check. She would have had to pay several hundred dollars to make up for such a mistake.*

You know how that could have played out if we had been dishonest folks. But praise God, honesty was firmly lodged in our hearts. We passed the test! How are you doing with the tests that crop up in your life? We must be truthful, not gossip or judge others, be honest and many other virtues if our hearts stay in fellowship with the Lord. He will be finding out just how we are growing spiritually.

Delight:   Romans 8:29    Romans 6:11-13

## November 5

*"All the ways of man are clean in his own eyes;
but the Lord weigheth the spirits."* Proverbs 16:2

    God looks into our hearts and contemplates the motives we harbor there. There is the taint of human pride mixed into all we do and expect. How could we ever think ourselves pure and good? Apart from our relationship with Jesus, we are hopelessly dead in sin. Sin is such an overwhelming powerful force that easily gets control over those who are not in the place of protection. That place is in the Lord Jesus Christ. As Christians, we are fully protected unless we stray away from closeness with Him. Like the wandering sheep finds, there are dangers out there which will do us in if we grapple with it alone. Just slipping away from a routine of spending time with the Lord in Bible reading and prayer will affect us more than we can imagine. Soon, there will be a different atmosphere in your home, and family. One backslidden Christian can do it. It is a costly thing if we turn a cold shoulder to Jesus. He loves us still, as always, but the Lord will not overlook our sins and bless us. We must confess and forsake them for the mercy of God to start pouring in on our lives again. *"He that covereth his sins shall not prosper: but whoso confesseth and forsaketh them shall have mercy."* Proverbs 28:13

    As we serve the Lord, we must prayerfully consider whether our motives are right and good. Ask God to enable you to have a pure heart for whatever work you are doing for Him at the time. If you never got an ounce of gratitude or praise for it from others, would you be glad you are serving God, for His honor and glory? With our naturally deceitful hearts, only the Lord can make it happen.

Delight:    I Corinthians 1:31    Colossians 3:17

Edna Holmes

# November 6

*"He that justifieth the wicked, and he that condemneth the just, even they both are abomination to the Lord."* Prov.17:15

In our society today, this has become a common practice. More and more in our country, there is an attitude of rebellion against the laws of the land. Those who have committed blatant crimes have gotten away with their wrong-doing; innocent people have been maligned until their lives have been nearly ruined. What can be done about a leading section of our society that is bereft of conscience? When in power, they can be a fearful force to deal with.

We can take comfort in knowing Who is ultimately in charge! That is Almighty God, our Creator, and Savior Jesus Christ.

*The Lord is exalted; for he dwelleth on high; he hath filled Zion with judgment and righteousness. And wisdom and knowledge shall be the stability of thy times, and strength of salvation: the fear of the Lord is his treasure.* Isa.33:5-6

God is not disturbed by men's attitudes or open acts of their rebellion. He inhabits eternity, and they are earth creatures. They in no way threaten God's authority. Vain creatures! *"Be not rash with thy mouth, and let not thine heart be hasty to utter anything before God: for God is in heaven, and thou upon earth: therefore let thy word be few.* Ecclesiastes 5:2 That statement should strike awe in our hearts. God is in heaven, and we on earth. We can't get to God unless we go through the Door which He has opened for us through salvation in Christ. What miserable creatures we would be without that hope from God.

Are we telling others about that Door? Are we pointing directly to it so others will understand and be convicted of its necessity? The Door! Don't miss the Door!

Delight:    Ecclesiastes 5:8    John 10:9

## November 7

*"...and I will wait on thy name; for it is good before thy saints."* Psalm 52:9

Patience is not one of the virtues of the saints, the born-again children of God. We *think* it is, but when it comes down to it, and we are tried, it proves to be otherwise. But the Lord has infinite patience and His name is *good* for all the promises in His Holy Word. The hard thing for us is *waiting on the Lord after we petition Him for the things* that are promised in His name. It's as sure as it can be that God will come through in answering our prayers...but He will work all things together for good...*while we wait.* We are so used to instant service in our daily lives in this modern world.

Everything has changed so much since my husband and I were children. The fast food places had not been invented yet! All we had was fresh food prepared the very day we ate it, and all made from "scratch." This generation hardly waits for *anything!* It is no wonder the Christians of this day are very impatient, even with God Himself.

Can we remember that the Word says that God's name is *good before thy saints?* He will not back down, or fail to deliver an answer of prayers prayed in *His name. Just wait! Along with waiting, however, we can look with assurance toward an answer. It will come.*

Your prayer life ought to be an exciting part of your work for God. Lost souls must be prayed for. Your brothers and sisters in Christ need daily prayers sent up for each other. We need prayer for the family and solutions to problems coming and going. Pray! But then wait and watch as God answers in a way far above what we could ask or think. May the Lord bless us with a revival in praying!

Delight: I Thessalonians 5:17  Colossians 4:2

Edna Holmes

# November 8

*"Walk in wisdom toward them that are without, redeeming the time."* Colossians 4:5

We are to redeem time as though it were a precious treasure in the house that we watch over to be sure of its safety. Time is simply our life...measured in tiny pieces called seconds and minutes and hours. We are to *redeem them, buy them up,* so we will have more to use in serving God as much as possible. That equals to so structuring our time and utilizing it that we have extra time left over, so to speak, and there's more for God's business in our lives.

We are walking in wisdom when we do that. The world needs us because we have the message of salvation to proclaim, and the Christians are the only ones who can do it. You must experience salvation to know how important it is to spread the good news. You long for the salvation of others because God gave you a new heart. We see the world through different eyes. We desire to "Walk in wisdom toward them that are without..." What the world sees in us will repel or attract them toward the gospel of Christ.

"Redeeming the time" may be difficult for many people. I'm not naturally an organized person. But the Lord gave me a husband who was, so I learned a few of his ways which helped me a lot. I'm most successful when I keep things written down in a handy notebook so I know what I'll do in each block of time, keeping notes of detail things that should not be forgotten. It is an invaluable tool and those who are most efficient in redeeming their time use that method or something similar. Use the *Mary Method* the first thing every day; that is sitting at Jesus' feet and listening to His words, talk to Him and in God's power and blessing you can accomplish all you planned in a day.

Delight:   Ephesians 5:15   Psalm 90:12

Delighting in the Lord

# November 9

*That at the name of Jesus every knee should bow, of things in heaven, and things in earth..."* Phil.2:10

We know that power and salvation is in the name of Jesus. It is the most powerful name on earth. There is something soothing and settling about that name when trouble comes and gets our minds in a turmoil. One lady, a friend, went about all one day speaking the name of Jesus aloud when her heart was deeply troubled. The mere mention of His name can bring conviction on hardened sinners, and half-hearted Christians.

*Shortly after my husband was saved, he began car-pooling with a group of men commuting to their jobs in the big city. Their language became very offensive at times, being vulgar and using the Lord's name in vain frequently. One evening, my husband spoke the name of Jesus, and told how wonderfully the Lord had saved him. That evening and for the duration of their driving together, the bad words stopped! That amazing power in the name of Jesus put the fear of God in those men enough to shut their mouths to vulgarity and the vain use of the Lord's name.*

Is there little wonder why we are instructed to *pray in the name of Jesus?* That's where the power lies. Jesus said, *"all power is given to me in heaven and earth..."* and we are *in Him* safe and secure as children of God. Pray in His name; expect answers! You can never make God's supply run low when asking a lot. His ability to supply our needs and numerous blessings is limitless.

Delight: Romans 14:10-11

Edna Holmes

# November 10

*"In God will I praise his word: in the Lord will
I praise his word."* Psalm 56:10

After David, at a young age, killed the giant Goliath the whole nation knew that he had great faith in God. It certainly was evident when he ran to meet the nine foot, heavily armed giant with a simple sling-shot and a few little stones, that David knew God and trusted Him to have victory. "Is there not a cause?" David said. God had already given David supernatural strength to kill a bear, and lion which were after the sheep he watched over. David *knew* by his great faith in God, that he would also have victory over the heathen giant.

Israel was God's chosen people, and here the army was cowering before a heathen giant who challenged one to fight him. The winner got everything! Israel would go into slavery again. No wonder David declared "Is there not a cause?" God had made the nation promises in His Word, and David was the only one among them that believed God's Word. And by that, he saved the nation that day in history. In time David would become Israel's most beloved king.

In various stages of his life, David wrote the Psalms which poured out of his heart, full of praise and thanksgiving to God. Untold numbers of repentant Christians have knelt with Psalm 51 before them weeping and repenting of sins as king David did. Many hearts are made to fill up with praise grazing through the Psalms as they worship the Lord in their quiet time with him. God used David to fill the needs of many hearts through the centuries with his inspiring psalms. The staunch faith of one person can affect the world.

Delight:   Romans 10:17   Ephesians 6:16

## November 11

*"The thought of foolishness is sin: and the scorner is abomination to men."* Proverbs 24:9

This verse makes us realize how utterly hopeless and helpless we are to live without the taint of sin on us. It is impossible for any of us, Christians and the unsaved alike to keep from having a foolish thought from popping up in our minds. The fleshly bodies with their senses love that sort of thing. We laugh at things we should not give a thought to and give ear to unsavory stories or jokes. We don't want to; but the flesh has a tremendous pull and persuasion for us to do so. We know too that our friends or relatives may think we are "self-righteous" or pompous if we object to something they esteem so lightly as *sin*. We don't have the courage to 'buck the tide' or walk away from temptation. People who think foolishness all the time and often act it out can leave a trail of devastation behind them.

*A young woman, who had just married into a family comprised of many pranksters, was permanently injured when a brother of her husband pulled her off a couch by her feet. She sat down hard on the floor on the very end of her backbone and sustained an injury which left her paralyzed from the waist down. We can't imagine the thoughts of the young lady, and just think what that brother had to live with knowing he destroyed normal life for his brother and his bride because he entertained foolish thoughts…and put action to them.*

Remember in Genesis 6:5, God said before He brought judgment to the earth with the flood. *"And God saw that the wickedness of man was great in the earth, and that every imagination of the thoughts of his heart was only evil continually."*
That is the utmost foolishness, letting the imagination of the heart run in an evil way. Soon violence and wickedness filled the earth: unredeemable. Beware of the direction of your thoughts!

Delight:   Genesis 6:11-13   Proverbs 15:14

Edna Holmes

# November 12

*"Confidence in an unfaithful man in time of trouble is like a broken tooth, and a foot out of joint."* Proverbs 25:19

You can't chew with a broken tooth. It hurts! It is useless to you. Likewise, you can't walk with a foot out of joint. Someone who turns out to be undependable in a time of crisis or trouble causes grief and misery. To be an absolutely faithful person when others depend on you in some way is a very good character trait. Such a one is of great worth in the service of the Lord, as well as appreciated by neighbors and friends.

We *count* on others to be faithful; our pastor will study and pray to be ready to preach and teach the Word of God to us.

The choir and music director will put in hours of practice to be ready to sing special music to honor the Lord in the worship service.

Blessed are those that clean the buildings faithfully.

Sunday School teachers must be faithfully ready for teaching. Those who fail to be faithful in the church work are indeed like broken teeth and a foot out of joint! It causes disorder and delays as others must hurriedly take care of the neglected responsibility.

*"Pastors' wives are usually ready for any kind of need which may crop up on Sunday. Many times, I've had to teach a SS class with no notice at all. A teacher is absent for some reason or quits on a whim...on Sunday morning! That happened once and I was handed a class to teach which lasted several months until another person volunteered to take it. It put more stress on me at the time, since I worked in every part of the music, which took lots of practice time, and drove our car out to pick up elderly women for every service, and also taught a Ladies Bible Study every Sunday evening. By God's grace He restored my attitude each time it got resentful. He enabled me to be faithful!*

Delight:   Psalms 31:23   Matthew 24:44-45

## November 13

*"...and there is no new thing under the sun."* Ecc.1:9

The verse following our text verse states, *"Is there anything thereof it may be said, See, this is new? it hath been already of old time, which was before us."* Ecclesiastes 1:10.

This may be a little baffling to those young in the faith, or those who don't read the Bible much. You will find that the more you read all the Bible, you can begin to connect the dots so that everything comes together in completeness. So, what does it mean that there is no new thing under the sun, when we have in each new generation numerous new inventions? We have mind-boggling new developments in technology every year. That's new, isn't it? Actually, no. It's just like God said in His Word, "...It hath been already of old time, which was before us."

When God created the earth, He created it *fully furnished.* All the fabulous discoveries of men on the top side of earth, in the earth, and in the atmosphere surrounding it, were there all the time. God allowed man to find it and utilize it for the needs of the inhabitants of this planet. God even allowed man to get as far in space as the moon, and they found nothing but a reflector of the sun's light on earth in the nighttime. They had to take life sustaining elements from earth to live while they were off the planet for a brief duration. Man is not going anywhere out in space, to live, without taking "earth" with him: air, water, food, human company. Only earth is suitable and perfect for man to inhabit. God made it that way in the beginning. No new thing under the sun!

Delight:   Job 28:1-2, 5   Genesis 1:1

Edna Holmes

# November 14

*"Truly the light is sweet, and a pleasant thing it is to behold the sun."* Ecclesiastes 11:7

We humans are greatly affected by the elements that rule our lives. The sun is the light in the little area of the vast universe where our planet is located. Planet Earth could not survive without all the unseen benefits the sun affords it, not to speak of the main thing, the light. It is the example we use in a comparison to Jesus, our Savior, who is the Light of the world of mankind. All souls are in spiritual darkness, without hope for eternal life, unless they come to the Light of the world, the Lord Jesus Christ.

Light affects us so; we can hardly do without it. In a rainy season which has cloudy, overcast days with no sunlight, many people fall into a gloomy mood which last until the light brightens the days again. As nature is our comparison to spiritual things in many ways, concerning the effect of sunlight on our outlook, our minds go to the way we are affected if we backslide ever so slightly from sweet fellowship with the Lord. We need His blessed presence and light more than we need anything else.

The Word of God is our sustaining element: spiritual food, water, joy and inward peace of mind. It is God talking to us. We need that. It prompts us to pray; that is talking to God. We need that! That is our power line to God. Stay faithful in those things and you will be encouraged with answered prayers! You will be thrilled at being close to the Lord. The devil will attack you daily to distract you from keeping that regular time at Jesus' feet; but stay faithful!

Delight:   John 1:1-4   John 1:14

## November 15

*"As newborn babes, desire the sincere milk of the word,
that ye may grow thereby."* I Peter 2:2

A sure sign that a sinner has trusted in Christ and been saved is his desire to read the Bible. If he cannot read, which in some cases has happened in past times, he will plead for someone to read it to him! His desire to know what God has spoken to him is so strong, he cannot rest until his soul is satisfied with that "milk of the word". That is the strongest desire a new Christian has. What happens to deter Christians from the book of books, God's Word?

Immediately, when a person trusts in Christ, the devil zeros in on him as a target. The spiritual warfare starts from that hour to keep a new Christian from being devoted to the Lord with the newborn fervor of first love. But if one is guided and taught to put the Lord first, no matter what, and stay faithful in reading God's Word, he is not likely to be defeated.

I cannot explain how crucial it is to know God's Word. It is our life! Yet, we let down the guard on our hearts, start being lazy about regular reading and study of the Bible. We only hurt ourselves, and others who depend on us for guidance, and it also grieves our Lord.

A noted scholar, commentator, made a most convicting statement. It stirred my heart. *"There is no wiser, no more knowledgeable being in the universe than the Author of the Bible. There is no more patient teacher than the Holy Spirit. The is no greater book than the Bible. There is no greater privilege this side of Heaven than to have a copy of the inspired Word of God. Yet we often let it gather dust."* Phillips.

The ignorance of Christians today about the Bible is truly appalling. Decide today to read the Bible more than anything else.

Delight:   Job 23:12   Proverbs 30:5

Edna Holmes

# November 16

*"For the time will come when they will not endure sound doctrine...having itching ears."* II Timothy 4:3

That time is on us full bloom. Never have we had so much "tickle itching ears" type of preaching. Isn't it a strange generation we live in as the clock of the universe is ticking away the day of grace? Now, everyone on earth can be saved if they only believe on the Lord Jesus Christ, and repent. But, sadly, hardly any, compared to the population of the earth, is being saved. They want, instead, to hear a watered-down message from the Bible which makes them feel good about themselves in their lost condition and tickles their ears. They are not concerned about where they will spend eternity.

On the contrary, when these same folks go to their doctors, they want to be told the absolute truth about their health condition of the body. They are being badly deceived by the devil, which will ultimately cause them to miss heaven and endure the unspeakable horror of eternity without Christ, eternal darkness and hell forever.

Christians oftentimes don't want to hear preaching that routs out their *secret sins* and brings conviction. When the Pastor touches on tithing, it offends those who don't obey God in that matter, and they leave in a huff. Social drinking and alcohol users do not like it if that subject comes into the message. Even mention of neglect of the Word of God can stir up a reaction, other than repentance! People want their ears *tickled* so they are not bothered when the Word is preached to them. If the Bible is preached, in its pure state, it will bring conviction to all our us. It is holy, and we are not!

Delight:    Hebrews 4:12    Jeremiah 23:29

Delighting in the Lord

# November 17

*"Acquaint now thyself with him, and be at peace: thereby good shall come unto thee."* Job 22:21

Through our Savior, Jesus, we have full access to God, but many never pursue a close acquaintance with Him. He seems very far off and so majestic we hesitate to pray like we know Him. We forfeit great peace by not learning of God and being comfortable in His presence. It comes freely to us through the Gift of salvation. Jesus paid all our sin debt, and now we can approach God. Let's consider one aspect of God's character and way toward His children which should melt our hearts, His *tenderness.*

God refers to earthly fathers so we will understand. A good father also pities his little children. The Bible tells us that God *pities us. There is love and tender feelings in pity.* We are not harshly judged the minute we succumb to temptation and sin. *"For he knoweth our frame; he remembereth that we are dust."* Psalm 103:13. God knows us through and through, and *pities* us in our human frailty, and loves us. The verse, following reveals the tenderness of God. *"Like as a father pitieth his children, so the Lord pitieth them that fear him."* v.14

Then there are mothers. *"As one whom his mother comforteth, so will I comfort you…"* Isaiah 66:13. No one can comfort like a mother. She can heal with a kiss, hug, or a word.

*In childhood, one of my brothers burned his hand. He was about five years old. While sitting on Mama's lap as she tended to it, his heart filled up with fear. He asked her in a trembling little voice, "Mama, am I going to die?" She looked at his hand thoughtfully, and said, "No, son, I think you are going to make it." He said he remembers the comfort and relief he felt at her words.*

God comforts and pities His little children…like a mother. He loves us so much. Can we not love Him back, and learn of Him?

Delight:   Psalm 103:17-18   Deuteronomy 6:5

Edna Holmes

# November 18

*"Keep thy heart with all diligence..."* Proverbs 4:23

We can't say enough about keeping our hearts. We should *work at it* and never let down our guard. The condition of the heart is also very discernable. *"A good man out of the good treasure of his heart bringeth forth that which is good; and an evil man out of the evil treasure of his heart bringeth forth that which is evil: for of the abundance of the heart his mouth speaketh."* Luke 6:45. **Listen!** We hear others verbally expressing themselves and instantly know a little, or a lot, about them from the content of their speaking. Jesus gave this exhortation to the people so they would know what is real and what is not.

Pretense in the matter of salvation will be exposed in time. Those who feed their relationship with Jesus, will have discernment and keener awareness of the true and false. I've met church members who were unsaved, and it was apparent. I could identify, because that was my case for many years. It's easy to learn the "language" of Christians, to an extent, and imitate prayers you hear. But the lost person, no matter where he is, always has an emptiness that won't go away. Only the new birth will fill the need of the heart. I finally saw it plainly when my husband was saved. He was totally changed, a new man, and I realized my heart had not been changed like his.

*"The great outlet of sin is the <u>tongue</u>; the great inlets of temptation are the <u>ear and the eye</u>; but of the whole body <u>the heart is the mistress</u>. Therefore, let <u>grace rule the heart</u>, and the whole man shall be subject."* Moody Bib. notes.

Obedience to God keeps the heart, by the Word and prayer. Listen to yourself speak; what are you hearing? Keep your heart!

Delight:   Matthew 6: 20-21   I Peter 3:15

Delighting in the Lord

# November 19

*"This is the day which the Lord hath made; we will rejoice and be glad in it."* Psalm 118:24

Every day is a golden opportunity. It is a new beginning of the rest of your life. In reference to Jacob's evaluation of his life when he was being introduced to Pharaoh by his son, Joseph, he mentions his length of life in days. *"And Pharaoh said unto Jacob, How old art thou? And Jacob said unto Pharaoh, the days of the years of my pilgrimage are a hundred and thirty years…"* Genesis 47:8-9. Jacob mentions the *days* before years because he must have marked them off eagerly when he worked seven years for Rachel to be his wife. The Bible says it seemed but a few days to Jacob, because of his love for her. That was some love!

Moses wrote Psalm 90 which has a reference to days: *"So teach us to number our days, that we may apply our hearts unto wisdom."* Psa. 90:12. Days are to be considered a very valuable segment of time in which we should accomplish all that God would have us do for His honor and glory on earth. We are wasting our life when we fritter away the days in careless neglect. I've done that at times and still regret the days I've wasted when they are so valuable. We learn by experience that to obey the Word of God brings more peace of mind and happiness to us than any other thing. We should use each day wisely as God intended. Start it right!

My best day starter is a "wake-up verse". If you only know one verse in the Bible, repeat it before you get out of bed, or as soon as your feet are on the floor. Say it aloud! Get God's Word in your head and heart before you start the day. Women have told me, that that one thing has changed their lives. You can tell a difference when you do or don't. Make it a rule of your life from now on.

Delight:   I Thessalonians 5:2   Ephesians 6:13

Edna Holmes

# November 20

*"Surely goodness and mercy shall follow me
all the days of my life..."* Psalm 23:6

They used to say in England, *"If a man walks, he must be poor. If he sometimes calls a cab, he is better off. If one footman rides behind him, he is rich. But if two footmen are back of his carriage, he must have a great inheritance."* God has no poor children; they all have a great inheritance; two footmen are always behind, *"Goodness and mercy shall follow me all the days of my life."* Moody.

We are timid about taking God's promises in His Word for what they are worth. You couldn't measure the worth of them by any earthly thing, such as gold or precious gems. Power generated by faith in His promises can turn the earth upside down in order to favor God's children. Miracles happen; that is a supernatural happening which is out of the realm of human capability. One such miracle happened on a foreign mission field.

*"A missionary's district, many decades ago, was suffering a state of famine; they helped the people with food until they had nothing left to give. He told the natives that God would hear and answer their prayers, and he led them in joining him for a prayer meeting every afternoon. So, they prayed. On the fourth day, he was called out of the prayer meeting to observe a dark cloud approaching and as it crossed the district, it rained heavily a deluge of little black seeds, so many they could be shoveled up in abundance. They were edible and such great supply, it sustained the people until harvest. It was later learned a storm had wrecked the storage place of this grain in Mongolia and carried the seed fifteen hundred miles to drop on the district of the praying Christians!* Treasures to Keep. EH

If we could only wrap our minds around the reality of the worth and great power in praying. God loves us, delights in us, but our own unbelief hinders us. Start anew today. Pray!

Delight:   I Thessalonians 5:17   Matthew 6:6

Delighting in the Lord

# November 21

*"Take thou away from me the noise of the songs; for
I will not hear the melody of thy viols."* Amos 5:23

There is a time when people should be repenting and turning to God, instead of singing to distract their hearts from the Holy Spirit's conviction of their lost condition. Lost people, especially unsaved church members, whose pride is a driving force that keeps them from turning to Christ for salvation, do various things to keep their thoughts from being serious when conviction is working in them.

They sing with gusto during the worship service, and during the invitation afterwards when the lost are invited to come to Christ.
At the same time, they may be hoping nobody comes on that "last verse opportunity" so it will be over soon. During the weekdays, the radio or TV is kept on so there is constant noise. They can't hear the voice of conviction in their hearts. People have invented many ways to resist the Holy Spirit calling them to repentance and salvation.

But here we see more clearly the great love of God, and His marvelous grace and mercy. He loved us from the foundation of the world. *"According as he hath chosen us in him before the foundation of the world, that we should be holy and without blame before him in love..."* Ephesians 1:4 These words are astounding to our hearts, and hard for us to grasp fully. But our God knows everything from the beginning to the end. How could He not? He is God. If you notice, it says that He chose us *in Christ* to be *holy and without blame* before Him in love. God would have those in Christ to become like Him. Transformed. Are you saved? Pray that you become more like Jesus.

Delight:   Romans 10:10   Ephesians 3:16-19

Edna Holmes

# November 22

*"Thou wilt keep him in perfect peace whose mind is stayed on thee…"* Isaiah 26:3

When you have tried and proven this verse of scripture, you will claim it as your own comforter for life. It never fails to calm your mind when you normally would be at the height of worry. When you rivet your thoughts on the Lord Jesus, worry goes out the window!

What do we think about as we focus on Jesus? First, we should meditate awhile on who He is. He is the only begotten Son of God, and God the Son. Jesus said, *"I and my Father are one."* John 10:30 So, Jesus was God dwelling temporarily in a body of flesh. He chose to humble Himself in that way so that He could die for our sins.

Next, give thought to the love He has for us. No love on earth has ever been so pure and deep as the Lord's love for us. So much, in fact, that He would die the most horrific death, enduring torture at the hands of the experts, the Roman soldiers. Think about that love.

Think on the twenty-third Psalm which tells of the Lord's care for us in all facets of our lives. If you memorize that short psalm, it gives you an edge for you can "read" it from memory to yourself. I love to do that and meditate on each verse.

Our text verse has kept me from worrying myself sick at times, especially when my husband had his open-heart surgery. I was afraid he would have a heart attack BEFORE the surgery could be done the next day. I ran that verse through my mind like a ticker tape in the night until I fell asleep with blessed relief from fear and anxiety. I've shared that blessed promise with many since then. Try it!

Delight:     Galatians 5:2     I Peter 1:18-19

Delighting in the Lord

# November 23

*"For thou wilt light my candle: the Lord my God will enlighten my darkness."* Psalm 18:28

How does the Lord light my candle? Man is made up of three components. <u>His spirit</u> is the door by which the Spirit of God enters and takes up His abode at the moment of the new birth. The <u>soul of man</u> relates to others, as it is the seat of the mind, emotions and will. Then <u>the body,</u> which holds the man, relates to the environment or has world-consciousness. When God lights my candle, He enlightens my darkness. *"Who hath delivered us from the power of darkness, and hath translated us into the kingdom of his dear Son..."* Re: Col.1:13 That's when the darkness goes out and the Light comes in at the moment of salvation. The Holy Spirit abides with our spirit in us.

Our enlightened spirit is the candle of the Lord by which He searches us. What is He looking for? *The things which must be removed so that we can grow spiritually.* The Lord already knows what is there in the depths of us, the search is NOT for His information. It is for ours so that we will realize there are hidden things in us that need to be gotten out and left behind.

God wants us to face the truth and then be wise and act on it. Psa. 51:6 *"Behold, thou desirest truth in the inward parts: and in the hidden part thou shalt make me to know wisdom."* Some of the hidden things are; pride, greed, stubbornness, desire to control others, spirit of revenge, independence, unforgiving attitude, anger etc. You know these things are sins, and they hinder us when they linger in our hearts. God shows us that and moves us to do a heart cleaning. God is merciful and loving; should we not love Him back, and obey Him?

Delight:    Psalm 27:1    Psalm 139:23-24

Edna Holmes

# November 24

*"A true witness delivereth souls: but a deceitful witness speaketh lies."* Proverbs 14:25

Christians only can be witnesses for the Lord, for they know Him personally. They have experienced salvation. They want other souls to be saved. Therefore, in various ways, soul winners reach out and witness to lost sinners. Some are bold in their witness for Christ, while others may be timid and shy. Some of the latter kind have won people who then reached untold numbers of souls for the Lord. In his great exposition of the book of Acts, Dr. Criswell relates some facts about the influence people wield as they endeavor to win souls to Christ, though they themselves are never known in the world.

*"A woman, whose name has been forgotten, gave a tract one day to a very bad man, Richard Baxter, who read it and was converted. Then Baxter wrote a book, The Call of the Unconverted, which brought a multitude to God, among them Philip Doddridge, who in turn wrote a book, The Rise and Progress of Religion. This book brought tens of thousands into the kingdom, among them, William Wilberforce. He wrote a Practical View of Christianity, which brought a multitude to Christ, among them being Leigh Richmond, who wrote a tract, "The Dairyman's Daughter, which has been the means of salvation for untold multitudes. Look how that began. A woman, whose name is forgotten, gave a tract one day to a very bad man, and the influence goes on and on. A man does not know what he does when he does something good for Jesus, speaking a word in His name, sowing the seed of the Word of God.*

Keep some tracts in your purse, or pocket and *ask God* to nudge you when He wants you to give one to a person or leave one somewhere. The Word of God has such power to save. Sow it! Selah.

Delight:   Psalm 126:6   Psalm 89:26

## November 25

*"Casting down imaginations, and every high thing that exalteth itself..."* II Corinthians 10:5

Not enough can be said about vain imaginations, and their detriment to our spiritual welfare. I have had to battle them through the years. I learned right away that it is a lethal weapon the devil uses a lot to distract those who are serving the Lord.

Vain imaginations can start with needing an "escape", a kind of mental vacation, so to speak to relax. Whatever is imagined in a brief period of time usually disintegrates *unless* we revisit the mental "website" and add additional thoughts to the same plot. That makes it stronger, and each time, if more imaginations are added, it soon becomes a stronghold which the devil rules, tempting us then to indulge the vain thoughts which continually will call to us and distract from faithfulness and the truth of God's Word.

Strongholds can be constructed by thoughts of bitterness, jealousy, envy, pride, anger and other evil attitudes of mind which people so easily fall prey to. All will fail the test of God's Word as how to think. God tells us how to think in Philippians 4:8. Read that carefully, and you will see the first condition is "whatsoever things are true". That rules out vain imaginations, for none of them are true! Vain means *empty, worthless, foolish: of no value or importance.* Imagination is the power of forming pictures in the mind of things that are not present to the senses. The danger in indulging such is that vain imaginations stir emotions into action. In that way, the devil can have great sway over our lives. Make a copy of Philippians 4:8 and put it in your private part of your home. Make it your guide every day.

Delight:   Hebrews 4:12   Proverbs 24:9

Edna Holmes

# November 26

*"...if there be an virtue, and if there be an praise,  
think on these things."* Philippians 4:8

Other than pure, right thinking, the thoughts come under the category of *vain imaginations.* Our thoughts are building material for strongholds in the mind. The devil gathers our vain thoughts and makes a fortress for him to rule and attack us daily.

The truth of God's Word will destroy every vain thing lodged in our hearts, if we will use the weapon. Hebrews 4:12 describes the nature of God's Word. *"For the word of God is quick, and powerful, and sharper than any two-edged sword, piercing even to the dividing asunder of soul and spirit, and of the joints and marrow, and is a discerner of the thoughts and intents of the heart."* Every stronghold that has ever lodged in my mind and heart has been torn down by the power in the Word of God. When I put renewed effort in reading and study of the scriptures, the walls began to crumble! We must keep Jesus the priority in our thoughts and reject the foolishness that constantly invades our thinking. Some strongholds are light, even silly, to others who are not struggling with it; but it can be a life of misery for the afflicted one.

*My husband's mother was deathly afraid of weather, even a gentle rain! She would walk the floor, wringing her hands, and kept close to anyone in the house with her. She always imagined it could turn into a destructive storm. She had added to that stronghold in her mind all her life from her childhood, so that fear was embedded firmly in her heart.*

Many Christians are plagued by vain imaginations, thoughts that waste time which they could be using in useful service. Use God's Word to stay out of that trap.

Delight:   II Corinthians 10:4-5   II Corinthians 4:15-16

Delighting in the Lord

# November 27

*"One dies in his full strength, being wholly at ease and quiet...
And another dies in the bitterness of his soul, and never eats
in pleasure." Job 21:23, 25*

    This describes the difference in a man who would not give up the bitterness of soul in forgiving others in his life, and one who kept a clean slate by confessing his sins and practicing forgiveness as necessary for peace and harmony in his life. Forgiveness is a source of emotional health and freedom. It has the power to set us free from the hurts of the past, whether it was ten minutes ago, or ten years ago. Well, what exactly is forgiveness, and how do I do it?

    FORGIVENESS is an act of our will in which we give up the right to hold another person accountable for the wrongs they have done to us. It means releasing that person from any obligation to ever make things right to me. In other words, turn it all over to God and let Him deal with it and be the Judge. After that transaction is done, when the same thoughts begin to invade our minds, we just tell the devil that we have turned it over to God, and He has forgiven us. We claim the Word of God and its protection. *"Submit yourselves therefore to God. Resist the devil, and he will flee from you."* James 4:7

    Obey the Lord in everything. Stay close to Him in fellowship and worship. Speak or sing His praise every day. Satan will flee from it. Put that to the test, and you will be pleasantly surprised that it is so. God's Word makes us willing to forgive and ask for forgiveness when it is necessary for us to do to be right with the Lord, and others.

Delight:    Romans 12:17-19    John 13:34-35

Edna Holmes

# November 28

*"I rejoice at thy word, as one that findeth great spoil."* Psalm 119:162

It is the treasures of knowledge in His Word that acquaints us with the person of Christ. It means spiritual growth which is invaluable to us. Finding out more about God, and our Savior Jesus Christ is done by reading the Bible. Consider how we pursue books in our interest realm. We should pray that God would put that kind of fervor in our hearts for His own Word.

I love the start of every New Year on the calendar. In that new beginning, I start through the Bible anew, making notes and learning new things as God reveals His Word and will to me as I read and study. Do we understand that the Word of God is His will? When we obey it, we are doing the will of God! To obey it in all the decisions of our lives will keep us firmly established in God's will and ways. *"Therefore be ye not unwise, but understanding what the will of the Lord is."* Ephesians 5:17. We are very unwise if we neglect to read and nourish our souls with the Word of God.

A word of exhortation, by a noted commentator, expresses the folly of Christians. *"Surely it is the height of stupidity to have in one's hand the very Word of the living God—inbreathed by the omniscient, all-wise Creator of the universe—and neglect to read it, study it, memorize it, and obey it! The angels must look at our foolishness in astonishment. We invest time and money to sit at the feet of those we consider to be learned. We buy their books, attend their lectures, apply our minds to master what they have to say. But we neglect our Bibles. What folly! What an exposure of our warped sense of values!* Phillips

Delight:   Psalm 119:130   I John 2:5

Delighting in the Lord

# November 29

*"And this is eternal life, that they may know thee the only true God, and Jesus Christ..."* John 17:3

For many years I can truthfully say that I believed the Bible was God's divine Word. I believed God was the only true God, that Jesus was the only begotten Son of God, that he died for sinners, that He was resurrected from the grave after three days, and He saved sinners. I thought people must be downright heathens not to believe those basic things about God. *But I was not saved!*

What was my problem? I joined the church as a child, knowing nothing of what the Bible said about salvation, and was in an ignorant state for many years as a good church member. I was not aware of my lost condition in reality until I witnessed the change in my husband's life and attitude when he was saved. The immediate change in him, especially with his instant love and interest in the Word of God, turned a light on in my heart. I *knew* my husband had experienced a change in his heart and soul that I did not receive when I "joined the church." Conviction started in me and lasted for some time before I had to humble myself and admit I was a lost sinner in need of salvation through the Lord Jesus Christ. I asked Jesus to save me. He did!

I tell this often because there are many others just as I was. They are lost and ignorant of it, or thy know it and are held by pride from confessing the need of salvation and coming to the Lord. Being raised in the church, being taught good morals, and upright living, makes you resemble a Christian, but nothing but the blood of Jesus Christ can wash away your sins and make you genuine, with your name recorded in heaven as a child of God. Selah...

Delight:    Romans 10:9-10    John 3:36

Edna Holmes

# November 30

*"This is the work of God that ye believe on
him whom he hath sent."* John 6:29

The people had asked the Lord what they could do to "work the works of God." Our text verse is His answer. "This is the work of God, that ye believe on him whom he hath sent." The people must have been amazed. They couldn't imagine how worthless their works for salvation would be. God made it so simple for us poor lost sinners. Not one should miss heaven. He gave Jesus as a sacrifice for our sins. We believe on Him!

*"Not by works of righteousness which we have done, but according to his mercy he saved us..."* Titus 3:5

The *works of God* as we think of it flows from "the work of God". All the commandments of the Lord in His Word are ours to obey and by that demonstrate the works of God as we serve Him on earth as His ambassadors. We are witnesses of our Savior, telling the lost sinners of God's work: that they believe on Him Whom He hath sent. God says we are "letters" which the world is reading. *"Ye are our epistle written in our hearts, known and read of all men."* "I Cor.3:2

The world reads us. Christians are an oddity to unbelievers; so, they watch our behavior and "read" us daily. Prepare *before* you leave the house each day to be read like a newspaper, praise God, have a song on your lips, and express thanksgiving for salvation.

*Once I was fretting with impatience waiting to check out at a store. At my turn, the clerk said so sweetly, "The Lord will bless you for being patient." The Lord rebuked me through her mouth! I repented that moment of the hidden sin in my heart. Soon it would have been on the front page.*

Delight:   Titus 3:8   John 6:40

## December 1

*"For unto us a child is born, unto us a
son is given..."* Isaiah 9:6

We are entering into one of the most hectic months of the year. Through the centuries, the month of Christmas has had traditions added, and now it is the world's most romanticized time of the year. Only Christians hold to honoring Christ in all the hassle, some in sincerity and truth, and some for tradition. We hardly understand the Lord's birth and the surrounding events that accompanied it. Many prophesies were fulfilled at that time, but few realized it. But the fact remains that the Eternal Son of God entered this world that cold dark night through the womb of a virgin, grew up among men as the Son of man, and ultimately gave Himself as a sacrifice for man's sin to save all that will put their trust in Him as their personal Savior.

The tradition of exchanging gifts with one another evolved, which actually adds stress to Christmas time. People get into a rut with the expected gift exchange, and they don't know how to get out of it.

*My husband and I often speak of the differences in now and our childhood so many decades ago. Our families were poor just coming out of the Great Depression. No one expected a pile of gifts! If we got one item, we were thrilled. The biggest treat was the big bowls or pans of fruit appearing under the tree on Christmas morning. We had no citrus fruit during the year, but Christmas was special! To this day, when I peel an orange, the smell takes me back in memory to those mornings, getting out of bed, and running to the tree for that fruit and candy on Christmas Day.*

Delight:   Luke 1:30-33   John 1:14

Edna Holmes

# December 2

*"He that trusteth in his own heart is a fool: but whoso walketh wisely, he shall be delivered."* Proverbs 28:6

This is another promise in God's Word which is often overlooked as a source of help. Most Christians, I would think, know that if we trust in our own hearts, we will make unwise decisions. Remember this advice to us; it is my mainstay: *"Trust in the Lord with all thine heart; and lean not unto thine own understanding. In all thy ways acknowledge him, and he shall direct thy path."* Proverbs 3:5-6.

We can't pry our way out of troubles, think our way out of difficulty, or scheme to make solutions fall into place. We desperately need the wisdom that comes from above...from God Himself.

When strongholds build up in our minds, and habits take roots, refusing to loose the stranglehold they have on us, *we need to be delivered, but how?* He tells us in our text verse: Trust in God, not in your own heart; walk wisely by asking for and living in the light of God's wisdom. James 1:5 tells us: *"If any of you lack wisdom, let him ask of God, that giveth to all men liberally, and upbraideth not; and it shall be given him."* That is so clear.

How do we know when we are on target, and walking wisely? If you obey the Bible, you are wise. If God's Word be your guide *in everything; you are wise.* The Ten Commandments will give us a powerful guide to follow. "Thou shalt not bear false witness..." that is, don't lie! Don't bend the truth, twist it, or otherwise make it out to be what it is not: *a lie!* Determine to be wise, today.

Delight:   Colossians 2:2-3   Hosea 14:9   Matthew 7:24

Delighting in the Lord

# December 3

*"Looking unto Jesus, the author and finisher of our faith..."* Hebrews 12:2

Jesus suffered such agony and shame in dying on the cross. His body was human flesh just like ours. He suffered every moment as He was tortured to death to pay for our sins, and when it was done, He said, "It is finished" and dismissed His Spirit from that broken body. He did it for love; He showed us how much He loves us. He did it for the joy that was set before Him: souls would be saved! Also, Jesus would go back to His Father in heaven.

Salvation in Christ, the new birth, settles your destiny for all eternity. Fellowship with God settles the issues of life, as in Proverbs. *"Keep thy heart with all diligence, for out of it are the issues of life."* Little or no fellowship with the Lord will deplete your peace and joy. How quickly the doldrums of backsliding come on us when we neglect the Word of God! If you belong to the Lord, you will never be happy without staying in fellowship with Him.

What does that mean, fellowship with Jesus? Essentially, it is the same thing as our fellowship with our brothers and sisters, the church. We love to talk to them when we meet to worship the Lord, and occasionally we have special events after the services where we eat together, and interact with each other, delighting in the company.

In fellowship with the Lord, we meet with Him every day at a set time if possible. We read His Word and He speaks to our hearts; we speak to Him in prayer, and the Bible tells us the Lord *"delights in the prayers of his saints."* Proverbs 15:8. Give time to meditate on that amazing fact: <u>*Jesus loves to hear us talk to Him*</u>. Don't neglect Him; delight Him!

Delight:    Psalm 100    Psalm 103:17-18

Edna Holmes

# December 4

*"He is not here: for he is risen, as he said.
Come see the place where the Lord lay."* Matt.28:6

We have a friend whose son died several decades ago. She was so grieved, she and her husband moved into a place where she can actually see the cemetery from a window and the grave where their son is buried. It has been a comfort to her through the years.

We should always be in the place of spiritual health whereby faith we can see the empty tomb of the Lord Jesus, our Savior. It is our assurance of heaven because we must believe in the resurrection of Jesus to be saved. Christians have a *living* Savior!

We are to *meditate* on the things of God, always reading the Bible, then thinking on it until we "digest" what we have taken in. One thing to give meditation time to is the wonder of the empty tomb of Jesus. Think on that! God raised Him from the dead just as He said He would. Jesus actually got up and walked out of the tomb with all power given to Him in heaven, and earth! What a Savior!

Beside the empty tomb, we should meditate continually on the unfathomable love that Jesus has for us. How could He love us so? We are unworthy of His love, His blessings, and His extreme care for us in minute details. I like to read Matthew Ch. 6, where Jesus tells us of His attention to the details of our needs. *"Therefore take no thought, saying, What shall we eat? or, what shall we drink? or, Wherewithal shall we be clothed?...for your heavenly Father knoweth that ye have need of all these things."* Matt. 6:31-32. Of course, we do think of the fact of these earthly needs, but we are not to *fret* as though we might starve or need necessary clothing. The Lord said He is aware of everything and He cares for us. Such love!

Delight:     Matthew 6:33     Matthew 7:11

Delighting in the Lord

# December 5

*"The wicked flee when no man pursueth ; but the righteous are bold as a lion."* Proverbs 28:1

Our conscience is a very strong part of our makeup. It houses the knowledge of right and wrong, with the tendency toward the right. If we violate our conscience, we have guilt feelings. Having sin registered in the conscience weakens us spiritually. Sin is *wicked*, no matter where, or how we attempt to conceal it. A *clear* conscience makes one bold to stand for what's right with strength.

I read of a great lady, a missionary, who was managing a girl's home in China in the days when Japan invaded that country. The soldiers were marching in devastating the country and ravishing the women as invading enemies usually do. Bertha Smith met them as they came marching up the lane to her girls' home. She spoke boldly with authority, telling them to leave the premises for it was a Christian girls' home. Her boldness and confidence could only have been in the strength of the Lord God Almighty. The soldiers turned and left without a word.

But most Christians are not "bold as a lion" because there are little things that they have done sometime in the past that is still a blot on their conscience. People slow down when they see a policeman on the highway! Why is that? We all have disobeyed a traffic law of some kind. The conscience reminds us when the "law" is in sight.

The only way we can keep our consciences clear is by taking account at the end of each day, asking the Lord to search our hearts and convict us of sin present in us, so we may confess and forsake it. Take a *spiritual bath* before retiring for the night as you may take your daily bath at night to be ready for the next day. Start the next morning with a *wake-up* verse as you get up and sing while you get ready for the day! You please the Lord and defeat the devil at once.

Delight:    Psalm 51    Psalm 139:23-24

Edna Holmes

# December 6

*"Let the word of Christ dwell in you richly
in all wisdom..."* Colossians 3:16

To be obedient to this verse, we have to *practice* faithfully each day in order to be skilled in taking in the Word of God. Yes, practice! Anything we do well is achieved by consistently practicing. Mostly, we think of musical instruments or singing; but in fact, it is anything we want to excel at for some purpose.

The great pianist, Rubenstein, once said, *"If I omit practice one day, I notice it; if two days, my friends notice it; if three days, the public notice it."* It is the very same way for a Christian in his zeal and determination to learn the Word of God. In his daily fellowship with God, he is *keeping his heart with all diligence. (Proverbs 4:23)* It shows up in his life if he starts skipping practice!

I know from experience, when I neglect a day of fellowship with the Lord, I notice it. I have a vague feeling of dissatisfaction, and diminished peace of mind. If I miss two days of quiet time with the Lord, others can tell there is something "not right" about me. I'm not happy as usual. It is probably because my guilty conscience is working me over and it's troubling.

Three days of missing *practicing* sweet fellowship with the Lord, feeding on His Word, and praying to Him, will affect your life and mine more than we would think. Then, the people that see us on a daily basis, will notice a different frame of mind showing up in conversation, and they do not know we discontinued faithful *practice.* They may just suppose we have backed away from our Christian profession of salvation. God forbid that we give such impression! Stay in practice!

Delight:   Acts 17:11   I John 5:13

## December 7

*"In everything give thanks: for this is the will of God in Christ Jesus concerning you."* I Thessalonians 5:18

Our nation was suddenly plunged into World War II when Japan attacked Pearl Harbor in Hawaii on this day in the year 1941. My father sat in our front yard visiting with relatives that Sunday afternoon. Our older sister came out crying and said she just heard on the radio that the Japanese had bombed Pearl Harbor. All the able-bodied men went to town the next day to volunteer to go "whup-um!" But they didn't take the farmers who stayed by the stuff at home and did their part by raising food and other things needful to sustain the country throughout the war years.

While the country was *in that war*, certainly, no one was thanking God for it. But *in it,* there were many praying and thanking God for His blessings poured out on this nation during very difficult times. This verse is misquoted by Christians. They will cite it as saying "for all things give thanks"; where obviously it does not say that. In, and for, are two different words and meanings.

Our nation and its allies won that war. Our God is Sovereign over the world. He decides who will be in power, not man with his schemes of aggression. *"For promotion cometh neither from the east, nor from the west, nor from the south, But God is the judge: he putteth down one, and setteth up another."* Psalm 75:6-7

We all have trials and troubles in life; no one is exempt in this world. In all things, the Lord says in His Word to give thanks. While it is happening to us...*give thanks!* Thanksgiving is like medicine; it has a healing touch to it. And remember, the Lord is worthy!

Delight:    Proverbs 3:5-6    Psalm 96

Edna Holmes

# December 8

*"...Forasmuch as this people draw near me with their mouth, and with their lips do honour me, but have removed their heart far from me..."* Isaiah 29:13

Recently, a church we know had its piano tuned. It had been neglected for many years, and though the need was obvious, the congregation didn't notice anything wrong with it. It had gradually become out of tune, and their ears had become accustomed to the sound of off-pitch notes being played. That's the case at times. The church offers up singing in worship accompanied by an instrument badly out of tune. The Lord mercifully listens to that discord.

Worse, we worship God in His house with our hearts out of tune and think nothing of how we dishonor our Lord. Sin causes discord in our lives and deceives us to the condition of our hearts: *badly out of tune!* We may muddle through for a while, but the Holy Spirit will one day stop us in our tracks and give us a "heart cleaning" to get us right with the Lord. *"He that covereth his sins shall not prosper: but whoso confesseth and forsaketh them shall have mercy."* Proverbs 28:13

After a heart cleaning with the Word, be consistent, or the enemy will come back. When you do spring cleaning and rid your house of dust-catching clutter, clean surfaces appear. Soon, we fill them up again, with *stuff.* Just so, when we get serious with and ask the Lord to give us a heart-cleaning, He will do it. The devil sees the Christian has a clean orderly heart; he works to get the trash of sin back in. We must keep a guard posted.

*Once when an old attitude was trying to get back in my heart, I left my Bible open on the nightstand at night after I'd read it. It gave* me comfort, and I *knew the devil was afraid of its power! We must exercise simple faith.*

Delight:     Psalm 95:1     Psalm 149:1

Delighting in the Lord

# December 9

*"For whosoever shall call upon the name of the Lord shall be saved."* Romans 10:13

On this day, decades ago, my husband trusted in the Lord Jesus Christ for time and eternity. It was very obvious in the following days and weeks that he had experienced a "new birth." As a good conscientious church member, I had diligently urged and pushed him to go to church with me, and when he did, the gospel messages he heard took root in his heart. The changes in him were so obvious, even though he was a "good" man before he was saved, in fact exemplary as a husband and father. But spiritual life in him made a different life altogether.

It didn't take long for the realization of the difference in "joining the church" and real conversion to Christ to make an impression on my heart. One night as I was watching him eagerly reading the Bible, marking almost every line of it as he pored over it, something registered in my heart, clearly. I didn't want to admit it, but I was lost! He had something new in his heart that I did not get when I joined the church at nine years of age. I struggled along three years with that knowledge, yet my pride and self-righteousness kept me back from salvation. Finally, God took hold of my heart and didn't let go until I confessed my need to be saved, and I experienced the same change that my husband did, on this date long ago. I began to eagerly pursue the Word of God, desiring to learn all I could about the Lord Himself. I simply could not understand it before and was not really interested. *Christ makes a difference!* Examine your self today. Do you like to read the Bible? Do you love to go to church? Is Jesus real to you...in your heart? Answer truthfully; *you will know.*

Delight:   Romans 10:9-10   Romans 6:23

Edna Holmes

# December 10

*"Confidence in an unfaithful man in time of trouble is like a broken tooth and foot out of joint."* Proverbs 2519

We share one more thought about this verse with its strong admonition to be faithful in this world. Most people learn this truth soon as they start life's journey as adults. It is very disconcerting to learn by experience that misplaced trust in another will be grievous when it's found out. Trouble comes and instead of helping, your most trusted friend forsakes you. That causes pain like a broken tooth and a foot out of joint! In our fickle world today, that scenario happens too often. Both love and dependability are shallow in this generation. We would be wise to always put our trust and expectation in the Lord first of all. He will never forsake us in time of trouble.

*"My soul, wait thou only upon God; for my expectation is from him."* Psalm 62:5.

We can't trust our own hearts, and it is most unwise to wholly trust another's heart as well. Remember Peter's confidence in his faithfulness to the Lord? He told the Lord he would lay down his life for Him. Jesus told Peter that he would, that very night, deny Him three times! Peter did, and he went out and wept bitterly.

Peter was the boldest and staunchest in the faith, yet, he denied that he even knew the Lord Jesus in a moment of testing. He was trusting in himself to remain faithful and dependable. He learned a hard lesson. *"He that trusteth in his own heart is a fool..."* Proverbs 28:26. There is only one whose Word never fails to be true. That is Jesus, the Lord. Take comfort in reading His Words. It is a mirror to see yourself in the true light. Correct the flaws. The Lord will deal with the ugliness of sin in all our lives.

Delight:   Luke 17:5    I Thessalonians 5:24

Delighting in the Lord

# December 11

*"And about the time of forty years suffered he their manners in the wilderness."* Acts 13:18

Can you imagine human beings being rude to God? The Israelites were so bad with their manners when they immediately began to charge God and Moses foolishly about water, food, and their very lives. They said to Moses and Aaron, *"for ye have brought us forth into this wilderness, to kill this whole assembly with hunger."* Exodus 16:3. What a terrible charge indirectly to God through Moses and Aaron. The people had just witnessed a few weeks before, how God divided the Red Sea and the people passed through on dry ground. They even sung a victorious song of praise to God at that time. Now they are complaining!

God gave them manna for forty years. It appeared each morning for the Israelites to gather. He furnished meat. He furnished water; it came gushing from a rock! It *followed* them! I Corinthians 10:4 tells us that the Rock was Christ! *"...for they drank of that spiritual Rock that followed them: and that Rock was Christ."* They even took that for granted as they did the other miracles that God performed in providing for them.

*Daily, He loads us with benefits.* Re: Psa.68:19. Are we grateful? I urge ladies to get a spiral notebook for listing blessings. Of the benefits He gives us each day, could we not name a few, even one? Counting blessings and thanking the Lord is one sure way to keep happiness fresh and vibrant in your heart. Depression may be nagging at you, trying to get a hold; get your pen and write down blessings, from salvation on. God is worthy of our praise. Write it; speak it; sing it! Just do it, and you will see what a great benefit it shall be to you.

Delight:    Isaiah 61:3    Psalm 150

Edna Holmes

# December 12

*"Wherefore come out from among them, and be ye
separate, saith the Lord..."* II Cor. 6:17

This chapter in the Bible has several warning verses for Christians concerning friendship with the world, or those outside of Christ and the church. The flesh loves to be out there in the world; it is comfortable. It is the presence of the Spirit of God which controls the flesh. We must totally surrender to the Lord. We must be committed, or the world can too easily draw us away. We will stay too long in it, and our feet will be stuck on that wayward path, and we can't free ourselves. We will be weaker, spiritually. Christians may not intend to linger in the world, but the devil can trap them easily.

*On the farm, it was one of those strange winter weather days, when a "Norther" or cold north wind blows in and changes 40-degree weather into 25-degree freezing rain in a matter of minutes. We were doing the evening chores in the barn when the freezing weather hit, so we hurriedly secured the animals in their places, and scattered the flock of ducks so they would fly to their roosting shed. All of them did except one; he perched on the fence and refused to leave, even though the freezing rain was covering his feathers and his feet. We soon gave up on him and hurried out of the cold into the house. The next morning the ground was covered with a thick coating of ice. As Dad, my brothers and I approached the gate, we noticed the duck still on the fence, his feet frozen solid to it. He was flapping his wings, frantically trying to escape the icy trap. With the duck resisting, we broke the ice from his feet and took him to the safety of the roosting shed, out of the weather. Dad said of the duck frozen to the fence all night: "He just stayed too long."* From <u>Every Single Day</u> by Max Holt.

We stay too long in tempting situations. We feel strong and confident. Mistake! Roost in Proverbs 3:5-6. It's safe there.

Delight:   I Corinthians 10:13    II Corinthians 6:14

Delighting in the Lord

# December 13

*"For the wages of sin is death; but the gift of God is eternal life through Jesus Christ our Lord."* Romans 6:23

In walking recently, I noticed a tree full of mistletoe near the road. The tree was rather scraggly compared to others around it. There was a reason. Mistletoe is a parasite; it attaches to and feeds off the life in the host tree. It slowly multiplies and spreads and will eventually kill the tree.

People don't think of mistletoe being a killer. It is pretty and has tradition attached to it. At Christmas time, some folks will decorate with it, tying little clusters of mistletoe with ribbon and suspending it over head. If a lady walks under it, she forfeits a kiss!

One can't help but think of sin as a comparison. Sin can look pretty, but it is a killer! Many people are brought low by the deceitfulness of sin. Families, and churches are destroyed. It will rob the heart of good fruit the Holy Spirit develops there, leaving it destitute of joy. Like mistletoe, sin attaches and slowly destroys.

The gospel of Jesus Christ will free a sinner from the sin that binds him. By the same way, a Christian caught in the web of sin can be freed. *"If we confess our sins, he is faithful and just to forgive us our sins, and to cleanse us from all unrighteousness."* I John 1:9. Don't wait if sin is draining you of peace and victory in your life. Tell Jesus! He is the only One who can beat the devil, forgive sin, and restore the joy of your salvation. Avoid the *mistletoe* effect of sin in your life. Confess and forsake it immediately!

Delight:   I John 2:15:16    Proverbs 28:13

Edna Holmes

# December 14

*"...written with the finger of God..."* Exodus 31:18

Only God could write in stone with His finger! That is how He wrote the Ten Commandments which he put in Moses' hands to take down to the children of Israel. Moses had been upon Mount Sinai for many days receiving instructions from God Himself. Then Moses came down with the greatest treasure one could imagine for the people. *"And he gave unto Moses, when he had made an end of communing with him upon mount Sinai, two tables of testimony, tables of stone, written with the finger of God."* Exodus 31:18.

At the foot of the mountain, Moses found the people engaged in worshipping a golden calf...Egypt's god! Abomination! It was a deplorable scene for Moses who had just spent days with Almighty God, the God of Israel. Read the following chapters to find out the reckoning for the sins of the people and Moses' powerful intercession on their behalf. *Exodus, chapters 32, 33, 34.*

The Ten Commandments is the source of the code of moral and civil behavior of mankind on earth. Peoples and nations may claim it as their own, but all good comes from God; man cannot bring such holy things out of himself and his thinking.

We live with the results of the Ten Commandments taken out of public view, including schools, monuments, and public places where they used to be displayed. The Ten Commandments are like a hammer that hits the conscience of those reading them. This generation hates them; men are bent on evil and do not want to be reminded of God in any way, but they cannot destroy this powerful document. The Ten Commandments are settled in heaven in God's Word...forever.

Delight:   Psalm 119:89   Exodus 20:1-17

## December 15

*"For the Son of man is come to seek and
to save that which was lost."* Luke 19:10

What was lost? The souls of men. Jesus must seek them for men are not going to come to the Savior without the Holy Spirit of God first stirring the truth of their need into their hearts. Conviction, we call it. Without conviction, there will be no salvation. Before Christ seeks him, a sinner is *dead in trespasses and sin.* He has no love for God, no interest in His Word, and no power to make himself a "Christian."

Before I was saved, I'd been a church member many years. I learned little tidbits of the Bible and would argue with others about things I knew nothing about. Later, when I was in a situation where the only book in the house was a Bible, it was obvious to me how totally disinterested I was in it. We'd lost all our possessions in a house fire, escaping with only the clothes we were wearing at the time. Afterwards, we had nothing but bare necessities. Someone gave us a Bible! We were not Christians; so, it was sadly neglected. I tried reading it, but it had no pictures or anything to draw me into it. I was lost! The riches in that Bible were buried too deep for me to see until Jesus sought me out and brought me to admit I was lost and needed His salvation. How thankful I am for the love, grace and mercy Jesus has for lost sinners!

After salvation, a Christian won't grasp every word of the Bible at first but understanding comes with consistent reading. It is a deep, deep mine of riches which cannot be exhausted. Just read it! You will learn and grow spiritually; it is your life!

Delight:    Psalm 119:18    Hebrews 4:12

Edna Holmes

# December 16

*"Train up a child in the way he should go…"*
Proverbs 22:6

At this time of year, the malls are teeming with women shopping for Christmas, usually accompanied by their little children. Occasionally, you hear an announcement from the loudspeaker that a child is lost, and the frantic effort to reunite mother and child gets underway. You may also hear the cries of a child that realizes it has lost sight of its mother in the crowd. Sometimes it is unavoidable, but more often the case is a lack of training like the Bible speaks of. A child has to be trained! Children will not grow up on their own and automatically have the habits and ways that must be taught to them.

Teaching your children to obey you is the most valuable thing you can do for them. They are more secure and feel loved when they know their parents will not allow them the "freedom" to disobey. There must be *fences* around your children, and as they will surely try the fence once in a while to see if it will "hold", then discipline needs to be exercised to keep them assured of your love and authority. When a child is trained to obey, he is much safer in all situations. I've seen a mother with children in public, shopping, and her offspring are clustered around her holding to the shopping cart! That was her orders in the store. Then I've seen the same scene where the mother can hardly shop for yelling at straying kids, and pulling them off the shelves, or stop them running in the aisles! Training!

We fare much better in life when we simply obey the Word of God. People are so easily misled by books and magazines touting the way to raise their children. Better to listen to God. Men are so foolish who think they can go around God and come out better. Mistake!

Delight:   Proverbs 29:15    Proverbs 22:15

Delighting in the Lord

# December 17

*"Train up a child..."* Proverbs 22:6

It is vitally important that children *are taught* to respect authority and obey their parents. If they *do not learn that*, grief is going to pile up and cause much suffering in the family, especially of parents. The Bible says: *"A wise son maketh a glad father: but a foolish son is the heaviness of his mother."* Proverbs 10:1

I've seen many women burdened by heaviness. They struggle with life which is clouded by *heaviness* of heart over wayward sons and daughters. Start training them as babies and be consistent!

One instance where having trained our two little children in a certain way spared us possible tragedy, is told in his book, "On the Road to Roxton, Texas," by our son. I'm quoting excerpts.

*"It is probably the dream of every little boy to leave his younger sister some place! Well, it happened long ago in our family when we left Jeanne at the church. She was about three years old and was very used to the church. We went every time the doors were open. My parents were very involved, and we usually took a carload of people to church with us. That was before church buses.*

*After services that day, the car was loaded to return our riders to their homes; each person was dropped off at his house, then Mom took inventory and found Jeanne missing! We immediately made a return trip to the church. As we arrived our Pastor was just leaving with Jeanne to bring her home. He had made a last round through the building and found her calmly sitting on the steps of the platform waiting for Dad and Mom to come back. She knew they would be back. Everything was alright."* Louis A. Holmes.

If our little girl had run outside and into the street, she could have been hit by a car, or picked up by a stranger. Even as a toddler, she trusted us and stayed calm. At that time, training was priceless!

Delight:    Psalm 127:3    II Timothy 1:5

Edna Holmes

# December 18

*"I acknowledged my sin unto thee...and thou forgavest the iniquity of my sin."* Psalm 32:5

When we know we have sinned, we should confess it immediately. It is inevitable that we will sin for we live in a body of flesh. The "flesh" is not saved and keeps us struggling with spiritual warfare every day of our lives. The only remedy is yielding ourselves to the Holy Spirit of God. He warns us of sin as it tries to get a place in our lives. The fact is we do, and shall always, sin! The thing is to confess it every day. *"The same moment which brings the consciousness of sin ought to bring also the confession and the consciousness of forgiveness."* Hannah W. Smith.

God makes it easy for His children, yet we scurry about on this earth, in the world, just halfway happy when we could have our hearts full of joy and peace all the time. We think like spoiled children, that we can disobey the Lord and somehow get away with it. Jonah had that attitude at first, and eventually he lost it in the belly of a whale. He didn't think it through; he just took off running away in rebellion because he didn't want to preach in Nineveh. That was the capital of Assyria; the people were cruel and heartless, and Jonah didn't think they deserved God's salvation. No one does! But our merciful God "so loved the world..." and that included Nineveh with all its inhabitants.

Forgiveness is provided for us...daily; for we need it. *"If we confess our sins, he is faithful and just to forgive us our sins, and to cleanse us from all unrighteousness."* I John 1:9. God is "just" in forgiving confessed sin because our Savior, Jesus, has "paid *it all, all to Him we owe...*".

Delight:   I John 2:12   Ephesians 1:7

## December 19

*"Unto thee lift I up mine eyes, O thou that
dwellest in the heavens."* Psalm 123:1

Someone has wisely said that if you want to be wretched, look within. If you want to be distracted and fearful, look around. If you want to be peaceful and happy, look up. (*Moody notes*)

It really does make a difference as to where and which direction you are looking. Several years ago, I learned by unhappy experience the truth of that saying. It was one of those political years where the whole country is thrown into turmoil until a new leader is elected. If one chooses sides and allows the ups and downs of the wrangling among the candidates upset them emotionally, he can be terribly distracted and distraught for the whole year. I let my mind wander into the fray too much and couldn't pull myself away from the newscast each day about the progress for this side or the other.

I became unhappy and distracted, I could hardly work and get my Bible lessons prepared for thinking on catching the next news about the political situation.

I was foolish to let anything take my attention away from God's Word and work. We are to pray for our country, and the leaders, whoever they may be. So, pray first. Next, we vote for those we feel are best qualified. But to be constantly looking around fearful and hopeful at the same time is an unhappy state. Satan will use anything to distract us from staying close to the Lord. Be aware! *Looking up* brings hope and joy to us from above. Almighty God is there, Sovereign over all the earth, and He will take care of His children, even as the world swirls with unrest and trouble. Look up!

Delight:    Psalm 138:7-8    Jeremiah 32:17

Edna Holmes

# December 20

*"As he thinketh in his heart, so is he.*
Proverbs 23:7

The mind is unique with man. God gave His prize creation, man, a mind. No other living creature on earth has the brain and mental capacity of a human. Animals can be tamed, trained, and worked with for a lifetime, but they cannot come up to the level of the mind of man. There is a warning to all of us from God's Word concerning the power and wonder of the minds He gave us. *How we think will determine how we will be in our life on this earth.* Remember that heart, mind, and soul are synonymous in the Bible. All are involved in our thought life.

*"The dictionary defines the heart of man as 'the seat of one's inmost thoughts and secret feelings', soul and mind. It is also defined as 'the conscience and seat of emotions.' So, the heart/mind /soul functions in the same framework of our innermost being."* Treasures to Keep.EH

Our safeguard for this marvelous setup in us is to run the Word of God through our minds every day. It is the only "cleanser" which will keep our minds clean and clear of the world's contamination which touches us whether we want it to or not. We cannot totally avoid it. There is too much out there being dumped through eyes and ears daily. Everywhere you look, there are billboards, magazines, TV programs and ads, and now phones with internet which can furnish poison for our minds. And what you see and hear is kept *permanently* in your mind. Don't you wish you could forget what you want to? All we can do is to fill our minds full of the Word of God. Keep the bad buried under the divinely Good, and that is our peace of mind.

Delight:     Deuteronomy 4:9     Philippians 4:7

## December 21

*"...and a word spoken in due season, how good is it?"*
Proverbs 15:23

December is the most "due" season for speaking a word about the Lord Jesus Christ. This time of year is consumed with Christmas, the traditional time of the Lord's birth on earth. For most, it is not done in a Biblical fashion, but worldly tradition.

1. People exchange gifts and don't think of giving Jesus anything, though it is regarded as His birthday!
2. People go into debt, putting the family in dire straits financially, in order to have a *good* Christmas.
3. Children, who already have everything they desire, are showered with more gifts by their parents.

After Christmas there is a big letdown for many. The glow of Christmas has fizzled out. That could be avoided if Jesus Himself is acknowledged. Celebrate as it was done at His actual birth.

Angels appeared in the night to announce his birth, and to praise Him. *"And suddenly there was with the angel a multitude of the heavenly host praising God..."* Luke 2:13-14.

The Shepherds worshipped Him and then told others about Him. *"And when they had seen it, they made known abroad the saying which was told them concerning this child."* Luke 2:17.

Later, Wise Men from the East brought Him gifts.
*"...the saw the young child with Mary his mother, and fell down and worshipped him: and when they had opened their treasures, they presented unto him gifts; gold, frankincense, and myrrh."* Matthew 2:11.

This Christmas tell at least one person about Jesus the Savior. Give Him a gift! Money, time, talent given in a special way in the name of the Lord will be precious to Him. That will make you happy too...*after Christmas!*

Delight:   Hebrews 1:2-3   Luke 2:7-14

Edna Holmes

# December 22

*"That seeing they may see, and not perceive;
and hearing they may hear, and not understand..."*
Mark 4:12

There are verses which are difficult for Christians to explain in the Bible, but we should always stick with basic unchangeable facts and pursue the study of such verses until we can understand it ourselves and teach others. Such a one is our text verse.

When you first read that section, you may get the idea that Jesus is saying "I'm putting these things in parables in order to hide the truth from them. I'm putting these things in parables so they will see and yet they won't really see; and so, they will hear and they won't really hear." But such interpretation is contrary to the mission of the Lord Jesus. He came to reveal the truth, not *hide* the truth from the ones He came to save. *"For the Son of man is come to seek and to save that which was lost."* Luke 19:10.

*"Jesus is referring back to a scripture in Isaiah 6:9, A description of the result in the life of people who refuse to hear the word of God. In other words, Jesus comes and gives people the truth, but if they won't see it, the time comes when they cannot see. If they won't hear it, the time comes when they cannot hear. As they refuse to know the truth, they lose their capacity to know the truth. Jesus was using the parable, or picture form of teaching to reach through their hardened hearts, but they could no longer see or hear".* Phillips Com.

There's a saying, "Use it, or lose it!" That is true for everything. Even our knowledge and study of the Word must be kept up. Our talents and various learned abilities can rust, so to speak. Ignore the Bible, and in time you *can't see and hear it like before.* God will not be forever mocked by those who treat Him and His Word as though it is nothing. Renew your heart in his Word today, afresh and anew.

Delight:   Psalm 119:41-44   Romans 10:17

## December 23

*"Then was Jesus led up of the Spirit into the wilderness to be tempted of the devil."* Matthew 4:1

Many have a wrong concept of temptation. A common view is that temptation itself is sin; it is not. To yield to temptation is sin. As long as a Christian fights against temptation, using all the Lord provides to have victory over it, he is not sinning…he is winning! Spurgeon gives an interesting fact about temptation in his Morning and Evening devotional.

*"A holy character does not avert temptation: Jesus was tempted. When Satan tempts us, his sparks fall upon kindling. In Christ's case, however, it was like striking sparks on water."* The Lord was in perfect obedience to His Father in heaven, a wonderful pattern for His children to follow. Yet we all remain very vulnerable to temptation, which has varied appearances and colors. Satan can easily fool us into thinking something that comes to mind, or in view, is harmless, when in reality there is a concealed trap waiting for a convenient time to spring on us.

Religious people have done bizarre things to gain favor with their "god", such as sitting on top of a great high pole in order to suffer in the flesh, and isolated from society, so they won't sin! That shows ignorance of the salvation of our God. It is also vain, because every human being takes his mind with him wherever he goes and that holds certainty that he *will sin*. *"The Lord knoweth the thoughts of man, that they are vanity."* Psalm 94:11. As we have said many times, running the Word of God through your minds daily will be your best protection in temptation, followed by fervent prayer in the name of Jesus. Prayer going through Jesus is powerful beyond understanding. Pray!

Delight:    Genesis 6:5    I Corinthians 10:13

Edna Holmes

# December 24

*"Though he was rich, yet for your sakes he became poor."*
II Corinthians 8:9

As our minds are engaged about Christmas and all the things that entails, we should stop and consider what Jesus left behind Him to come down from Heaven and live among men as a man, the Son of Man. He did so according to God the Father's plan from the beginning to redeem Adam's race from the fall into sin. Jesus, the Son of God, born of a virgin, the Lamb of God born to be the supreme sacrifice for our sins was born in a stable...where lambs are born. We have all heard the story and read it over and over knowing all the facts lying on the surface of God's Word. But do we really grasp it?

How could we possibly know how rich our Lord was when He came? And He was no less rich when He returned. The Bible gives us a few helpful clues.

*"For by him were all things created, that are in heaven, and that are in earth, visible and invisible, whether they be thrones, or dominions, or principalities, or powers: all things were created by him and for him,"* Col. 1:16.

Everything in the universe and beyond is His! By Him all things consist (hold together). Can we get a tiny picture of His eternal wealth and riches? But the Lord's most precious possession is His blood-bought ones, those who have trusted Him for the salvation of their souls. We cannot imagine the place called Heaven. Men make it out to be like a glorified earth, a recreated garden of Eden. We know for sure that the Lord Jesus Christ will be the main attraction. We will praise Him forever and ever. He saved us and brought us there.

Delight:   I Peter 3:22   John 1:14

Delighting in the Lord

# December 25

*"...and when they had opened their treasures, they presented unto him gifts..."* Matthew 2:11

The wise men were rich men, and they brought Jesus kingly gifts...because they *knew* He was a King! They saw His star in the east and followed it to find Him so they could see and worship Him. They came, guided by that amazing star which went before them in the heavens, until at last it shone down on the house where Jesus was. Mary and Joseph did not stay in the stable...they found a house to dwell in until God told Joseph to leave and go into Egypt for the protection of the Baby Jesus. Tradition puts the Wise Men at the manger, but it just isn't so. It only makes a pretty picture. They came a long way to bring Jesus gifts. Have you given Him a gift today?

**The Gift**
Give a gift to Jesus? What does one give to a King
Who has untold treasure, the universe,
and myriad angels who do His bidding?
I'm least among His servants...what could I give?
Yet, there is one thing He desires of mine.
I'm thrilled, but frightened, and tremble at the thought
Of laying such a gift at His feet.
But His love constrains me.
So I take this tattered, rather roughened thing:
Dull with lack of courage,
Shriveled from lack of nourishment,
Slippery with a spidery web of deceit,
And I hold it out to the King...with fear and trembling.
*Lord, I present to you this unworthy gift:*
*I give to you...my heart.*

Delight:  I Peter 1:18-19  Hebrews 1:1-2

Edna Holmes

# December 26

*"...but this one thing I do, forgetting those things which are behind...I press toward the mark..."* Philippians 3:13-14

Immediately after the Christmas holidays is a favorite time of year for me. It's a turnaround, get re-organized for the next year, which also gives me a new perspective. The Apostle Paul's words meant that he wasn't going to let anything in his life that had happened to him stop him or slow him down in his goal to serve the Lord Jesus fervently with every ounce of his being. He would never forget that meeting with Jesus on the road of Damascus. He left all the sufferings and trials, and victories, behind and pressed forward toward the prize of the high calling of God in the Lord Jesus Christ. He concentrated only on that goal.

When we turn our calendar to January, we can better manage our lives if we get a mind-set like Paul. Leave all that has hindered and put a drag on your life behind you. Drop it; go on.

The new year before us has no mistakes, burdens, or failures in it. Clean slate! Now, what we add in the future will make it a struggle or a blessing. Of course, we can't make the right choices ourselves. Jesus must be our consultant and counselor. Talk to Him as though you have another person, present, you are conversing with, *all day long.* It's amazing how we try to cope with things before our hearts turn to the Lord out of desperation. Why not at first, when a problem surfaces? Pray that this new year will find you depending on the Lord with all your heart. Watch Him work, and you won't fret.

Delight:   Proverbs 3:5-6   Philippians 3:14-15

## December 27

*"Favour is deceitful, and beauty is vain: but a woman that feareth the Lord shall be praised."* Proverbs 31:30

Outward beauty does not count for much. There are few natural beauties in this world, that is, those who are strikingly beautiful without any makeup on. Most women become experts, keeping up with all the "helps" out there, in making themselves as physically attractive as possible. I'm sure that men appreciate the trouble they go to look "pretty." But there is more to attractiveness than mere looks. Someone has said of dating; "Charm may get you by for the first fifteen minutes, but after that you better know something."

A woman who "fears the Lord" will receive words of praise and appreciation from those who know her. Why? She will possess a kind of beauty that comes from above, not from jars and bottles taking up space on bathroom shelves.

The *fear of the Lord* is an awe and reverence of God that causes obedience. It is not a dreadful fear expecting a blow from the Lord at every mistake. Fear of God is a healthy attitude. Joseph had that attitude when Potiphar's wife tempted him to sin. He said "*...how then can I do this great wickedness, and sin against God?*" Genesis 39:9.

To look your best, have a clear conscience, and to be the best company to others, even your own husband, do these simple things. <u>Put God's Word in your mind</u> every day without fail. <u>Develop your prayer life</u> by using God's promises in His Word. Amazing results will happen. <u>Confess sins daily;</u> if you haven't been perfect all day in attitude, thoughts, words, and actions, you have sin to confess. Pillow your head at night with a clear conscience. God has provided.

Delight:   Deuteronomy 10:12   Psalm 31:19

Edna Holmes

# December 28

*"For other foundation can no man lay than that is laid, which is Jesus Christ."* I Corinthians 3:11

These few days between Christmas and New Year's Day can be the most beneficial for our lives. We can use the lull in normal activity the holidays caused to give our hearts to revival in our souls. Set up a memorial as Israel did at the Jordan river.

When the Israelites crossed over the Jordan river, God parted the water. He had Joshua set up twelve stones *in the midst* of the river where the feet of the priests stood on dry ground with the Ark of the Covenant. He also had one man from each tribe of Israel to carry a stone out of the river into the place where they first camped near Jericho. The stones were stacked up as a memorial, a testimony and witness for their children when they would ask in the future, "What do these stones mean?" The people taught their children how God delivered them by His mighty power and miracles and brought them to that good land. Sadly, in time, they forgot the importance of it.

We need choice stones as reminders; they won't move as the winds of trials and temptations try to lay us low. We can stand firm.

First of all, <u>get a new firm hold on the Word of God.</u> Remember when you read…*'this is the very words out of God's mouth…pay attention! Listen! He is talking to you!'*

<u>Pray</u>; you have the privilege. Talk, talk to Him. He loves it. *"…but the prayer of the upright is his delight."* Proverbs 15:8.

<u>Serve in your church faithfully</u>. It's God's family. Love them, participate with them. They will help take care of each other. These are choice stones of a firm foundation. Polish these up in your life.

Delight:     Joshua 4:19-24     Proverbs 15:8

Delighting in the Lord

# December 29

*"As the cold of snow in the time of harvest, so is a faithful messenger to them that send him..."* Proverbs 25:13

In the days of the Roman Empire, the wealthy Roman noblemen might refresh the guests at their tables by bringing snow from the mountain peaks to ice their drinks. It took enormous cost and speed to afford that rare treat. Perhaps Solomon had such a practice for he was the richest king known to the world. He could have afforded it! The "cold of snow" when snow was out of reach of common man, was such a luxury, and so rare.

A faithful messenger, whom one could confidently trust was of great value; and it is so with preachers of the gospel of Christ. The most precious treasure ever to be brought from afar, is the gift of salvation. Jesus brought it down; He loves mankind, was able to do the work of salvation, and had the power to cause it to be! Jesus provided for lost humanity "at the table" of life waiting to be refreshed with God's salvation. So, one that faithfully proclaims the gospel is of great value to those who believe on the Lord Jesus Christ.

*"The early fall months can be as hot as summer before the weather turns definitely toward winter. As a farmer's daughter, I experienced days when we pulled cotton in sweltering heat, which was miserable, and suddenly a "cold front" would blow through bringing a "cold of snow" breeze with it. How delighted we were! It doesn't say "snow", it says <u>cold of snow</u>. We would take off hats and bonnets and turn our faces to that cold wind for refreshment."*

In the new year coming toward us, pray that God will make you such a welcomed messenger, that you can witness to lost souls, one at a time, that some might be saved before it is too late.

Delight:    Romans 10: 9-10, 13    John 3:16-17

Edna Holmes

# December 30

*"And the Lord direct your hearts into the love of God, and the patient waiting for Christ."* II Thess.3:5

The spiritual warfare will not slack off in the New Year. In fact, it is sure to intensify because Satan's time is running out. Though he is doomed, and he knows it, he will still try to hinder the Lord's work on earth. He doesn't let up. He hates Christ and Christians. But in following the Lord, we can look ahead with confidence. He is with us.

Looking Ahead
You may notice the valleys are deeper
And the mountains loftily high,
And our steps more plodding with effort
As time rushes crazily by.

Hear the tireless roar of the devourer,
Though toothless and fangless he be.
In spiritual warfare that rages,
There's a psychological part you see.

There is always rattling of the chains,
Though truth has set us free.
It is disquieting to our souls,
And renders us fearful, doubting victory.

But there's a calm in the heat of battle,
Where the conflict ceases to be;
It's a secret place known to few
Directly at Jesus' feet.

Courage and strength are reinforced.
Resolve is polished to a sheen,
And love drives out fear and doubt,
Just lingering in that place with Him.

(Edna Holmes)

Delighting in the Lord

# December 31

*"...be ye steadfast, unmoveable, always abounding in the work of the Lord..."* I Corinthians 15:58

This year is leaving us today, and a new one begins. Let's stop and reflect and ask ourselves a telling question. "In view of eternity, what did I do this year for the Lord that amounts to anything?" Jesus said, *"But seek ye first the kingdom of God, and his righteousness; and all these things shall be added unto you."* Matt.6:33. When He comes, will He find us scurrying around like ants tending "all these things" ignoring what should be first with us, the kingdom of God, the Lord's business?

It is necessary to take care of physical life; we will naturally do that. But growing spiritually and serving the Lord should be in a first-place category. Doing an honest checkup on ourselves is beneficial as we go into a new year. Are we serving God like robots, doing our duty when our hearts are far from Him? Jesus said this: *"This people draweth nigh unto me with their mouth, and honoreth me with their lips; but their heart is far from me."* Matt. 15:8. I've had to repent of "robot service" before. It's miserable when we realize we have lost ground, and our hearts desperately need sweet fellowship with the Lord again.

Do I know any more of God's Word than I did a year ago? Do I pray? Have I told anyone lost about Jesus in the past year? Am I a good example of a Christian, in private, and out in public? A good 'start the year' prayer is Psalm 139:23-24. Let God do the searching because He won't miss a thing!

May you be blessed abundantly in the New Year.

Delight:   Galatians 6:9-10   Ephesians 3:16-21

## ABOUT THE AUTHOR

Edna Holmes grew up, a country girl, the third one of ten children. The rich and varied experiences of her childhood are often referenced in her writing.

She married her *soldier home from the war* at an early age, and five years later, they both became Christians through a personal faith in Jesus Christ. Their focus changed immediately. Years later, her husband became the pastor of a church in Grapevine, Texas. He would serve faithfully in that pastorate for forty-two years.

Within those decades, the church grew to be strong in their mission outreach: contributing to the support of many missionary families serving all over the world. Edna was privileged to travel with her husband to many countries as he visited the missionaries, encouraging them in their work. She learned from experience that Christian women all over the world, in all cultures, have the same basic needs and desires of the heart.

Edna, and her husband Louis, are enjoying their older years as they continue to serve the Lord in speaking, encouraging young pastors and their wives in the ministry, and generally being of help where they are needed. Their chief joy otherwise is their family; children, grandchildren, and great-grandchildren.

Edna has written two other books, already available at www.amazon.com: The first book of **Treasures To Keep** – 365 Daily Devotionals, and **Poems and More,** containing poems and stories about her large family, including nine brothers and sisters. All her books are available in both paperback and Kindle editions. Plans call for her books to be translated into Spanish, the process beginning soon.

Delighting in the Lord

A Delightful way to begin your day is to spend time with the Lord, through His Word. You will discover truths you've never noticed before. When you make time to Delight in the Lord, it will always make difference in your life. In a world full of controversy and uncertainty, your daily time with Him will give you the peace to face whatever the world brings your way. As Psalm 37:4 says, "Delight thyself also in the Lord; and he shall give thee the desires of thine heart."

www.ingramcontent.com/pod-product-compliance
Lightning Source LLC
LaVergne TN
LVHW081352060426
835510LV00013B/1782